Finlay's River

R. M. PATTERSON

VICTORIA • VANCOUVER • CALGARY

Copyright © 2006 the estate of R. M. Patterson
Foreword copyright © 2006 Janet Blanchet
First published in 1968 by William Morrow & Co., New York

First TouchWood edition

All rights reserved. No part of this publication may be reproduced, stored in a retrieval system or transmitted in any form or by any means—electronic, mechanical, audio recording or otherwise—without the written permission of the publisher or a photocopying licence from Access Copyright, Toronto, Canada.

TouchWood Editions
#108 – 17665 66A Avenue
Surrey, BC V3S 2A7
www.touchwoodeditions.com

Library and Archives Canada Cataloguing in Publication
Patterson, R. M. (Raymond Murray), 1898–1984.
   Finlay's River / by R. M. Patterson. — 1st TouchWood ed.

Includes bibliographical references and index.

ISBN-13: 978-1-894898-38-6
ISBN-10: 1-894898-38-9

   1. Patterson, R. M. (Raymond Murray), 1898-1984—Travel—British Columbia—Finlay River. 2. Finlay River (B.C.)—Description and travel. 3. Finlay River (B.C.)—History. I. Title.

FC3845.F55P38 2006   917.11'87   C2006-900627-X

Book design by Frances Hunter.
Cover design by Fraser Seely.
All photos courtesy of the estate of R. M. Patterson unless otherwise noted.

NOTE TO READERS: In order to preserve the authenticity and the history of the period in which this book was written, we have chosen not to alter the text to reflect modern-day attitudes.

Printed in Canada

TouchWood Editions acknowledges the financial support for its publishing program from the Government of Canada through the Book Publishing Industry Development Program (BPIDP), Canada Council for the Arts, and the British Columbia Arts Council.

This book has been printed on 100% post-consumer recycled paper, processed chlorine free and printed with vegetable-based dyes.

Contents

Acknowledgments   v
Foreword by Janet Blanchet   vii
Introduction   ix

Part One: *Southern Approaches*

Chapter 1	The Setting	2
Chapter 2	Summit Lake	10
Chapter 3	Crooked River	20
Chapter 4	Warburton Pike	26
Chapter 5	Ignatieff	37

Part Two: *Men Travelling into a Far Country*

Chapter 6	Finlay Forks	48
Chapter 7	Samuel Black	53
Chapter 8	Pete Toy	64
Chapter 9	Butler	66
Chapter 10	Selwyn	72
Chapter 11	R. G. McConnell	80
Chapter 12	Inspector J. D. Moodie	84
Chapter 13	The Police Trail	88
Chapter 14	Fleet Robertson	91
Chapter 15	Swannell on the Mesilinka	94
Chapter 16	Haworth	104

Part Three: *To the Headwaters*

Chapter 17	Deserters Canyon	108
Chapter 18	Swannell on the Ingenika	129
Chapter 19	Prairie Mountain	151
Chapter 20	The Explorer	175
Chapter 21	Thutadé	193
Chapter 22	Bower Creek	208
Chapter 23	The Surveyor	231

Part Four: *Downriver*
    Chapter 24   Deserters Portage   252
    Chapter 25   The Black Canyon   269
    Chapter 26   The Finlay Rapids   282

Maps   xii-xiii, 14, 28, 56-57
Appendices   292
Bibliography   295
Endnotes   297
Index   299

For Marigold

Acknowledgments

First and foremost I should like to thank Mr. F. C. Swannell for the free use of his 1913 and 1914 *Diaries*, for the photographs which he has provided, and for the many hours of his time that he has so kindly given me. Any gaps in the record have been filled in by Mr. G. V. Copley, Mr. Swannell's assistant of 1913-14, and Mr. Copley has added one or two touches of his own that bring to life that arduous survey as though it were a tale of yesterday.

Then I wish to thank the Hudson's Bay Record Society for permission to quote from their Volume XVIII, *Black's Rocky Mountain Journal*, the account of the first exploration of the Finlay. Of this permission I have made full use—and I am also grateful to the governor and committee of the Hudson's Bay Company for various information from their archives regarding Fort Grahame. Parts of the chapter on the Black Canyon of the Omineca have appeared before in the Hudson's Bay Company's magazine, *The Beaver*, and permission to reprint them here has been kindly given.

To Mrs. Leon H. Wallace of Bloomington, Indiana, I am indebted for permission to make use of her father's book, *On the Headwaters of Peace River*—and I am equally grateful to Mrs. Helen Ignatieff for the details of her late husband's career and of his plans for the development of the fertile areas of the Rocky Mountain Trench on the lower Finlay.

Once more I have had the run of the British Columbia Provincial Archives and the assistance of the staff in my search through old survey reports for the lively detail that alone can clothe the bare bones of bygone journeys. And in Ottawa the quiet of the Public Archives of Canada has been disturbed on my behalf by Mr. Courtney Bond, searching for photographs of surveyors at work in the high mountains. For his help, so generously given, I thank him.

My friend, Mr. Palmer Lewis of Seattle, delved in no archives: he went straight to the original sources. On a day that was turning to rain he went, with Art van Somer, up the Finlay and into Long Canyon specially to photograph, from dangerously close quarters, the island rock that Samuel Black named "the Old Man." Great must have been his faith in this book (it was still unfinished) and to him be a thousand thanks.

Finally I am indebted to Messrs. Chatto and Windus Ltd. of London, England (publishers), for permission to use as motto the quotation from Norman Douglas' *In the Beginning*—an apposite commentary on "progress" as it is thrust upon us today.

Foreword

My father's journey on the Finlay River with his young son Alan began at Summit Lake, north of Prince George, in July of 1949. Their craft was a 17-foot Prospector canoe—"a thing of beauty," in RMP's view—that had been built in Fredericton, New Brunswick. From Summit Lake they travelled along the Rocky Mountain Trench, down the Crooked River to the Parsnip River, then continued down the Parsnip to Finlay Forks, the junction of the Finlay and the Parsnip. At Finlay Forks the two rivers, flowing in opposite directions within the Trench, joined to form the Peace River, which turned east through the Rockies and flowed towards Hudson's Hope and Fort St. John. Alan and my father continued travelling northwest up the Finlay past Fort Grahame to Fort Ware, where the Finlay swings away from the Rocky Mountain Trench and turns west. Alan flew home from Fort Ware at the end of the summer, and RMP continued westward on his own, returning to Finlay Forks in September.

A map is essential to understanding this account of river travel and exploration, particularly in view of the changes that have occurred in the area. In the mid-20th century, there was a fine scheme to make use of land in the Trench close to the Peace River Gap for the purpose of planting specific grasses and raising seed, thereby encouraging settlement. This whole area is now under water: the construction of the Peace River Dam, begun in 1961 and completed in 1967, resulted in a great, three-armed reservoir that covers Finlay Forks and the old headwaters of the Peace and extends a considerable distance, both northwest along the Finlay and southeast along the Parsnip. The head of the Peace River is now deemed to be at the smaller Peace Canyon Dam, downstream from the main dam. Much of the country through which RMP and Alan travelled has vanished forever.

Finlay's River is much more than the story of a summer canoe trip in northern British Columbia; using his journey on the river as a framework, RMP recounts much of the area's fascinating history. Before the W.A.C. Bennett Dam was built, the Peace River Gap was a gateway into the Rocky Mountain Trench country from the east, and numerous travellers passed through it.

Samuel Black, chief trader for the Hudson's Bay Company, followed the Finlay to its source in 1824, travelling in a birchbark canoe. He left a vivid account of his journey and the incredible risks his party took. (Some years later, at Kamloops, he was murdered.)

William Butler and Warburton Pike travelled the country in the late 1800s, mainly for the purpose of exploration. Pike barely survived his journey; he and his companions were starving by the time they arrived at Twelve-Foot Davis' trading post at the end of December 1890.

Other early visitors to the area included the North West Mounted Police, who made two attempts to build a viable trail through the Peace River Gap to the Klondike. That scheme failed.

Then came the surveyors. In the summers of 1913 and 1914, Frank Swannell and his survey parties worked on the Finlay's tributaries, and each summer they used a dugout cottonwood canoe as their means of transport. With this relatively heavy and clumsy craft they navigated the rivers and encountered some truly hair-raising situations. Fortunately, RMP had an opportunity to talk to Frank Swannell and obtain a first hand-account of his experiences in the Finlay country.

RMP weaves all these tales and more into his account of the summer of 1949, and his own knowledge of the hazards entailed in canoeing wild rivers and running rapids greatly illuminates his accounts of journeys past. After Alan's departure he spent some time exploring further on his own, then drifted down the Finlay to the Omineca River, where he turned and travelled upstream to the Black Canyon, a place he had read about when he was 12. There he happily spent four sunny days before travelling to Finlay Forks, where he met my mother, Marigold, in early September. Together they took the canoe through the Peace River Gap, then downstream on the Peace in the softly gathering dusk, as the mountains closed in behind them.

Janet (Patterson) Blanchet

North Vancouver, British Columbia
January 2006

Introduction

Until now no book dealing with the Finlay from mouth to source has ever been written. P. L. Haworth's book of 1917 makes the nearest approach to this, but it stops short at the entrance to the canyons of the big bend, leaving untouched all that wild stretch of river from there to the birthplace of the Finlay in Thutadé Lake.

I have been fortunate enough to know some of the men who have travelled, explored and mapped much of that upper country—and I have also had the opportunity to see a considerable part of the country and the river for myself. Hoping, therefore, that I shall not be dismissed as an armchair historian, I have compiled what, I suppose, might be called a Finlay River anthology, based on my own journey through the Finlay country and my own experiences on other rivers.

Given similar conditions of climate, flowing water working in loose material can be counted on to do always the same things. A cutbank or a sweeper, a bar, a snye or a riffle—these are invariable on certain types of river: when you have seen them once you have seen them for all time. The only rapids that vary are those that are cut in the solid rock, for there the possible combinations are infinite. So, after years of experience on wild rivers, one can confidently visualize other men's adventures almost as if they were one's own. I hope that, in these pages, some of the stories that I have read, or have heard from those who were actors in them, will come to life for the reader.

As a limit to this account of travel on the Finlay I have taken the year 1916. That year saw the arrival of the outboard engine on those rivers of the Northwest; and since then travel has changed out of all recognition and many of the old skills have disappeared. I have overstepped the 1916 boundary only in two places: firstly my own journey, and secondly the experiment planned by Nicholas Ignatieff, which, if fate had allowed it to proceed, could well have made a country of established farms where now there will be nothing but the windswept waters of an inland sea. I have not, however, gone into any detail regarding the old settlement of Finlay Forks, vanished many years ago as its inhabitants, one by one, got tired of waiting for the road that never came. Somebody else, I am told, is writing the story of that settlement—and, in any case, this book of mine does not pretend to be a complete history of the Finlay.

My first trip to the Finlay was purely to see, and I remember it as a happy summer and one that led, later on, to some very interesting historical work. Furthermore, it was not a hunting trip: I had grown out of the urge to shoot things except for the pot, or, as the mining regulations used to put it, "in case of dire need." If a fine head of mountain sheep had crossed my path, I would have taken it. But no such thing happened and no shot was fired.

Cause and effect have always interested me, and one of the more remarkable instances of this process occurs in this book. Without knowing the full story it would be hard to imagine why, simply because an Irish captain in the British army almost died of fever on the Gold Coast of Africa in 1874, the then-director of the Geological Survey of Canada should make a canoe trip down the Peace River in 1875. Yet these things actually occurred in logical sequence (to my great pleasure) and here present themselves, linked together for the first time, for the edification of the reader.

For the rest: the bibliography contains the titles of the few books that touch on the Finlay, however briefly—sometimes only a single paragraph or a few lines. It contains also the titles of the more relevant government reports.

Following F. C. Swannell's practice, I have accented the final "e" of some of the place names to show that that syllable is pronounced: e.g., Thutadé, which should rhyme with "faddy."

I think there are no peculiar, esoteric words in this book except, perhaps, "snye"—which means the back channel of a river behind an island or a bar. It is thought to derive from the French-Canadian *chenal*, which means a channel, a narrow waterway.

The title, *Finlay's River*, calls for some explanation. All the rivers that were named after the early explorers were originally given the possessive form: Fraser's River, Thompson's River and so forth. Gradually these came to be superseded, in the latter part of the last century, by the present-day forms: Fraser River, Thompson River. I have retained the older form here on account of its slightly archaic flavour—thinking it to be well suited to what is largely an account of old-time travel.

R. M. Patterson

Victoria, British Columbia
September 1967

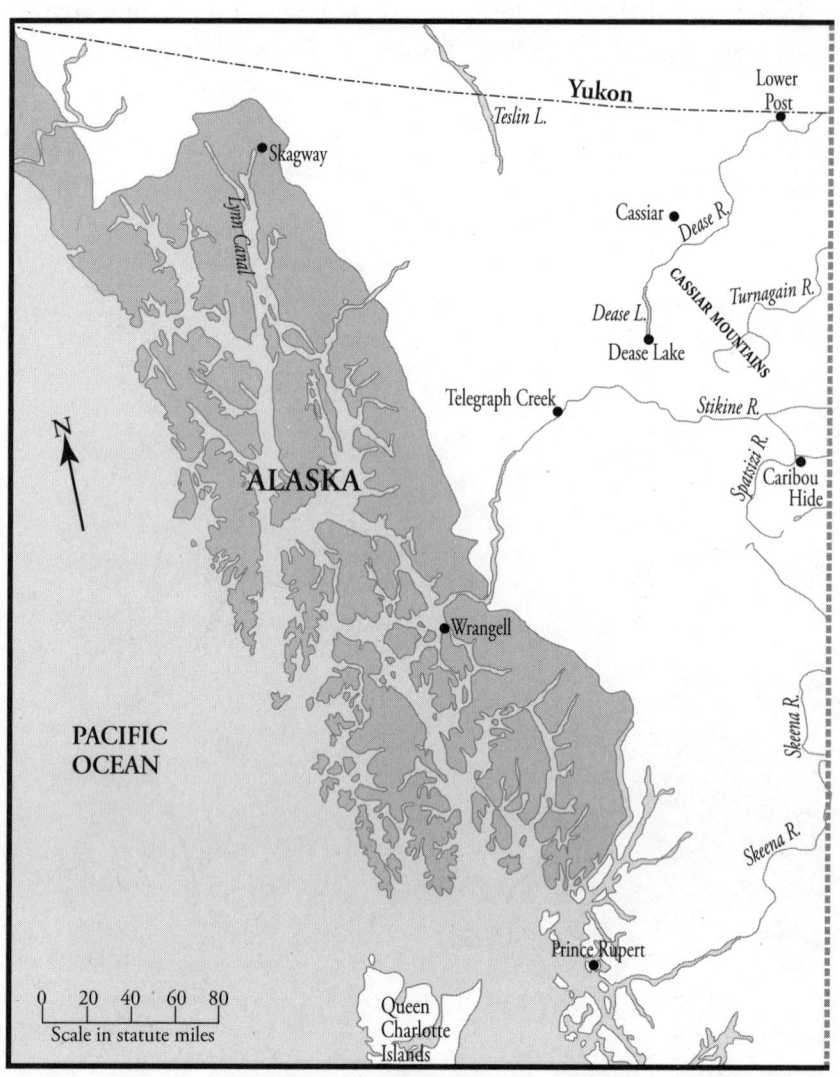

xiii

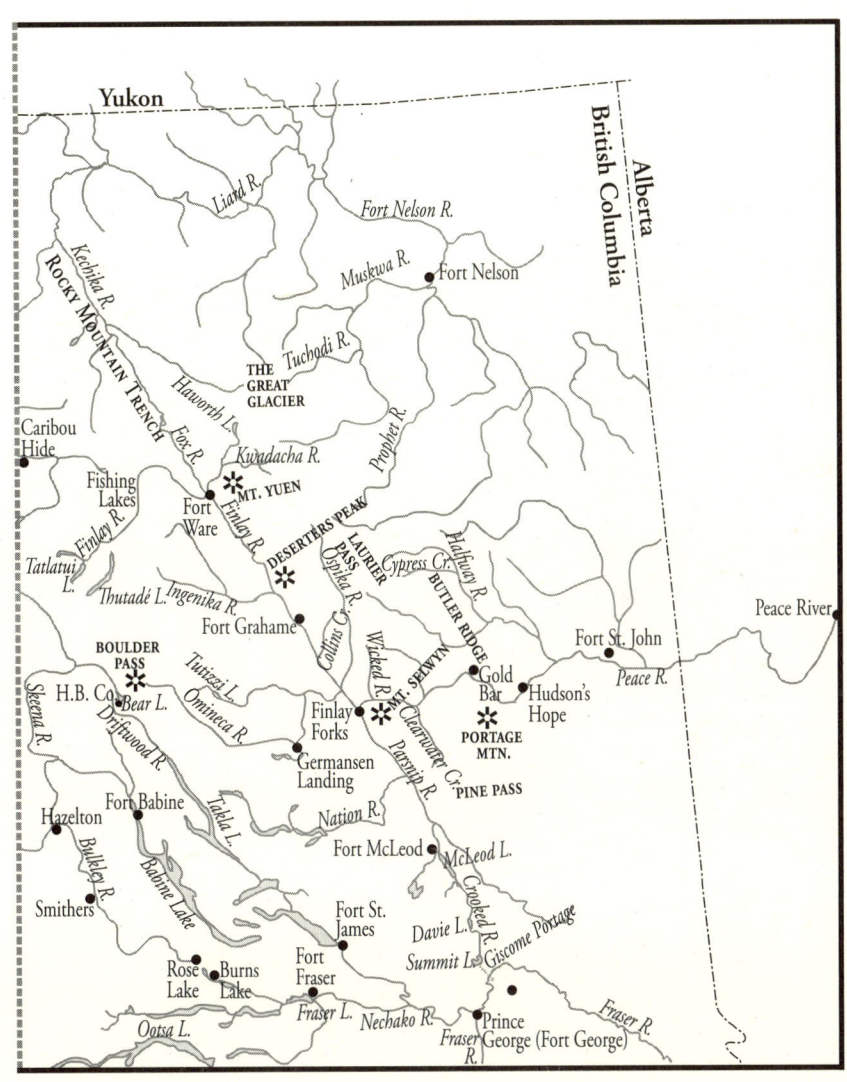

PART ONE

Peace River

I foresee the day when ... every fair spot has been scarred by their hands and deformed to their mean purposes, the rivers made turbid and hills and forests levelled away and all the wild green places smothered under cities full of smoke and clanking metal.

In the Beginning by Norman Douglas

I

The Setting

In the vestibule of the provincial museum in Victoria, the capital city of British Columbia, the visitor will encounter a large-scale relief map of the province. Let him stand there for a few minutes and look down upon it.

There it lies, in its case of heavy glass, its surface wrinkled with mountains, furrowed with valleys. It has been carefully painted with the varying greens and yellows that indicate the different kinds of forest, parkland and tundra. The mountains above timberline are a pale yellow, then white where their summits vanish into snow and ice. In the west the coast is lapped by the blue Pacific, and in that blue are set the mountainous islands of the sea. In the centre of the southern half of the map, walled around by the mountains and the dark, evergreen forest, and shut off by them from the open Pacific, are the dry lands of the Interior Plateau. These are held high above the ocean by the towering buttresses of the Coast Range, and they are shown, as is fitting, by a tawny, sun-scorched brown. In among all these greens and browns and yellows, shining pools of blue are to be seen: these are the lakes, and there are many of them. Yet these are only the larger lakes: hundreds more must remain unseen, too small to mark in relief, even on a map that is five feet wide by seven long.

Deeply incised into the chaos of the mountains and cutting great trenches in the Interior Plateau, one perceives the rivers. The crazy pattern of them is bewildering: some flow determinedly northwestward as if embarked on a journey to a known destination; then suddenly they change their minds and swing around in great arcs to flow in the very opposite direction, southeastward for as many miles again, only to turn west in the end and break through the mountain barrier to the Pacific. They do odd things, these rivers: they are to be found rising upon the Plateau and flowing, not *away* from the Coast Mountains, but straight *into* them, cutting their way down in roaring canyons to the sea. Some have been turned aside from their proper courses by flows of molten lava, and others, in less fiery periods of British Columbia's past, by crawling masses of ice. True it is, as John McLeod, the explorer of the South Nahanni River, wrote in 1824: "The courses of these rivers is very various."

Faced on the map with this intricate tangle of lakes and connecting waterways, even the native is sometimes puzzled, while the mind of the stranger reels. Far away in the northeast, beyond the Rockies, the waters flow in comparatively orderly fashion towards the Mackenzie and the Arctic Ocean; but west and southwest of the mountain barrier their capricious wanderings can only with difficulty be followed, even by the practised eye. Instinctively, in this maze, one searches for some feature that can be easily grasped, for something that will serve as a baseline, as it were, from which to trace out and comprehend the pattern of the rivers. And there it is: a long, dark trough in the eastern part of the province, a furrow ploughed by a giant at the western foot of the Rockies and running northwestward for some nine hundred miles, from the Montana line in the south almost to the Liard River and the boundary with the Yukon Territory in the far north. Geologists have a name for this great valley: they call it the Rocky Mountain Trench.

As yet, however, they have been unable to fathom the reasons for its existence: parts of it can be explained, yet no one set of explanations can be applied to its whole length. Meanwhile, there it runs, an enigma awaiting solution, a trough with the slightest of curves in its middle portion, but otherwise as straight as it is possible for a natural feature of this magnitude to be, and averaging about thirty degrees west of north. It cuts through this land of mountain and flood with all the drive and purpose of a Roman road, and no less than five of the major British Columbian rivers rise in it, flow in it, or are modified by it. From south to north they come in this order: the Kootenay and the Columbia; the Fraser, the Peace and the Liard. It is with the headwaters of the Peace that we are concerned here, and particularly with the main head—the Finlay.

This river takes its rise in a number of big lakes in the Stikine Plateau, and the chief of these lakes is Thutadé. Since the Finlay is the true head of the Peace, and since the Peace is larger than either the Liard or the Athabasca, that lake in those lonely mountains is the true source of the great Mackenzie, into which all these waters finally come. From the lake the Finlay starts on its turbulent way in a general northeasterly direction. Soon, however, it turns north—and these two legs of the journey together make up some fifty miles. Then, true to form as a British Columbian river, the Finlay changes its mind: it decides to break into the Trench from the west. Having gathered strength from the Firesteel and Toodoggoné rivers and from a thousand nameless creeks and rills, it flings itself at the southern ranges of the Cassiar Mountains and breaks through them in a great arc of some thirty river miles. Ten more miles of ordinary fast water remain, and then, below the open slopes of Prairie Mountain, the Finlay picks up Fox River, which enters from the northwest in a rush of whitewater—and from that point it becomes a river of the Trench, flowing southeastward in the great valley. In its headlong and tumultuous passage through the ranges that tried to bar its way, it has dropped almost a thousand feet from the level of Thutadé.

Other things and other men come into this story, but it is of this, the big bend of the Finlay, that I particularly wish to write: how Samuel Black made his way round it in 1824; and how Frank Swannell followed him, ninety years later, with his crew of three and the heavy cottonwood dugout that they had hollowed out and shaped with their own hands at Fort Grahame. How R. G. McConnell, that great traveller and geologist, came to it in 1893; and how P. L. Haworth and Joe Lavoie, in 1916, made their way on foot into the mountains north of the bend; and then, in order to return to their cache at Prairie Mountain, how they ran dangerously down the Finlay from the Split Rock on the good raft, *Necessity*, that they had built. And I wish to tell how Emil Bronlund prospected there, and how I, bypassing the cataracts of the river, cached my canoe and walked through the mountains in the loop of the bend to the upper Finlay and the Fishing Lakes.

The Setting

Rising from the lakes of the Stikine Plateau, the Finlay twists and turns its way among the mountains, gathering strength as it goes.

From the mouth of the Fox River the Trench runs southeastward in a dead straight line, and down it goes the Finlay. On the east—that is, on the left as one runs downstream—is the wall of the Rockies: a line of peaks which become lower as one approaches the Peace River Gap. On the west the ranges are more broken but the boundary of the Trench is no less clear. On the floor of the big valley, cutting and recutting its bed in the ever-shifting alluvium, the Finlay twists and turns. It maintains always the same general direction, since in all the hundred and fifty river miles down to the Forks there is no escaping from the Trench. Picking up river after river as it goes, the Finlay gains in size and strength—no longer now a clear stream, but coloured a milky blue from the glacial flood of the Kwadacha. A fast-sliding, driving river, undermining the cottonwoods and the tall spruce of the banks and sweeping away whole islands, only to build them again downstream in the eddies below huge driftpiles, the debris of the wrecked forest. Upon these islands seeds will fall and trees grow—trees which, when their time comes, will be undermined in their turn and carried away on some raging June high water. An endless cycle.

Running down the Finlay in a canoe, one can look forward and one can look back—and there, in each case, is the clear horizon, unbroken by any mountain. Yet on the right hand and on the left, the walls of the Trench run on as far as the eye can see, becoming lower and fainter as they fade from view over the curve of the earth. It would seem, indeed, that the river must go on forever. But at the Forks the Parsnip River appears, flowing in the Trench from the southeast. By a twist of the Finlay the two rivers avoid a head-on clash—but only just: they merge, and the clear, brown water of the Parsnip is swept away by the blue, glacial flow of the larger river. Together they form the Peace.

When two rivers collide in the Trench they must immediately find a way out, for there is nowhere else to go. When for example, further south, the Columbia meets Canoe River, their united waters break out of the Trench to the west by way of the Big Bend of the Columbia. That is normal procedure. But when the waters of the Finlay and the Parsnip have united to form the Peace, they do an odd thing: they launch themselves straight at the Rockies and break through—through the mountains and the foothills to the eastern plains. Just how they have

The Setting

contrived to do this tremendous thing is not material to the story of the Finlay, but the fact remains that nowhere else does any river escape out of the Trench to the eastward: this is the only navigable, water-level gap in the Rockies, from their faint beginnings beyond Santa Fe in faraway New Mexico to their end south of the Liard River in northern British Columbia. And that is a distance of 2,000 miles.

There is one more strange thing about the Finlay, and that is its name. In a year which may have been 1797, a certain John Finlay made a voyage of exploration west of the Rockies for the North West Company. In the course of this expedition he and his men went some distance ("a few days," according to Samuel Black) up the northern branch of the Peace. They may have got as far as the Ingenika River, some eighty miles above the Forks. Then they turned downstream again—and no record remains of that exploration, though Samuel Black writes that he had studied Finlay's chart. Nevertheless, in spite of this small and rather futile effort, the name of the first White explorer has clung to the river. The fur traders spoke of it as Finlay's Branch (of the Peace); later and more rarely they called it Finlay's River.

Twenty-seven years later came Samuel Black in command of a Hudson's Bay Company expedition. Black had a large birchbark canoe and a crew of ten—later augmented by various Sikanni Indians who attached themselves to the party. Had the explorer's name been almost anything but Black (with the possible exception of White) it would, no doubt, have been given to some main feature of the country and Black would have been remembered. As things turned out, this man who overcame the hazards of the Big Bend and penetrated to the very source of Finlay's Branch—and then went on, on foot, far to the northward until he fell on a river that flowed to the Liard—this man became almost completely forgotten except as a turbulent character in fur-trade history.

That tributary of the Liard from which Black turned back he named, very appropriately, the Turnagain. He never saw the mouth of it and he never knew that, lower down, it entered the Trench from the west. However, John McLeod, the explorer of the South Nahanni country, passed by its outflow into the Liard in 1831. He knew, from Indian report, that this was the same river as the one by whose upper reaches Black had camped in 1824: he therefore named it for Black, as they named rivers in those days: he called it Black's River.

This large river that McLeod christened is the most northerly river to flow in the Trench, which here dies away. It lines up, in its upper reaches, straight as an arrow with the other rivers of the northern part of the Trench, Fox River, the Finlay and the Parsnip, being separated from them by the low divide of Sifton Pass. The course of Black's River, until the guiding walls of the Trench diminish and sink beneath the surface of the earth, is the regulation course for a river of that great valley—thirty degrees west of north.

Here, as on the Finlay, the floor of the Trench is alluvium. Meandering in these soils and gravels, Black's River brings down in flood time a heavy burden of silt—so much so that the trappers and prospectors of a later day came to call it the Big Muddy. Well into this century it was still on the map as the "Black, Mud or Turnagain River." Then the Canadian Board on Geographical Names must have observed it—though probably not from the ground. From some eagle's aerie in Ottawa, perhaps. They evidently decided to tidy things up a bit, "for," they must have said, "there are already enough rivers in Canada called 'Black' simply because they are muddy." Under this wrong impression they searched for, and found, an Indian name for Black's River: they rechristened the river of the Trench, calling it "Kechika." The name "Turnagain" they quite properly relegated to the tributary reaches west, and outside, of the Trench. However, I found in 1949 that the river of the Trench was still called, in local parlance, the Big Muddy—and so, at one stroke, the good intentions of the Board were defeated and all traces of the name of Samuel Black were swept from the map of the Northwest.

Only one more slighting of Black remains to be told—but that was the unkindest cut of all. Black's official report of his exploration of 1824 lay in the Hudson's Bay Company Archives in London, unpublished till 1955. His draft of the report was in three parts, which became separated; and of the three only the last one was signed. The first part (and each one had its own peculiar history) somehow cast up at Cumberland House on the Saskatchewan, where it was vouched for by Chief Factor James McDougall as a part of "the journal of John Finlay

(H.B. Co.)." On this assumption, learned and distinguished men made extracts from it, and thus the error was perpetuated for over a hundred years. And so John Finlay's name has remained, and will now always remain, attached to the true head of the Peace and the Mackenzie—the name of the man who spent "a few days" of the summer of 1797 on the lower part of Finlay's Branch.

That is the river—and the setting of the river, and something of its history—which we are going to travel. My own personal acquaintance with the Finlay had its beginnings one winter's day in Alberta; and the place was the trophy room of the L7 ranch house in the foothills of the upper Red Deer River.

2

Summit Lake

It was on a January afternoon that the idea came to me. The low winter sun was shining through the big window, lighting up the rows of rare books, the pictures and weapons on the walls, the heads and the horns and the tusks of ivory. Had the room not been of a great size one would have felt overwhelmed by all these treasures, and by the trophies of Canadian and African game up aloft, sombre and aloof or glaring savagely. But as things were, it was a friendly room and the smell of it was a kindly blend of books and leather, tobacco and woodsmoke; there was no sense of pressure there.

I laid down Haworth's book, *On the Headwaters of Peace River*, and looked towards the Rockies. It was over twenty below zero that afternoon. Southwest, beyond the glittering foothills, wind-driven snow was smoking off the peaks. Behind me, in the big room, a log fire was crackling cheerfully, and my host, the Colonel, was over beside it, cleaning his guns.

"That Finlay River country must be worth seeing," I said. "Sheep country, too. Now, supposing one took a canoe—"

"You take my tip," the Colonel broke in, "and leave the Finlay alone. A bad river. You'll go fooling with a canoe once too often."

We argued—and as we talked the sun dipped down below the mountains and the golden light on the snow became blue and cold. Then, as the dusk crept into the big room and the flicker of the fire became stronger, the silent faces of the beasts came alive again, wrinkling and snarling in the moving shadows, watching us with shining eyes from the walls. That was always the magic hour in that

Patterson's friend, the Colonel, seen here with some of his trophies, warned against chancing the Finlay, a "bad river."

room: when it was lit only by the burning logs and the afterglow of the sunset. That was the hour that could lead a man to dream of distant rivers, and then plan to make those dreams come true.

Sound advice met with the usual fate of sound advice; and, as spring wore on into summer, plans to see the Finlay country were completed. A sunny morning in mid-July of 1949 found us—my wife Marigold, my son Alan, and myself—driving a heavily loaded car northward from Prince George in central British Columbia. The road was climbing a little, and soon a far view opened out before us: a vast sweep of forested country sloping away into the north, backed by blue mountains, still snow-streaked and far distant—the Rockies. The almost imperceptible height of land that we were crossing was the Pacific–Arctic Divide, and we were approaching Summit Lake, one of the furthest sources of the Peace River. As we drove over the water parting it seemed to me that, suddenly, the clear blue light of the plateau had become clearer and more blue. Once again, I thought, there had come that old feeling of elbow room, as though one had been given the freedom of a whole new world.

A truck had gone ahead of us that morning from Prince George, and we found, when we came to the lake, a canoe and a large wooden box lying on the shore. The canoe was a new one, a Chestnut "Prospector" from Fredericton, New Brunswick; it was seventeen feet long by thirty-seven inches wide, and in depth it was fourteen and a half inches. It was close-ribbed and that probably added another ten pounds to the standard weight: in all, about ninety pounds when dry. We unpacked the canoe from its straw and burlap and slid it into the water, where it floated gracefully. A canoe, made in the shape that the Indians first of all men imagined, uncluttered by outboard engine or drums of gas and without the disfigurement of a square end, is a thing of beauty in the same way that a yacht has grace and beauty. To sail the one, or to paddle, pole or track the other, demands various natural skills of hand and eye. There is a satisfaction in these abilities, as there must be in the performance of any physical feat; and the difference between travelling on a river "under one's own steam," and roaring over its surface to the din of an engine, bellowing at one's partner instead of conversing with him, resembles, in its small way, the difference between climbing a mountain on one's own feet and being freighted to the summit, as a sack of oats might be freighted, in a helicopter.

Empty and dry, the canoe floated out into the lake on the end of the trackline; it sat there, barely touching the surface of the water, with all the lightness of a sea bird. We turned it this way and that and admired it—then we drew it in and loaded it to the gunwales with stuff from the big box and the car. We took this first instalment out to a small nearby island; and in two more trips we had camp established there. Then the car was taken to a friendly house close to the landing. This was the only house in sight, and there the car was left in the shade of some trees and near an enormous house trailer with a Texas licence.

Summit Lake

The wooden box came out, on top of the last load, to the island, where it was promptly turned upside down to serve as a table. Once more we were at home.

The following day broke bright and sunny, and we used it to sort the outfit for the trip. The grub box was made up, and thin, dry, driftwood poles were cut for the floor of the canoe. On these, laid lengthways, the big tarpaulin and the load would sit, raised by them a little so that the rain and any water we might ship would drain freely towards the stern. I cruised around the island, looking for a tall, slim spruce that would do for a canoe pole. That proved to be a hopeless search, since the spruce here were all wind-twisted, tapering and knotty—too thick at the butt and fining down too soon. Summit Lake is almost as high above the sea as Dease Lake, from which I had started north the year before, and the altitude of Dease Lake is 2,500 feet. Both lakes lie just on the Arctic side of the Divide, and each one is a place of storms, long winters and slow tree growth. Neither, I found, could provide me with a good canoe pole anywhere near its windswept shoreline.

Poking around in the bush, looking for something that wasn't there, I finally made the best of a bad job: I cut a dwarfish, ancient spruce and trimmed it and peeled it. Then I went at it with axe and drawknife to whittle it down to something resembling a pole. And then I smoothed it with the rasp and drove on the steel point—the "shoe"—that I had brought with me. The result was a pretty desperate version of a pole—something like Harry Lauder's walking stick for straight, but smooth and strong. At least I could pole the canoe up a riffle with it, or check the canoe when racing down the little rapids of the Crooked River, the stream which flows out of Summit Lake.

That evening we celebrated what we thought was the last night's camp on the island before starting for the Finlay: a bang-up dinner with a plum pudding, smoking hot, at the end of it. That is the first and only time I have eaten a plum pudding in mid-July—the pudding's self being richly garnished with slapped and dead mosquitoes.

Camp consisted of one square tent for Marigold and two little "bug tents" for Alan and myself. All three were firmly set up, sheltered by the bush and strongly guyed to trees. The bug tents were miniature peaked tents with ends and roofs of Egyptian cotton, and with wide eaves,

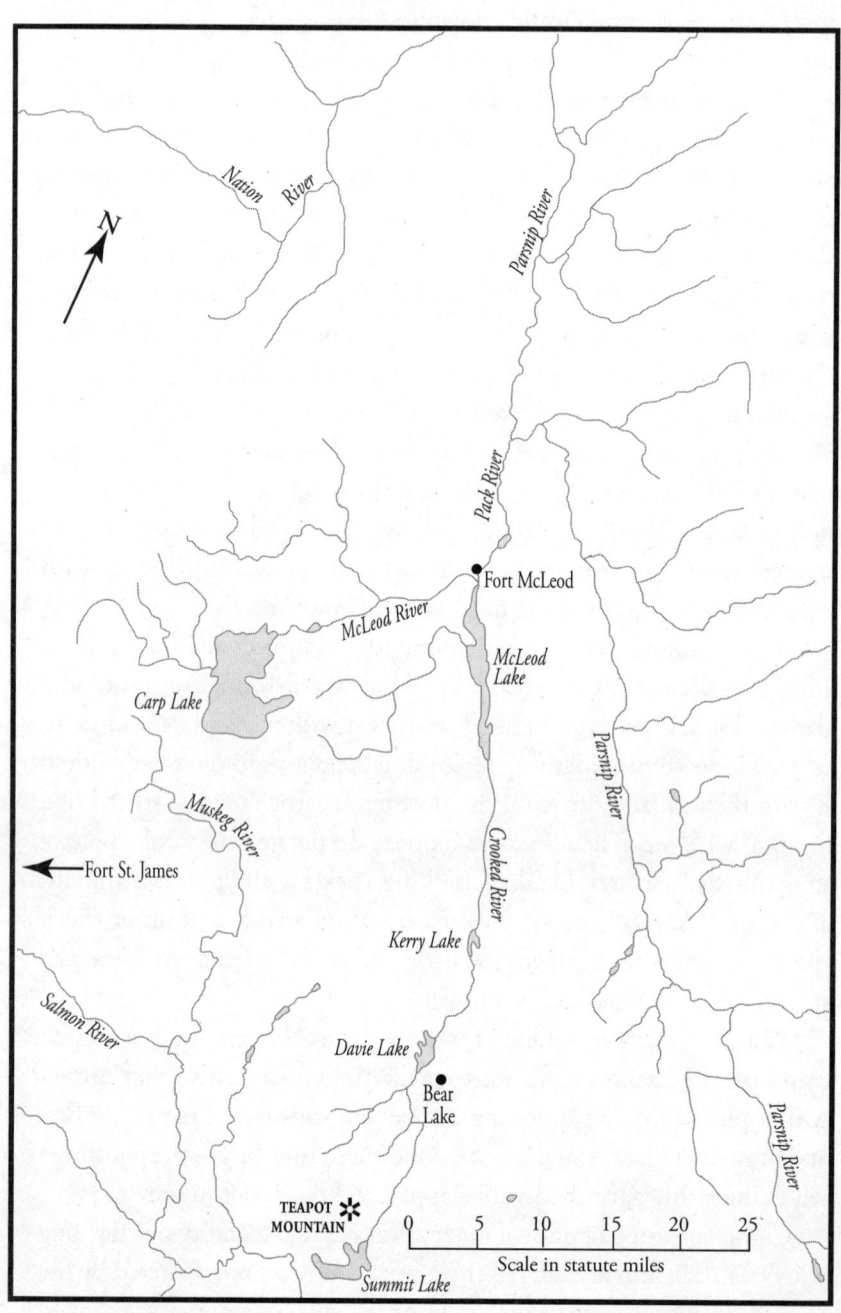

reaching almost to the ground, of the same material. The sides were of mosquito netting, and the tents were rainproof and mosquito-proof, light and compact. The only thing wrong with them was the amount of dew and condensation that the hard, impermeable Egyptian cotton roofs could collect, both inside and out.

Angry clouds had been gathering in the west through the latter part of the afternoon and into the evening. Now, as we were going to bed, they towered thousands of feet into the blue—great masses of cumulus, black, white and purple. Long black clouds were snaking across below and in front of them, slim as serpents and driven, one could see, by a fierce wind. Yet no breath of air was stirring here: the lake was without a ripple, calm as a sheet of glass. The evening deepened and the mosquitoes rose to the occasion, as they never fail to do before a storm. Full of plum pudding and good cheer, the three of us got things snugged down, pulling the canoe up into the willows and tying it there, weighting down the tarpaulins that covered the outfit, putting rocks on any possessions that might take wing and fly with the wind. At last, when all was secure, we hurled ourselves into our tents and eiderdowns, killed the mosquitoes that had come in with us, and fell into the sound sleep of tired bushwhackers.

Some time in the night I was awakened by the roar of the rain on my bug tent and the rush of the wind through the trees. I must have been sleeping like a log, for the storm was already in full blast: the crash of the thunder was like the sound of heavy guns. By the flicker of the lightning I could see the other two tents: they were rigid and straining against the wind but showed no signs of parting. Alan's tent was the closest to the shore of the island, and from that quarter there came a steady roar, as of an angry sea. That was the pounding of the waves on the beaches—and I looked anxiously to see how the canoe was taking it. There it lay, a dark, glistening shape that might have been a stranded whale, securely tied among the wind-flattened willows. Well—we had done what we could, and no man could do more than that. Hoping that the rest of the outfit was still under cover, I turned over, pulled my eiderdown over my head and slept.

The storm continued into the morning and we rose late to a calm and rain-washed world. One thing, we found, had gone wrong: a flap of a tarpaulin had been pulled out by the wind from under its rock, and rain had driven into our personal sacks. Nothing was damaged, but some stuff was wet; soon a variegated assortment of clothing was spread on the willows along the shore, drying in the sun. Then Marigold's tent and various other heavy items had to be carefully dried out before they could be folded up and put in the car. These would not be needed again, for Marigold was leaving us and driving the car with the surplus gear back to the Coast and home to Vancouver Island. She would return around the tenth of September and join me at the McDougalls' trading post at Finlay Forks; and then, together, we would run down the Peace through the Rockies, through the foothills, and beyond to the plains and the town of Peace River in Alberta.

That this was possible was due to the monthly mail service into the Finlay country. This was by plane, and the plane was a *Beaver*, the go-everywhere, do-everything workhorse of the North. The service was based on Prince George and was monthly only in name: in practice it worked out at about eight planes a year, since none could land on the river when it was either freezing up or breaking up; nor could any land with safety during the June flood, when the Finlay was at its game of uprooting forest trees and picking up all the old, stranded spars and roots off the shingle bars, covering its surface with a dangerous assortment of drift. According to the load of mail carried, two or three passengers could come in or go out on these planes; around mid-August Alan would be one of them, leaving from Fort Ware so as to be back at school early in September.

As we worked, drying the outfit, another mass of thunderheads began to bank up in the west. We went at it like beavers: we had to hurry, yet nothing could be left damp or it would go mouldy, packed tightly in the car in the hot country to the south. Finally we got Marigold and her outfit freighted over to the mainland and unloaded on the beach. Then we strolled up towards the house to get the car; and as we rounded a little clump of trees, talking strenuously and all at the same time, according to family custom, we were suddenly stricken dumb. The night's storm had fetched down a tall spruce, a good eighteen inches in diameter near the base, and had dropped it plumb in the centre of the roof of the Texans' large and expensive car—a disaster of the first magnitude, though fortunately the palatial trailer, which stood close by, was unharmed. Viewed as a means of transport, the car was a dead loss: not one of the shattered and twisted doors would open and the general effect was that of a soft and luscious cushion on which somebody has let fall a heavy canoe paddle. The wrecked car bulged at each end—and not without reason.

Our little Chevrolet was standing nearby and a branch from the big tree had bent the front number plate, missing the radiator by inches. Reverently I bent down and straightened the number plate—which, thank God, is no functional part of a car, but merely a government receipt for cash extorted from the owner by intimidation. Then we drove the car down to the landing, packed Marigold and her outfit into it with all possible speed and watched her disappear into the woods, headed south.

There was still work to be done on the island, and now the second storm was fast approaching. There was no hope of getting out of the place before it struck, so we went hard at it and once more got everything packed away and snugged down. Then we pulled up and retied the canoe and I got some sort of a simple supper ready. There was no time even to put up a lean-to; we just bolted our food standing up and with one eye on the weather. As we finished we saw the wind hit the extremity of the western arm of Summit Lake, four miles from our island. It came as an onset of whirlwinds, and one of these, in advance of the rest, came spinning along the full length of the southern shore. The water was still without a ripple around the island and we could see and hear the tall trees crashing down right and left before that wind. In four or five minutes the lake mounted from dead calm into a raging turmoil of white: no canoe could have lived in that or got to shore. Then the wind and the first great drops of rain and the whole uproar of the storm smote the island like a giant hammer. Alan and I, complete with books and fruit, dived for our bug tents and scrambled in. And that was that for fifteen solid hours of wind and deluge ...

The storm passed on to the eastward, and peace and sunshine returned to the camp around ten the next morning. Nothing had suffered any damage. There was a little drying out to do, and Alan's bug tent, which did not have the extra-large eaves, had had spray and rain driven through the mosquito-screen walls by the wind. We hung the tent out in the sun and Alan's eiderdown with it—and made a mental note to pitch that bug tent well in the shelter for the rest of the trip. Then we cleared up camp and experimented with the loading of the canoe till we had it about right for the shallows and the little riffles of the Crooked River. When all was done we paddled over to the landing to take up to the house a forgotten dunnage bag that should have gone with the car, and to say goodbye. And then we swung the canoe's nose into the north and started for the Finlay.

A four-mile paddle brought us to the outlet of Summit Lake at the end of the northern arm. We made an early camp there by a tree-ringed lagoon that lay to the east of a dome-shaped hill known as Teapot Mountain. The shallows were pitted with moose tracks; the lagoon itself was covered with golden water lilies, and through the lily pads ran a clear lane of dark brown water, the trail of the riverboats and the canoes to the beginnings of the Crooked River. We might have gone further on that perfect evening, had the riverboats of the Finlay still been using Summit Lake as a year-round base of supply. But a road was feeling its way northward towards the Parsnip River and the Pine Pass over the Rockies (the Hart Highway of today) and, while Summit Lake had remained till now the main base for launching boats in the spring and for pulling them out in the fall before freeze-up, this summer the river freighters were getting their supplies hauled over the new road to Davie Lake, some twenty river miles further downstream. That meant that few travellers would have been using the upper reaches of the Crooked River—and I was wondering what the recent storms had achieved in the way of blocking the channel. The Crooked, I knew, was nothing but a little trout stream at the start: one good-sized tree could span it, and the way trees had been falling in the last couple of days we might be in for some trouble. Here was a good camp and it would be best not to start downriver in the late afternoon.

In any case we had time to kill. The riverboats that did the freighting on the Finlay were owned by Dick Corless of Prince George. I had arranged with him by letter that we would make our own way by canoe to the trading post of Finlay Forks, a few miles up the Finlay River. There we would be picked up about the end of July by one of his boats and taken, with the canoe and outfit, upstream to Fort Ware, a couple of miles below the mouth of Fox River and about a hundred and fifty river miles upstream from the meeting of the Finlay and the Parsnip. However, our dates had been changed slightly. Dick Corless had later sent word that there would be some delay: part of the freight for Fort Grahame and Fort Ware had been held up, and so his boat would probably not arrive at the McDougalls' trading post before the second of August. Delays, especially on rivers, are a part of the northern scene. The only thing that one can do about them is to fill in the time as pleasantly as possible. We now planned to do exactly that—and we had a couple of weeks to play with.

3

Crooked River

In the morning, in brilliant sunshine, we followed the trail through the water lilies and slipped over the last gravel bar into the little stream that calls itself the Crooked River. Immediately, the current took hold of the canoe; one could feel it quicken. We found ourselves travelling in only a few inches of water: we could look down and see the canoe's shadow very close, flickering over the rounded pebbles of the river bottom as we gathered speed. The canoe was heavily loaded and once in a while we would touch, doing no harm but grating a little on some small rolling stone. The trees leaned out over the winding river and the dense jungle of the willows leaned forward from the low banks. Slipping silently along, we would pass from sunlight to green tree shadow, then back once more into some dazzling pool of light on the edge of which clusters of small blue butterflies would be sunning themselves on the wet sand below the willows. The navigable channel would often be no more than five feet wide: it felt as though we were following some narrow wagon trail that went winding through the bush, twisting and turning as old Indian trails twist and turn. Not for nothing did this trout stream bear the name of Crooked.

In spite of the recent storms the river was low, and it was also going fast downhill, down riffle after riffle. Soon we came to the first of the famous "wagon roads" of the Crooked. These had been made gradually over the many years that the river had been used as a highway into the Finlay country—a bit of work here and a bit of work there by all concerned: fur traders, freighters, miners, surveyors and the few homesteaders who had taken up land near the meeting of the big rivers.

Frogging their riverboats upstream in some droughty summer or in the low water before freeze-up, wading against the swift current, pulling and shoving, these men had rolled the larger boulders out of their way, arranging them in long, even lines on either side of the channel. This effectively marked the way for the stranger—though that was probably the last thing the builders had in mind—and also seemed to concentrate the flow of the river into the long chute so formed. Haworth, in his book *On the Headwaters of Peace River*, likens his passage down one of these wagon roads to rushing down a steep flume—and the description is apt. Careering downhill on the flashing water with a straight, regular line of rocks, obviously man-made, flitting past on either hand is a most exhilarating form of travel, and one that is quite often repeated on this river. Outside the channel, between the boulder line and the banks, the water would be all over the place, often only ankle-deep or less, sparkling in the sun as it flowed over the stones.

Besides rocks and shallows there were other obstacles to travel. The passage, through some hundred and fifty years, of generations of rivermen had been insufficient to convince generations of beaver that it was a waste of time trying to dam this little river. In one place we shot through a recent, man-made breach in a sizable beaver dam that was just wide enough to let a riverboat through. Further down, and again on that first morning, we swept round a bend right onto a newly built dam that stretched clean across the river. The dam was not yet very high, so there was no need to damage it. We selected a good place, stepped out into the water and unloaded one or two heavy pieces. Then we gently slid the lightened canoe at an angle across the dam, taking care to support the keel against any strain. The canoe slipped easily back into the water below the dam; we brought it to shore, reloaded the portaged pieces and went on our way. A large spruce, recently fetched down by the wind and now lying in the water right across the river, was similarly dealt with: I cut a gap in the branches and smoothed with the axe a level place over which to slide the partly laden canoe. Then, to slick it up, we splashed water onto the tree—and the canoe slid easily over as if on greased skids.

Progress was slow, for there were numerous trees across the channel: off some of them I cut the tops so that we could ease the canoe around them; others I cut through in the centre so that they sagged into the water and we were able to float over them; others, again, lay across the river waist-high, and off these I cut the lower branches, making narrow gaps beneath the heavy tree trunks through which we could slip in the canoe. The usual afternoon thunderstorm broke over us and down came the rain in torrents, but we went on, soaked and somewhat bothered by mosquitoes. At last the river widened, and we came to a series of calm reaches where, again, the golden water lilies grew and the late afternoon sunshine winked at us off the flat green lily pads as the ripples passed over them. In this slack water families of ducks scuttered downstream ahead of the canoe or hid under the willows till we passed, waiting to make their way back to their own feeding grounds.

Finding a good campground was the problem in this part of the world: the jungle on the banks made it impossible to land. A gap in the greenery suddenly appeared; it was on a quiet stretch of the river that was narrow and swift-flowing and under big dark trees. We shot past it, both exclaiming, "There's a place! That's us for the night!" I grabbed the pole and stopped the canoe, then poled back upstream again. We landed—and there was an old campground, unused for the last year or two. The underbrush had all been cleared away and the whole area lay under a soft carpet of spruce needles. In the centre of the cleared space there stood, as so often in old campsites, a vast, ancient spruce with a spreading tangle of branches through which not a drop of rain could penetrate. The lower branches of these old trees have a drooping habit of growth and are very dense. Even the heaviest rains are thrown away from the centre to the outside, whence the water drips on to the ground. We used to call spruce of this kind "umbrella trees." This was perfect—and soon a fire was going with the tea pail singing over it and the two sodden voyageurs steaming beside it. Soon the inevitable hummingbird appeared; there always seemed to be one hummingbird around these early camps and it was not till we were well down the Parsnip River that two came to visit us.

Over long stretches of river these cleared campsites were the only places at which one could land with any ease. We were later told that they used to be more numerous and much closer together. That was in the days when river travel was by means of pole or paddle, trackline or frogging, and when men had to be content with much shorter distances

Alan demonstrates how to wash hair camp-style.

as a day's journey. Later, as road construction reached out to Summit Lake, and Giscome Portage from the Fraser fell into disuse, gas and oil became more readily available and the outboard and the inboard arrived on the headwaters of the Peace. With them, longer distances could be covered in the day, and consequently certain of the campsites ceased to be used. Soon the bush crept in again. Soon those less convenient camps vanished behind the screen of the willows, leaving in use only the better ones and those that were well sited for the longer day's travel.

One way and another we managed to take twelve days running down from Summit Lake to the meeting of the rivers and the birthplace of the Peace—a nice bit of timing and one that left us (we thought) with two days in hand to pole up the few miles of the Finlay to the trading post and visit with the McDougalls. The distance as the crow flies is a hundred and ten miles; though, as an Arctic grayling would swim it, heaven knows just what it might be—probably not far short of a hundred and fifty. Looking in my old trip diary to find out what we did with the time, I see that a lot of it went in fishing. Alan did the fishing; I acted as gillie, held the canoe where it was needed and netted the fish. Haworth waxes ecstatic about the fishing in the Crooked River and we certainly had no complaints to make. It was most exciting: in that clear water one could plainly see the fish, deep down, moving slowly over sand or gravel. Down to them would come a spinner (Haworth recommends one of medium size with a few orange beads on it) or a fly with a shot or two on the lead. Up would come a fish to investigate. A couple of times, perhaps, he would flick away from the lure; then his mind would be suddenly made up and you could see him go for it, all out. Flash and swirl—and he would be on and the little reel running out and the top joints of the steel rod bending. The fish that we got were, in order of preference, rainbow trout, Arctic grayling and Dolly Vardens. There was no ritual about this sort of fishing and little science. Indeed, not much science was needed: on the Pack River, about three miles below McLeod Lake, Alan caught a beautiful rainbow and then a good Dolly. Then he caught a small Dolly and, as we didn't have much use in this sort of water for small fish, we carefully returned it to its native element. Undaunted, it came again—and again we put it back. But there was no saving that fish: in under two minutes it was in the canoe for the third time and as it seemed to want to be with us all that badly, we kept it. The same thing happened with another small Dolly that very same day—except that we caught it only twice, and then decided twice was enough.

Along this waterway, as far as Fort McLeod, there is no definite western wall to the Rocky Mountain Trench: here the Trench is breached and opens into the Interior Plateau through a scattering of hills, the highest of them not more than a thousand feet above the Crooked River. Through these hills the river system threads its way towards the Parsnip, passing through five lakes, the largest of which, McLeod Lake, is twelve miles long. From Summit Lake on the Plateau to the meeting with the Parsnip is about sixty miles as the crow flies and the general direction is fifteen degrees west of north. Between McLeod Lake and the Parsnip the name of the little river changes: it is known as Pack River. At its mouth it is picked up by the much larger Parsnip and the combined waters flow on together to meet the Finlay, northwestward and in the Trench, which is, below McLeod Lake, once more contained by a western wall.

With all these lakes and the small rapids and the long stretches of slack water there was plenty of variety in our trip downstream. Twice we camped on islands, on one in Kerry Lake and one in McLeod Lake—and always through the lakes we kept a wary eye on the weather. The sudden fury of those two storms on Summit Lake had been a revelation to me. Now, in the afternoons, we would anxiously watch the blue-shadowed masses of cumulus rising in the north and west, shining white where the sun's rays caught them, silver-rimmed against the summer sky. Towards evening the daily deluge would descend on us, but never again did the wind strike as it had done back on the Continental Divide. We made our islands safely—and got off them eventually, late and after storms of rain, thunder and lightning that continued far into the morning.

It was shortly before we got to Kerry Lake that we met the Texans coming back upstream. They were in one of Corless' long, open, red-painted riverboats, and they had been down the Peace into the Rockies to camp and fish in the canyon of the Clearwater, a notable fishing place. Bill van Somer and Bob Henderson were in charge of that expedition—and since none of them knew what had happened up at Summit Lake and we had no wish to spoil the strangers' trip by telling them that their car had been squelched by a falling spruce, we just pulled in to the bank and gave them the river.

The two guides waved to us as they roared by. The Texans (we never knew their names) made no sign. They were sitting amidships, hunched up and motionless, and they were wadded up with enough heavy clothing for late October. We on the other hand, were paddling our canoe and putting all the beef we could behind it. What we wanted to do was to get to Kerry Lake and get camp made and a pan of trout into us before the evening rain came down. We were clad in open shirts and we were hot. This, quite unreasonably, gave us a feeling of superiority and we eyed the dudes with contempt. This was both illogical and wrong of us: we should have looked on them with compassion. After all, they were strangers, away north of their home range and strayed into a province so vast that you could drop Texas into it and still have room left for Wyoming.

4

Warburton Pike

A day or two later we were away down the Parsnip, and, just as Haworth did, we made our noonday fire near the mouth of the Nation River, a tributary that enters from the west. Opposite the mouth of the Nation and on the right bank of the Parsnip there is a high cutbank, a sand-and-gravel cliff honeycombed in its softer strata with the holes of sand martins and kingfishers. A little below the mouth of Pack River, and also on the right bank of the Parsnip, we had passed a similar high gravel cutbank—and around these two cutbanks there has gathered a tale.

It was more than just a tale; it was very nearly a tragedy. On December 8, 1890, that restless wanderer, Warburton Pike, hit the Nation River some distance up from its mouth and turned upstream with his party of four, being under the impression that he was turning up McLeod's River, the old-time name for the Pack River of the present day ... This was the end of a long road for Pike—a well-educated Englishman, and one possessed of a devil in the form of a passion for travelling in the more inaccessible and uncharted regions of the North. On this particular trip he had left the railroad at Calgary in June 1889, driving north in a buckboard to Edmonton, and from there in a wagon to Athabasca Landing, the point of departure for the river steamers that ran downstream to Fort Chipewyan, Great Slave Lake and the Mackenzie.

The following sixteen or seventeen months Pike had spent making two trips, fall and spring, into the Barren Lands, celebrating the intervening Christmas at Fort Resolution on Great Slave Lake. He had seen, and killed for food, animals that were new to him: the wood

After a halt by the Parsnip, Alan is ready to resume paddling.

buffalo, the Barren Land caribou—even the muskox. But—and this was of even greater importance to a man of his stamp—he had travelled far and had rarely slept twice in one place. He had penetrated, by canoe and on foot, into the wide-open country beyond the limit of trees: he had seen the Great Fish River and camped by the upper reaches of the Coppermine. In spite of hardships and privations, and the burden of coping with blockheaded and untrustworthy half-breeds, Pike had put in a wonderful year. A wonderful year, that is, from the point of view of the born wanderer. For the safe man, the man whose ideal is a safe job with a pension at the end of it, it would have been a year's absolute hell.

And now, at the end of 1890, Pike was on his way out. Together with two Indians and a Hebridean engaged servant of the Hudson's Bay Company, Murdo McKay, he had come up the Slave River from Fort Resolution to Fort Chipewyan on Lake Athabasca. "By this time," he writes, "it was well on in September and eight hundred miles had to be travelled to reach the Rocky Mountains, and when these were sighted there were still three hundred miles to McLeod's Lake, the farthest point I could reasonably hope to reach by open water." Quite plainly there was no time to lose, and so the party began the ascent of the Peace.

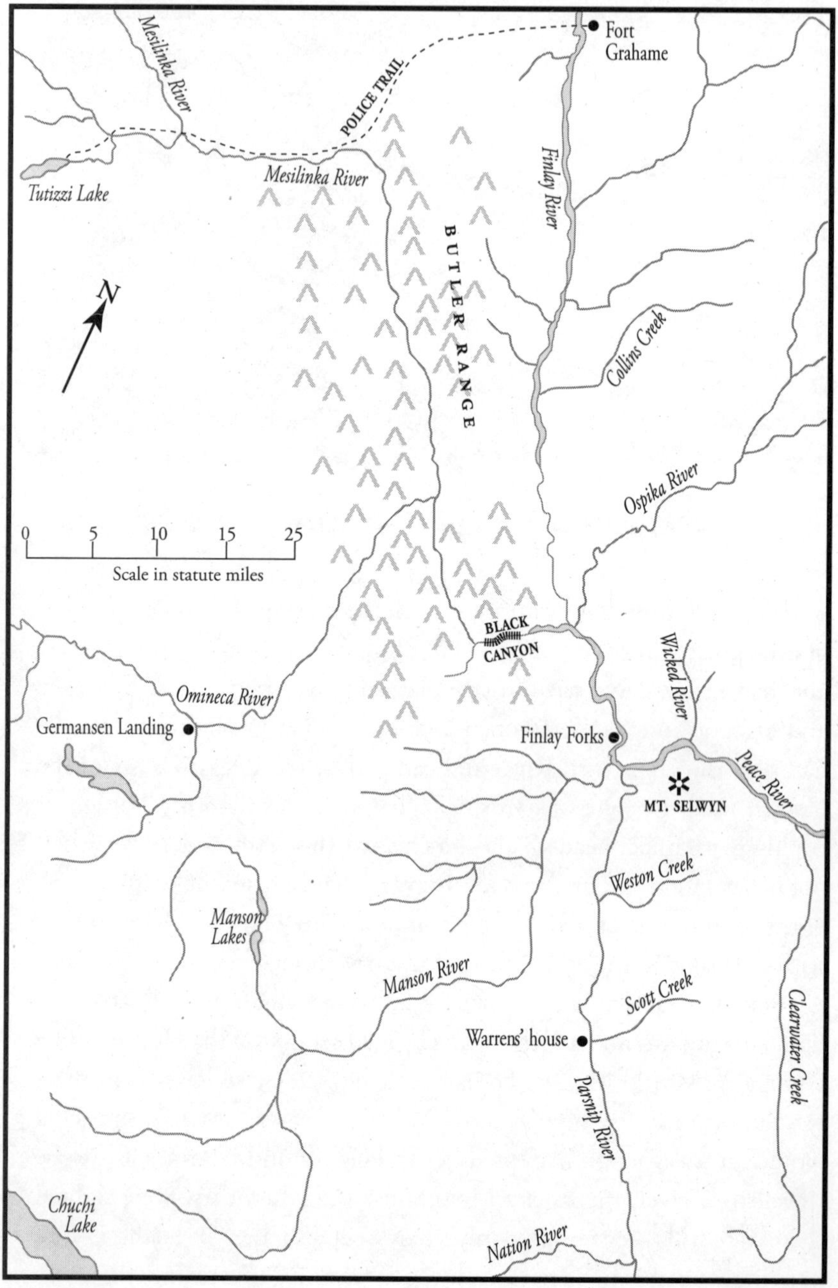
Fort Grahame
Mesilinka River
POLICE TRAIL
Tutizzi Lake
Mesilinka River
Finlay River
BUTLER RANGE
N
Collins Creek
Ospika River
0 5 10 15 25
Scale in statute miles
BLACK CANYON
Wicked River
Omineca River
Germansen Landing
Finlay Forks
Peace River
MT. SELWYN
Weston Creek
Manson Lakes
Manson River
Scott Creek
Warrens' house
Clearwater Creek
Parsnip River
Chuchi Lake
Nation River

After eleven days of steady tracking and poling they came to Fort Vermilion. There the two Indians left Pike, departing downstream again to their homes, taking with them the canoe as previously arranged. The only craft now available was a heavy skiff, too large for Pike and Murdo to handle without help. This is an important point, since it was owing to the unwieldiness of this skiff that Pike took a third man into his party—a strong, well-built Englishman, but one who proved to be so lazy and so utterly useless on a river that Pike will not even mention him by his surname in his book, referring to him simply as "John." The only pleasure that Pike and Murdo got from their new companion (of whom they could not rid themselves, since he was so well known that no fort en route would undertake to harbour him for the winter) was when they first sighted the Rockies and John, "in his admiration for the scenery, slipped off a narrow ledge of shale along which he was tracking and fell with an oath into the river. The snowy peaks were forgotten in the joy that greets other people's misfortunes in this sort of travelling."

The weather on that trip up the Peace, except for one day's snow, was perfect, and Pike arrived at Hudson's Hope at the east end of the Rocky Mountain Portage on October 27 with a warm chinook wind blowing out of the southwest, soft as a summer breeze. At "the Hope" he was compelled to waste eight days of good travelling weather, waiting for the independent trader[1] who was on his way in with the winter outfit of goods for the little trading post at the head of the portage.

Eventually the trader appeared: it was the man whose name was to become a legend in the Peace River country—Twelve-Foot Davis. When I first heard this name, back in the early twenties at some stopping place on the Fort Vermilion trail, I naturally concluded—as many another had done before me—that its owner had been a giant. And, like many another, I was mistaken. Davis was exceptionally strong, but he was no giant: he was a short, stocky man—the ideal build for a packer—and it was nothing for him to pack a two-hundred-pound load over a long portage. He had come by a long, roundabout road to the Peace: from his native Vermont to the California diggings, and from there, like others of the forty-niners, to the Cariboo and Omineca goldfields. It was on one of the rich Cariboo Creeks that he acquired his nickname: an official survey revealed the existence of a twelve-foot fraction between discovery and the adjoining, equally rich, claim; and F. H. Davis was the man alert enough to stake the fraction and get in first to the mining recorder's office to file. From this small patch of ground he took $12,000 and his lifelong title to fame.

From gold mining Davis drifted into fur trading in independent opposition to the Bay, and now, in this November of 1890—himself being at the age of seventy—he was headed down the Peace, outfitting his string of posts along that river for the winter's trade. The first of these posts was the one at the head of the portage, on the big, eddying pool just before the Peace narrows and dives between the rocks into the canyon. A White man, Thomas Barrow, was to be left in charge there while Davis bustled the balance of the outfit over the portage and went on downstream.

Davis' trade goods had come from Quesnel in British Columbia by way of Summit Lake, the Crooked River and the Parsnip. As soon as he had got his stuff over the twelve-mile portage trail he would be able to dispense with two men: Charlie, a half-breed from Quesnel, and Pat, a Sikanni from Fraser Lake. These two would be free to hit the trail for home as soon as the job was over—and thus it was here that they joined Pike's party, as guides. A long, narrow canoe, a cottonwood dugout, was now available at the head of the portage; and Pike was all set to go when suddenly, and as often happens after an excessively warm chinook, the climate reversed itself and winter struck. They woke on November 6 to find snow driving down and ice forming in the river.

That seemed to settle it. Baptiste Testerwich, an Iroquois half-breed hunter with whom Pike had struck up a friendship, told him it would be madness to proceed at this season by canoe. The best thing he could do now would be to camp and wait for the Peace to freeze—in the meantime hunting and making sleds of birch on which he and his party could haul their outfits over the ice.

So they camped and hunted—but they could come across no big game, though they managed to live well enough on rabbits and bush partridges. And they searched for birch with the proper curves to it, and they built their sleds.

But the days went by and the river did not freeze—and then a chinook with all the warmth of Indian summer in it came roaring down out of the mountains, licking up the snow and taking out even the little ice that lingered in the eddies. This was too much for Pike: his demon took possession of him and on November 25 he decided to start on the morrow by canoe and damn the consequences. Pat and Charlie swore they could recognize the little river that led up to McLeod's Lake Fort, and Pike figured that if the weather would just let them get through the main range of the Rockies by canoe, and so to the meeting of the Parsnip and the Finlay—then, even if winter caught them and the Parsnip froze, they could still make the fort on foot in about four days. It sounds like a mad action, starting out in late November by canoe, but chinooks have been known to hold through most of the winter: there was a chance that this one might give them the needed days.

It did not. They started on the twenty-sixth and the tracking was perfect, both on that day and the next. Then, on the second night, the chinook died away: a heavy snowstorm came in on the east wind, and it froze hard. And still they slipped and staggered forward, water freezing on the paddles and the trackline heavy with ice and frozen, forcing their way against the running ice in the heart of the Rockies. "Our moccasins," Pike writes, "from constant wading turned into heavy lumps of ice." How they managed to travel upstream at all under these conditions, slipping and falling on rocks coated with ice and frozen snow, baffles the imagination.

At midnight on the sixth day, and after a desperately dangerous day's travel, they made camp above the Finlay Rapids and in the Trench. The Rockies lay behind them and they hoped that the Parsnip, flowing from the south, would give them open water. But in the small hours the sounds of the running ice ceased, and daylight showed them both the Finlay and the Parsnip jammed with piled-up ice and silent. Winter had shut down on the land and the rivers were closed to them.

Near the meeting of the rivers they built a cache. Into it they piled everything they could do without, including Pike's shotgun, for which he had only twelve cartridges left. They left thirty pounds of flour there also, starting out with each man "carrying his blanket and a small load of provisions, kettles and necessaries." They took all their beans and rice. The going was slow, and owing to the piled-up confusion of the ice they found they had to get away from the river and travel high up on the benches, forcing their way through the thick bush and the deepening snow. Pat and Charlie, the two guides, laughed at the idea of getting lost: all that was needed, they said, was to get across the Parsnip and follow it up on the west side till they reached McLeod's River. Then, from its mouth, a fifteen-mile journey would bring them to McLeod's Lake Fort, and to food and men and the trail south towards Quesnel. So they made a risky crossing of the Parsnip on a jam, wondering as they did so whether the ice bridge over the deepest water would not give way beneath them. By the grace of God, it held.

They found better going away back from the river on the ridges—and five days went by as they slowly plugged ahead. They could not fail to be near McLeod's River now, they thought. Their beans and rice were finished and they made up the last of the bread. Then they began to abandon their cooking pots and even their blankets, sure that the fort was within their grasp. Pike sent Murdo and Charlie ahead without loads while he and Pat came on slowly, staying behind with John, who was clumsy and awkward and already losing heart. Soon John abandoned his pack, leaving it hanging on a tree—and, shortly after that, the three of them saw, far below, a tributary stream flowing towards the Parsnip from the west, "a stream that Pat instantly declared to be McLeod's River." They got down to it, found the advance party's tracks and followed them upstream till darkness fell, when they made camp. It was a cheerless camp, especially for Pike, who stayed awake by the fire all night while John was comfortably rolled up in a blanket that Pike had carried all through the day. There was nothing to eat—but they were not too worried about that, for they were sure of a good breakfast when they reached the fort in the morning.

In the first grey light they started up this new river—which seemed to Pike to have a remarkably fast current for a much-used waterway of the fur trade, one up which scows were regularly tracked. Towards noon they saw ahead of them "a thin blue column of smoke rising from a cabin in the woods; a cheering sight." But soon they could see from the tracks that something was very wrong: Murdo and Charlie had been further up the river, and then had returned. They found the two men in the cabin: they had been upstream as far as a strong rapid, which even the self-styled "guide," Charlie, knew for certain did not exist on McLeod's River. Now Murdo broke the dread news to Pike: "Charlie says it is the wrong river; we are lost, like damned fools."

They were now in a terrible fix. Pat and Charlie were obviously useless as guides: neither of them could remember ever seeing or hearing of this strange river—which was the Nation. As for John, he later admitted to Pike that he had been very drunk when he left McLeod's Lake some years back: he could remember nothing. Pike himself went on upriver to make certain that there really was a rapid barring the way that would be impassable for scows. Then he returned to the cabin, his mind made up to beat a retreat downstream. Perhaps, he thought, they had passed the mouth of McLeod's River when they were travelling through the bush on the east side of the Parsnip; and in any case they could not go on with no food, merely *hoping* that McLeod's River lay ahead. Whereas, by going downstream, if they failed to find their river they would at least be nearer to the Forks and the thirty pounds of flour in the cache ... They camped in the cabin that night. They still had tobacco and they gathered Labrador tea in the bush. As the main course they boiled and ate some strips cut off the moosehide they had brought with them for mending moccasins.

It was the tenth of December when they left the cabin and headed down the nameless river towards the Parsnip. At the mouth they were confronted with the great yellow cutbank, a notable landmark on any river; but Pat and Charlie "both put on a hopeless, blank expression and said they had never seen it before in their lives." This confirmed Pike in his idea that McLeod's River had to be somewhere downstream from where they were. Actually, some forty miles travel *upstream* would have brought them to McLeod's Lake Fort. But, instead, they were starting on a march of about one hundred and fifty miles.

A dreadful journey ensued. They were forced high up above the Parsnip in ever deepening snow and, that night, the bottom burnt out of their one and only lard pail—so they "had to give up the small comfort of moose-skin and wild tea" and just crouched empty over their fire. On the following night they reached the camp where they had abandoned some of the blankets and the cooking pots—but still there was only the moosehide and the Labrador tea. A whole desperate week passed before they reached the cache at the head of the Finlay Rapids, and the only real food they had had in all that time had been the scrapings off a flour sack that they had thrown away at their "Sikanni coffin camp" on the way up—a place where a dead Indian had been wrapped, according to custom, in birchbark and slung high up, between two trees. They scraped off about half a pound of flour and, by good fortune, pounced on a mouse that must have decided to winter on the abandoned sack. In no time at all it was killed, singed and flung whole into the pot with the flour—an appetizing gruel, the best thing they had tasted for days.

It was on the evening of December 17 that they came anxiously to the cache, wondering if any wolverine had got at it, knowing that, if it had, they were finished. But the cache was intact and they ate cautiously of the flour ... Ahead of them lay the great gap by which the Peace enters the Rockies. The winds and the drifting of the snow there are terrific, and these people were travelling without snowshoes, in clothes that were now rags, and in worn-out moccasins. Their only axe had been carelessly left overnight in the embers; it was now almost useless and firewood had to be gathered by hand by weakened men. John took good care to lag well behind, never taking his turn at breaking trail, never coming into camp till the fire was blazing and the wood stacked. It was in this poor shape that they went on—down the big river into the high mountains, breaking trail step by step in the cross-drifted, crusted snow. So bad was the going that *in two days' travel* from the cache they reached only the foot of the Finlay Rapids—a distance that a canoe can make in seven or eight exciting minutes. They were always cold now, and only Pike and Murdo were still able to hold and strike the matches to light their many fires.

A blizzard swept through the pass, straight in their faces, and a day went by when they just sat by the fire, unable to face the storm. More blizzards came, and again they lost a day—but gradually the going improved as they came out of the mountains to the eastward. But by then Murdo was going a bit off his head with hunger and weakness: he had always disliked John; now he "developed a passionate hatred to Charlie and Pat" who, at one camp, had stayed behind on some pretext and had eaten, at one sitting, four pounds of the communal flour that had been entrusted to them. This, in these desperate straits, was the unpardonable crime. It was the equivalent of murder in normal life, and

Pike, while he was boiling up the evening gruel, considered shooting the pair of them. However, there was still about seven pounds of flour left, and in the end he figured they might all just make it on reduced rations. Nevertheless, his unspoken thoughts were already running on: it was now coming to the point where, if a man dropped and could not get up, his life might have to be taken so that his companions might live.

They did not come to that, though now "a mutual distrust was prevalent; hatred and the wolfish madness of hunger ruled the camp; and to this day I cannot understand how it was that the fatal spark was never struck, and no tragedy of murder and cannibalism enacted on the banks of that ice-bound river." That was written of Christmas Eve; and on Christmas Day, Pike shot a grouse, the only one they had seen since leaving the cache. That justified having carried the gun all that way, for it may have been that one small bird that provided the last spark of life that drove them on ... The end came on December 27. In the moonlight they crawled up the steep bank to Twelve-Foot Davis' trading post at the head of the canyon of the Peace. With the last of his strength Pike pushed open the door—to see an expression of horror come over the faces of those within as they slowly recognized the ragged, blackened skeletons that tottered painfully over the threshold ...

Gradually, under Barrow's careful nursing, their strength came back to them. Pat, the Sikanni, stayed on with Barrow through that winter. The rest of them slowly dispersed, Pike leaving at the end of January for Lesser Slave Lake, and arriving at Calgary in the middle of March, 1891. Before he left the trading post, on a day when he and Pat were out after grouse together and setting rabbit snares, Pat told him the story of the stolen flour. It seemed that Charlie (who had a most scoundrelly record) had talked Pat into it, telling him that the flour they were carrying would be kept solely for the benefit of the three White men; if they wanted to live they had better help themselves while they had the chance. Pike was inclined to believe this story as Pat had, in various ways, behaved very well under stress "and had always done more than his share of work in making camp and breaking the trail."

That is Pike's story of his ill-equipped, ill-starred venture through the Peace River Gap by canoe in mid-winter. Seventy-five years have passed since those five men set out for McLeod's Lake Fort—time enough for the tale to become a legend and for the legend to gather to itself a few accretions. So much so that it has now come to be accepted, on the headwaters of the Peace, that Pike's guides had been misled by the resemblance between the high gravel cliff opposite the mouth of the Nation and the very similar high gravel cliff near the mouth of the Pack—or McLeod's River. Mistaking the one for the other they turned up the Nation, only to find themselves lost.

This story did not take long to become established. Haworth heard it in 1916, probably from Joe Lavoie, and he sets it forth most circumstantially in his book. It has been told to me several times. Yet a careful reading of Pike's book shows that there is not a word of truth in it. Pike's people never saw the big cutbank till they came back *down* the Nation—and then Pat and Charlie stared at it blankly and said they had never set eyes on it before.

Who starts these tales? And why do people never question them? Pike's party could not have known about the two cutbanks without knowing that one of them marked the entrance to a second river, the Nation, which flowed into the Parsnip well below McLeod's River. With that knowledge, and on finding themselves up the wrong river, they would have realized they were up the Nation and would have acted accordingly: they would have travelled on up the Parsnip, knowing that McLeod's River lay upstream. Four or five days' travel and starvation instead of that desperate seventeen.

The whole disastrous venture was the result of poor staff work on Pike's part—since, surely, anybody at Hudson's Hope could have told him that the Nation River existed and would have to be avoided. But even more does it demonstrate the will to survive, the force that drives men on to achieve the impossible. On nothing, and with nothing but sheer willpower, Pike, Murdo and Pat lifted themselves and two useless bodies over those ghastly miles and through the dead cold of that December. In spite of every setback, *they went on.* And those three simple words could well stand as the motto of that great company of men, that tattered buckskin-and-mackinaw army—the explorers, adventurers and traders of the old Northwest.

5

Ignatieff

Alan and I threw the embers of the noonday fire into the river and packed the lunch things into the canoe. Then we slipped away downstream past the high cutbank, now warmed by sun and alive with bank swallows, at which Pat and Charlie had gazed so hopelessly in the December snows of 1890. Fifteen sunlit miles went by—and then the afternoon thunderstorm came at us out of the northwest and we could see the grey, trailing curtain of the rain sweeping over the forest, blotting out the mountains. On these occasions one gets less wet standing on shore than one does sitting in a canoe; so we landed, put on our slickers and climbed up the low bank. We found ourselves on a level, fertile flat that was almost bare of trees but covered, in places, with an almost tropical growth of the giant cow parsnip from which the river gets its name. The stuff grew up to seven feet in height and was topped by its spreading umbels of white flowers. The din of the rain on the huge leaves was like the rush of a tremendous wind.

The afternoon cleared into a perfect evening with every rain-washed leaf glittering in the sun. Five more miles went by and then the river swung straight into the west in a two-mile reach. Away down at the next bend something peculiar was showing against the dark trees: it just caught the sun and it looked like the sharp-peaked roof of a house built for a deep-snow country. But we knew of no house in these parts: it must be, we thought, a couple of storm-blasted trees, half-fallen and lodged together. Yet, as we drew nearer, a house was what it proved to be—a neatly built house painted a dull red with white trim, and having a green, steeply pitched roof. Boats were tied up at the landing, and close by the house and reaching out over the river there stood a derrick—a heavy beam and block-and-tackle swinging from a tall, strong upright of spruce. People were coming down to the landing to welcome us.

The house was occupied by the Warren family; and two other men, George New and Len Melcher, had put in there on their way upstream shortly before we came. We were immediately asked to stay, and that raised the number for supper by a further two. We slept that night on the floor in the screened-in veranda, very comfortable and protected against the rain and the mosquitoes.

The trapline, of which the house was the headquarters, was now held by the Warren brothers. It had formerly belonged to a man by the name of Scott who had once been a cowpuncher in Routt County, Colorado, and whose memory is kept alive by Scott Creek which flows down from the Rockies to enter the Parsnip just below the bend. Scott had come to the Parsnip in 1912 and was the builder of the house. Opinion was divided as to whether or not he had found it advisable to get out of Colorado in a hurry. I asked what the derrick was for— and I was told that in 1926 Scott had decided to build himself a real boat, a boat that would take him down to the Arctic, to the mouth of the Mackenzie, where he would sell her and then work his way back upstream. So he set to and built the boat in Prince George. And he got her hauled over the Divide to Summit Lake, and somehow took her down the little rivers and home to Scott Creek. But there were several things wrong with the design of that boat, the main fault being that she was built with a deep keel, as for the sea or for a fully navigable river or canal—useless on a shallow headwater stream except at high water. And not of much use then, for her lines were not right and she was hard to handle. Perhaps she was just naturally a sort of nautical bronc—a cowpuncher's boat.

Somebody told me that Scott did once take her down to the Forks, but Dick Corless, who should know all that took place on that waterway, says no, Scott never ventured down that far with her. It was Scott who built the derrick; and in the fall he used it to lift the boat onto the bank by the house, out of reach of the river ice. Unfortunately, in that operation her back was broken, and there on the bank she remained for good, painted and cared for, upside down on skids in the open at first, then under cover. The inboard engine, a Universal, was taken out and mounted in the workshop where it, too, was cared for and its oil changed regularly, and where eventually it generated the electricity for the place. One can picture Scott tending that engine—fancying, probably, in the clatter of machinery and the whiff of the exhaust, that he was running downstream on the lower Mackenzie, headed for Herschel Island and the Beaufort Sea. End of a cowpuncher's dream.

About twelve miles below Scott Creek another stream comes down out of the Rockies—Weston Creek. This commemorates Scott's nearest neighbour, Weston, also a trapper; and, when traplines are in dispute, a mere twelve miles, in a country as big and as lonely as this section of the Trench used to be, can easily amount to overcrowding. All men who live much alone are apt to be set in their ways and resentful of what they consider to be interference. That was true of both these men—and Scott was a peculiar character in his own right: apparently it was impossible to tell whether one would meet with a welcome at his house or be coldly requested to keep on travelling. High up in the gable of his house there was a small loophole from which he could see far up the river with a glass. Who was it, people wondered, who he thought might be coming from the south? Somebody whom he feared? Somebody who was on his trail?

Scott and Weston had quarrelled over trapping rights and fur—and finally, so the story runs, Weston set out to settle the matter once and for all. He left a note in his cabin: "I am going up to see Scott. If I don't come back you will know where to look for me."

Weston never came back—and the British Columbia Provincial Police looked for him, as he had suggested, but no trace of him was ever found. It was freely alleged that Scott had shot him and shoved him under the ice, but, though things looked black for Scott, there was never any proof of that: men travelling up a river on snowshoes can quite easily break through a snow bridge and vanish into the icy waters without any outside assistance. Scott's weapons were impounded for a year or so by the police—but then they were returned to him, for a man cannot live indefinitely in the wilderness without firearms and no good reason could be given for withholding them. And there the matter rests: only the Parsnip River knows what happened and it has kept the secret ...

In the morning Alan and I walked with Milton Warren up a steep trail that led back from the house to the summit of a little butte that rises to a height of fifteen hundred feet above the river. Clouds and a weather haze were already creeping in from the west, but we were in plenty of time to get a splendid view up and down the Trench. We could see the Rockies all the way from near McLeod Lake to Fort Grahame, and we could see the break in the mountains where the Peace River escapes through the Gap. Away to the north, towards the Gap, one small butte, much like the one we were standing on, broke the level plain of the great valley. To the northwest a small stretch of horizon, dead level and with no mountains visible, showed where the floor of the Trench faded over the curve of the earth; and then, west of that again and running northward from the Omineca River, there rose the blue, foreshortened outline of the Butler Range—named for Captain W. F. Butler, who narrowly escaped disaster there in the Black Canyon of the Omineca. Southwestward from the Butler Range we could see the low trough of the Mesilinka River (in English, the Stranger River)—and then, to the left again and running out of sight from the southeast far into the northwest, came the western wall of the Trench, at this point going by the name of the Wolverine Mountains. Patches of snow still streaked those rocky summits, and the nearest of the peaks lay only fifteen miles back from this bend of the Parsnip River at Scott Creek. Truly this butte was so well sited for the fire warden's lookout that the Forest Service proposed to establish there.

Black clouds hid the sun before we started on the downward trail: soon the rain was falling and it was with ease that we were persuaded to stay a second night with the Warrens. But there followed a perfect morning—a real traveller's day, and soon after breakfast we were once more running down the Parsnip.

We made camp towards evening a mile or so below the big horseshoe bend and about two miles above the meeting of the rivers. A long, open, flat-bottomed skiff had passed us a little before camping time. Long before it caught up with us we could see a man in it, standing up, running the engine and steering. Then, as it drew near, we could see that there was a woman in the boat—and also a couple of young men, variously draped over the load. This proved to be Nicholas Ignatieff, then Warden of Hart House, University of Toronto, with his wife and with two of his former pupils from eastern Canada ...

The germ of Ignatieff's project had been a chance meeting back in the thirties. On one of his speaking tours for the Canadian Clubs, he had been told, by Judge Wilson of Vancouver, about the waterways of the British Columbia Interior and about the skill of Dick Corless as a riverman. He stored this information away in his memory. Then, for four years, he taught Canadian history, a subject in which he took a passionate interest, at Upper Canada College—and for three of those summers he took a number of boys on tours into the West, "to show them that Canada was something more than just Bay Street, Toronto." Horse trips in the Rockies helped to drive that point home—and it was when that was over and done with that Ignatieff recalled the stories he had heard about Dick Corless and the rivers of the Trench.

Over the years Dick built several riverboats for him—and in them Ignatieff discovered for himself the wide-open landscapes of the great intermontane valley around the meeting of the rivers. It fascinated him,

Famed riverboat builder Dick Corless is seen here in the stern of one of his vessels on the Parsnip River.

that big, sunlit country between the Rockies and the Wolverines, and he came to see a tremendous future for it.

One of Ignatieff's guides on those early trips into the Finlay country was Slim Cowart. Slim and his partner ran a trapline based on the Wicked River, a thirty-mile torrent which flows into the Peace from the north about ten river miles down from the Forks. They had acquired title to the homestead at the mouth of the Wicked, close under Mount Selwyn, which towers from the opposite shore. I see that I have called it a homestead. Officially, in the books of the Land Registry, it is a pre-emption. Actually, both words are meaningless. This place where the great river enters the high mountains has a magic to it: the mind is caught and held by it, and the weight of the countless ages during which the Peace cut down the Rockies as they rose in its path can almost be felt here as a tangible thing. Camp here, as I have done, beneath the stars and the slender sickle of the young moon, and you will know the full meaning of the words, "all majesty, might, dominion and power." It was a place, you would have thought, where nothing could ever change—a firm oasis in the shifting desert of time. And how wrong you would have been ...

As soon as Ignatieff set eyes on this spot the spell was on him and he knew that, for him, no other site in the whole wide Northwest could ever mean a thing. It was the only holding of land in the Gap of the Peace, and there was something about the place that satisfied him, both from the wild beauty of its setting and also, as the years went by, as a place for the experiments he wished to make. Some day, he thought, Slim Cowart might come to sell that homestead—and he asked him for the first refusal of it.

Through the six war years, in Intelligence at the War Office in London as head of the Russian and Scandinavian section, Colonel Ignatieff kept his vision of the Peace River Gap and the brawling torrent of the Wicked. Then, as soon as he could get out west again, which was in 1949, he bought the homestead from Slim Cowart. "He felt," Mrs. Ignatieff writes, "that it was one of the most beautiful places in the world."

A dreamer, you will be saying ... Yes, but a practical dreamer, one of that select band of men who transmute their dreams into action—

men who have occasionally changed the course of history or altered the face of the earth. A London-trained civil engineer, Ignatieff had always been an enthusiast for sane and well-planned immigration schemes—and now more so than ever with the misery of overcrowded, war-torn Europe fresh in his head. What he wanted to do was to bring skilled and capable settlers into this emptiness and see them prosper and make homes. And he had a plan.

In those first postwar years the government at Ottawa was concerned with the failure of alfalfa and various grasses to set seed in the older seed-growing districts of the West. An isolated country, virgin land and a new beginning seemed to be the immediate answer—and here, in the Finlay and Parsnip valleys it was estimated that 600,000 acres of agricultural land lay waiting. This was the largest area of unexploited land west of the Rockies—a bonanza in mountainous British Columbia, but still unknown and neglected and, in a province that was still poor in actual cash, without road or railroad or much hope of getting them. In all this lay the opportunity.

Discussion with Vladimir Ignatieff, the brother of Nicholas and a soils expert, and with numerous western raisers of fine seed made the whole thing seem feasible. The plan had the blessing of Ottawa, and the British Columbia Department of Lands voluntarily put a couple of thousand acres near the meeting of the rivers under map reserve for the purpose Ignatieff had in mind. And now here he was, headed down the Parsnip towards Wicked River ...

No vast amount of that homestead was level, and at low water it lay behind a landing (if you could call it that) of enormous rounded and polished boulders—the finest place imaginable for breaking a leg while carrying a load from boat to shore. But Ignatieff loved it, and there, with his wife or with some of his students on a summer trip, he would proceed with his researches. A small plot near the cabin was carefully levelled and in it one could see, in later years, strips of the different varieties of grass that he was testing. Here if anywhere, he thought, with the well-drained, loose-textured soil of the district, with sunshine and sufficient rainfall, and with no interference in the shape of imported weeds, crop diseases and the farming activities of men, he should be able to get clean and accurate results. Besides the plots at Wicked River he had isolated patches of grass, grown from selected seed, scattered here and there in the mountains in places where the soil had been sampled and tested. Ignatieff's vision, the dream that led him on, was of the fertile portions of the floor of the Trench laid down to grass and raising seed—a valuable product and not a bulky one; a product which could stand the costs of transportation to the outside world by plane or riverboat, and which would promote and sustain settlement till road or railroad reached this forgotten valley, this stepchild of British Columbia. Meanwhile other varieties of grass, tested in the mountains and proved to be suitable, would be employed in converting other areas of the Trench into pasture land, building up the sod and the humus without which men and animals cannot live. "All flesh is grass"—and it was a wise man who wrote those words.

A detailed plan was worked out, a prospectus was drawn up, the desired capital of $350,000 was subscribed. Unfortunately, the dream remained nothing but a dream—one that now can never come true. In 1952 Ignatieff died an untimely death and his plan had to be abandoned. Now only a vast, stormy lake with an ugly shoreline will take its place, for the Gap and wide areas of the Trench in those parts are doomed to vanish beneath the waters of a monstrous dam ... [2]

We drifted together for a while, the riverboat and the canoe, introducing ourselves and talking. Then Ignatieff went on and we made camp on an open beach that faced east and would catch the morning sun. And for the first time on that stormy trip I slept confidently in the open without tent or mosquito net.

The meeting of the waters, to which we came next morning, must be one of the most dramatic places on the river map of Canada. As one slips quietly down the last slack reaches of the Parsnip, the roar of the Finlay Rapids, a couple of miles down the Peace, breaks upon the ear in a slow crescendo. On one's left, in August water, is a great waste of shingle. On the right hand are the foothills of Mount Selwyn; and the mountain itself, when at last it can be seen, towers almost 6,000 feet above the valley floor. Ahead, and beyond the big shingle bar, fast water is playing strange tricks in the dancing mirage: it is of a new colour and it is moving from left to right, shearing off, as with a knife, the sluggish current of the Parsnip. And that is where the Peace is born, offspring of the darker, clearer water in which the canoe is riding and the driving, silty-blue flood of the more powerful Finlay. The Gap in the wall of the Rockies opens up a little, but it is still four miles distant in the northeast—and in any case you have no eyes for it since the onrush of the new river is now within a few feet. Quickly you step out into the shallow water on the point. A strong shove sends the canoe flying out into the Finlay. Coil by coil the trackline pays out through your hands; then comes the tug as the canoe fetches up at the end of it. A very slight adjustment of the double line sets the canoe at the proper angle to the current to hold it away from shore; and then, leaning a little and with both arms taut to take the strain, you start the long walk upstream. Obediently the canoe follows, a little behind you and some fifty feet out from shore into the racing water of Finlay's Branch.

In our case the walk was pleasantly shortened. Upstream, in the distance, a boat appeared, running down at great speed. That was Ignatieff, going all out for Wicked River. He had been up to the McDougalls' trading post, some four miles up the river from the old, and now abandoned, settlement at the meeting of the rivers. As he passed by he shouted to us the welcome news that Roy McDougall would soon be coming down to pick us up and tow the canoe in to the post. So we lunched

Patterson's canoe follows obediently as he tracks it upstream.

in the shade of some trees, and then we tracked on to the head of the bar—and from there, with pole and paddle, we made our way up into a deep eddy. There McDougall found us, and soon the little canoe was hitched to the side of his large boat. A pole was then lashed crossways on the canoe and adjusted to hold the two craft apart so that the water would slip easily between them instead of boiling up and flooding the canoe. Then the outboard roared again and the big boat shuddered as it gathered speed against the strong current. Close in to a long, curving cutbank, where the water boiled dangerously through the sweepers, we made our way until, in the distance, there showed a vast shingle bar on the west shore. That was Pete Toy's Bar. Boats were tied up in the snye behind it, and on the bank the outlines of buildings could be seen among the trees. That was McDougall's post of Finlay Forks, and the first leg of our journey was at an end.

PART TWO

Men Travelling into a Far Country

6

Finlay Forks

We woke the next morning in a cool, quiet room that led out of the store. It was log-built and it smelt pleasantly of Indian-tanned moosehide and moccasins; traps hung from the walls, a keg full of axe hafts was standing near to where I had slept on the floor; all the tools and outfit of a northern trading post stood or hung around the storeroom in orderly disarray. For a moment, after a week or two of bug tents and the bush, it was puzzling: then I remembered …

Roy McDougall had come to this valley for the first time in 1925. He had battled his way up the Peace against the summer flood and it was on June 6 of that year that his boat emerged from the Gap. The whole sweep of the Trench, from the Rockies to the Wolverines, lay before him—a wide country, and his to choose from. Since that time the settlement at the meeting of the rivers, already on its last legs, weary of waiting for the road or railroad that never came, had died completely—and now the post office and the radio station, though still marked on the 1947 map as being in their old positions at the head of the Peace, had migrated some four miles up the Finlay to McDougall's post. The name had followed them, and this now was Finlay Forks.

It was more than just a trading post: it was a stopping place and a refuge for all who passed up and down the Finlay. Here everybody came—surveyors, trappers, geologists, Provincial Police, freighters on the river and casual wanderers like Alan and myself. Here all were sure of a meal and a night's rest—and this might be extended for days in times of running ice or bad flying weather. And here nobody was allowed to pay. That was the only trouble—trying to find some way in which to return the open-hearted hospitality of Marge and Roy McDougall. Some small service, or a gift of a book or photographs—that was all one was allowed to do. In Marge's view this was the northern way of doing things, and that was that.

There was a book published about this time, a book which related the experiences of a couple who, seeking for nature in the raw with a view to writing about it, spent a winter in a valley of the mountains west of Finlay Forks. These people located on the main trail between two old-established trading posts—but the impression given was that "few White men had ever ventured," and more to that effect. The two intrepid winterers came through this ordeal with their lives— and it certainly paid them well, for the book contained exactly the right amount of saccharine and sentimentality and thus had a roaring success with all who knew nothing of the North. It must have made a packet ... But it fell flatter than a pancake with Marge McDougall. She knew too much, and she could strip that well-decorated tale bare of all its camouflage just as easy as skinning a marten. And she spoke of it always with contempt. "Did you notice," she would say, "where those fellows were stuck and had to camp overnight with those two wonderful pioneers? And the pioneers actually *charged* those two men for their meals—did you ever *hear* of such a thing?" That sets forth Marge's attitude towards travellers on the trail, and it was into this sort of hospitality that we, a couple of homeless strays, had dropped.

And the sun was shining and breakfast was at eight, over at the house. Reluctantly I rolled out of my comfortable eiderdown and looked at the humped-up bundle on the floor that was Alan sleeping ...

That morning, from a spot just downstream from the post, I took a colour photograph of the Peace River Gap. The slide is before me now: a brilliant sun illuminates the scene; a few white clouds are floating across the bluest of summer skies; the river is a paler version of that blue, streaked with the tawny sand ridges of the lower end of Pete Toy's Bar. In the foreground there is grass with a scattering of some yellow flower; then, looking down through the willows of the riverbank, one can just see the water of the snye where the boats and the canoe are tied. The far bank is green with coniferous forest of varying age.

Dead in the centre of the view is the Gap in the outer ranges of the Rockies. It lies almost due east and four or five miles distant from McDougall's post. Somewhere in those miles, unseen and beyond the green monotonous forest of the further shore, lie the turns and loopings of the rivers as they manoeuvre for their onslaught on the Rockies. To the right of the Gap towers Mount Selwyn, still with a patch or two of snow sheltering between its barren ridges. Through the Gap other stony summits can be seen—grey, distant sentinels looking down on the escape of the river.

On that still morning one could hear, from the direction of Mount Selwyn, a noise like the steady pounding of surf on an open beach. That was the Finlay Rapids making themselves heard across three miles of bush and sandbars. To a crew of voyageurs toiling up the Peace, having already carried around the canyon at the Rocky Mountain Portage and having successfully lined their craft up the Ne Parle Pas Rapids in the eastern foothills, these rapids by Mount Selwyn were the last obstacle

Sheer walls meet whitewater in this view of the majestic canyon of the great Peace River.

before entering the wide valley of the Trench. Up this roaring slope of water came—first of all White men—the Northwesters: Alexander Mackenzie in 1793, John Finlay in 1797, Simon Fraser in 1805. But at the Forks only Finlay turned up the river that bears his name: the other two were looking for a way to the western sea and they ascended the smaller river, the Parsnip. Mackenzie missed the mouth of Pack River and made his way by a difficult and dangerous route to the great river that was to become known as the Fraser, but which he then hoped might be the Columbia. Twelve more years were to pass before Simon Fraser reached McLeod's Lake by way of its small dark river—suggesting afterwards, as he checked his own journal against Mackenzie's, that his predecessor must have missed its outflow into the Parsnip while enjoying a nap.

In 1805 and 1806 Fraser explored the new territory, and it was in those years that he built McLeod's Lake Fort, Stuart's Lake Fort—which later became Fort St. James—and Fort George at the outflow of the Nechako River into the Fraser. Behind him, east of the Rockies and where the Peace, swerving away from the Butler Ridge, sweeps in its canyon round the foot of Portage Mountain, he had already built the post of Rocky Mountain Portage. Only then, with these things seen to and with his communications established through the mountains, was he able to launch out on his quest for a route to the ocean.

Each man, in a sense, achieved his object. Each one reached tidewater on the Pacific—Mackenzie in one terrific journey in that one year of 1793, Fraser by way of his own river in 1808 by one of the greatest feats of canoe travel of all time. And each one also failed, for neither had found what he was looking for—a practicable fur-trade route to the sea, preferably by way of the Columbia River. But where Mackenzie went and returned, leaving in the mountains only the ashes of his campfires, Fraser, profiting by his fellow explorer's pioneering voyage, established the trading posts and organized the district of New Caledonia for the North West Company. The highway into the West was now open.

But over the byway of Finlay's Branch there still hung a large question mark. From the Forks the great valley faded out of sight into the northwest and no White man had seen the end of it. Did it have an end, the fur traders wondered, an end like that of any ordinary valley—in some lofty coulee, blocked by encircling mountains? Or did it, rather, run on over the horizon, straight into the summer sunset, perhaps to the Riviere aux Liards or even beyond—an avenue between two mountain walls, a flightway for the birds and a passageway for men? If only one were able to go and see ...

The pioneers were probably the free Iroquois hunters and trappers, who traded with the North West Company's posts. These people, by now over 2,000 miles from their homeland, exiles and wanderers, were west of the Rockies by the early years of the nineteenth century. In the tradition of their nation they were fighting men, and it was all in the day's work for them to brush aside the Sikannis of the Finlay country, a downtrodden race, hounded and penned in on all sides by enemies—and, according to Samuel Black, "laizie and indolent," a people who "will not move a step over their usual rotine and will rather eat Grass than use exertions to live better." Because they were rovers, the Iroquois had no interest in maintaining a good stock of fur in any country that they hunted: rather did they sweep it clean before moving on—and that applied to the game animals as well, for they killed regardless of season, sex or age. Skimming the cream off the country as they went, they penetrated deep into the mountains of the big bend of the Finlay, perhaps even to the Fishing Lakes on the upper river where, at certain seasons, the tracks of the game can make those muddy shores look like a corral churned and trampled by a mob of cattle in the June rains. Eventually the Iroquois settled once more, taking to themselves wives of alien blood and making new homes in these far-western mountains. It was a descendant of these same free hunters who, in 1890, befriended Warburton Pike at the Rocky Mountain Portage.

It was inevitable that an expedition would be sent, sooner or later, to explore Finlay's Branch to its source. But at first neither the Northwesters nor the Hudson's Bay Company could spare the men: the two companies were fighting each other, and no matter how far to the westward the more active Northwesters penetrated, they would eventually find the Bay following slowly on the trails that they had made. In 1820 the traders and voyageurs of the English company came through the Gap for the first time and reached "the Forks of Fraser's River." The Northwesters at Stuart's Lake Fort were on the alert and ready for them—but then the union of the companies in March of 1821 put an end to the wasting struggle.

7

Samuel Black

The time was now ripe, and after various delays Governor George Simpson of the Hudson's Bay Company confided the enterprise of the Finlay exploration to the former Northwester, now chief trader, Samuel Black. Black was to spend the winter of 1823–24 at Fort St. John on the Peace River, collect all the information about the country to be explored that the local Indians and the Iroquois hunters could give him, and then, as soon as the Peace was free of ice in the spring of 1824, set out by canoe for the Finlay.

This man whom Simpson had chosen as leader of a hazardous expedition is no vague shape, dimly seen through the mists of some hundred and forty years. From writings both hostile and friendly—from Simpson's rancorous description in his secret *Character Book*,[3] and from the old *A History of the Northwest Coast* by the retired fur trader, A. C. Anderson, who knew Black and respected him—one can form a clear picture of the one-time Northwester.

He was a man of enormous stature with a slow and imposing manner of speech. He was strong, vigorous and active, very cool and "resolute to desperation." He was wary and suspicious, hard to pin down to a direct answer, and "fancies that every man has a design upon him." In appearance he reminded Simpson of Don Quixote. As regards mental capabilities, Simpson conceded that Black was tolerably well educated and, at all times, a hard student. Anderson is more generous: in his opinion Black was "a man of great mental as well as literary attainments," though lacking "the advantage of a critically correct education." He was also a keen amateur geologist, while the geography of the unexplored Northwest "received through him many additions." Best of all testimonials, he had the universal respect of his colleagues—though they sometimes indulged in quiet smiles at his eccentricities. Furthermore, his closest and lifelong friend was the well-educated, gay and laughter-loving Peter Skene Ogden, equally prominent with Black in the war between the companies and thus equally obnoxious to Simpson. A man is best known by his friends, and Ogden was no ordinary man.

Black was a great reader, particularly of books on exploration, and one can see from his *Journal* that he had acquired some knowledge of classical mythology. There was leisure for reading during the long winters of the fur country, while the books and the odd magazine, such as *Blackwood's*, which found their way to the isolated trading posts were few but good, and well suited to the sound Scots education of those days.

That paints the picture of the man. But on this strange fur trader who had the gift of words, further light is shed by the pages of his *Journal*. Surely, in all the archives of the Hudson's Bay Company there can be no record of a wilderness exploration that can equal this one for sheer exuberance. Simpson had written to Black: "I will feel obliged by your giving me a full and particular account of everything worthy of remark that may come under your observation." He got that—and much more besides—for Black, emboldened by these and other equally vague instructions, felt free to let himself go.

He was a native of the parish of Pitsligo in County Aberdeen in Scotland. There seems to have been a little irregularity about his birth, for the register of baptisms in that parish contains an entry: "1780 May 3 John Black in the Parish of Tyrie and Mary Leith in Bodichell had an illegitimate Son Baptized named Samuel." Then, in the marriage register for June, 1781, we read that John Black and Mary Leith "having been contracted and claimed were married." Their only son came to Canada in 1802 and by 1804 was a devoted and loyal member of the North West Company. He flung himself into the struggle between the rival companies with all the zest of youth. "Zeal" was his favourite word—one meets it again and again in his letters and reports—and it was with both zest and zeal that he proceeded, over the next seventeen years, to make life interesting for his opponents in the Hudson's Bay Company, including in this category the future governor, George Simpson, thereby arousing an enmity that was to affect his whole later life. During those stormy years, and apparently at any time afterwards when the occasion demanded it, Black went fully armed with dirk, sabre and pistols. There is a story of an affray off Fort Chipewyan on Lake Athabasca between two North West Company canoes and one canoe of the Hudson's Bay Company: the Northwesters were dragging Indians out of the Bay canoe and into their own, and the voice of the Bay employee in charge, Hebert Lemas, was loudly raised in resentful protest. Black silenced him with a ferocious threat which Lemas evidently thought he was quite capable of carrying out: he drew his sabre and shouted to the speaker to hold his noise. Any more words, he said, and he would send Lemas' head flying off his shoulders and into the lake. It was usually enough for this giant of a man, "raw boned and lanthorn jawed" and doubly fearsome when roused to anger, to threaten. Simpson himself wrote that Black's word could be depended on, and nobody else seemed to be in any doubt on that point, particularly when it was a matter of pistols or the slashing of sabres.

After years of this sort of thing it is not surprising to find, in the settlement of 1821 that followed the surrender of the North West Company, that Black and his close friend, Ogden, were specifically excluded from service with the Hudson's Bay Company. But their exclusion did not last long: it was not good business to leave two men of such energetic character and long experience in the fur trade lying around idle and available to any opposition that might arise in the Columbia country. Far better would it be to get the two warriors under Company control and discipline. So that was done in the course of the winter of 1822–23, at which time Black and Ogden made a trip to London—and Black, presumably, also to Scotland to visit his mother for whom, throughout her life, he never failed to make provision out of his salary.

In 1823 the two former Northwesters, now admitted into grace, returned to Canada and started their new careers with the Hudson's Bay Company, each one with the commissioned rank of chief trader. The next thing to be done, from Simpson's point of view, was to get

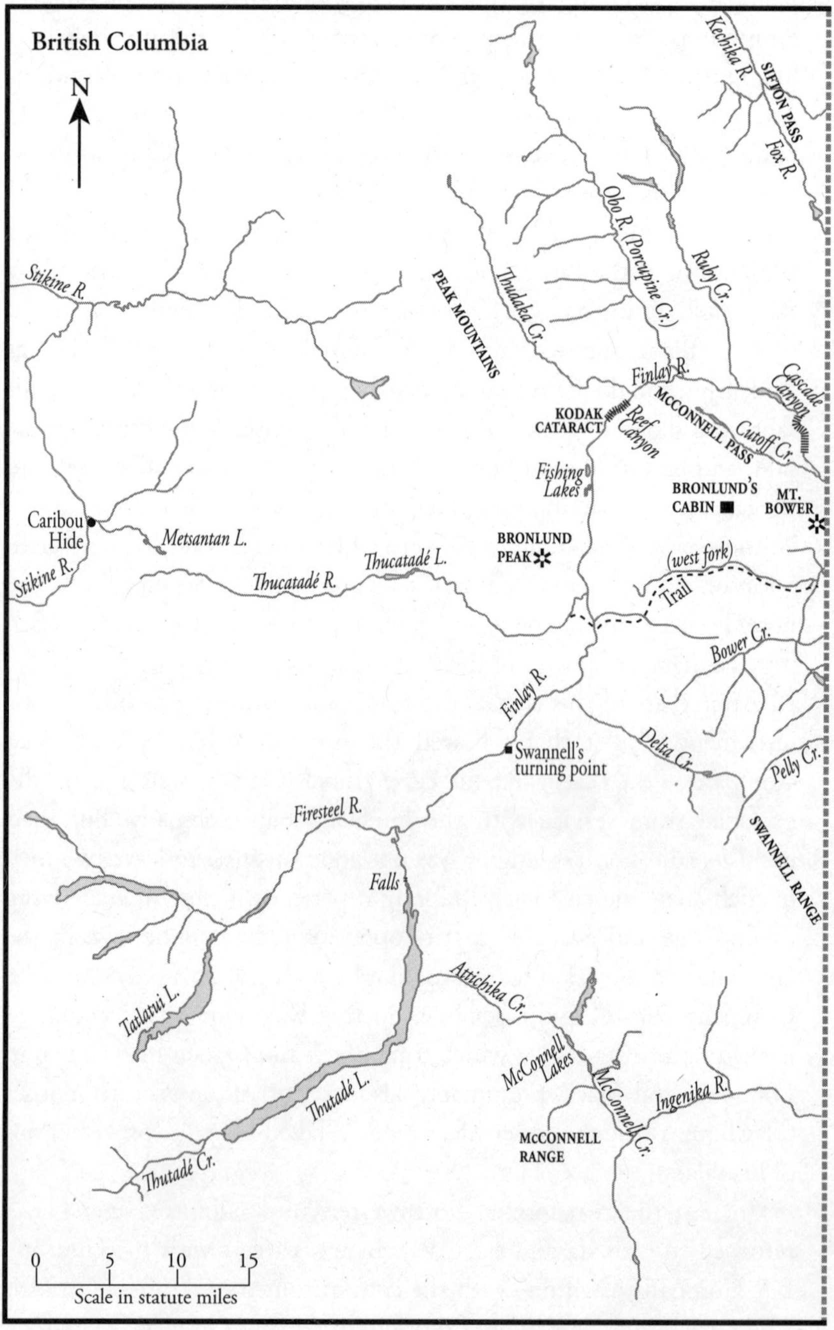
British Columbia
N
Kechika R.
SIFTON PASS
Fox R.
Obo R. (Porcupine Cr.)
Ruby Cr.
Thudaka Cr.
PEAK MOUNTAINS
Stikine R.
Finlay R.
Cascade Canyon
KODAK CATARACT
Reef Canyon
McCONNELL PASS
Cutoff Cr.
Fishing Lakes
BRONLUND'S CABIN
MT. BOWER
Caribou Hide
Metsantan L.
BRONLUND PEAK
Stikine R.
Thucatadé R.
Thucatadé L.
(west fork)
Trail
Bower Cr.
Finlay R.
Swannell's turning point
Delta Cr.
Pelly Cr.
Firesteel R.
SWANNELL RANGE
Falls
Tatlatui L.
Attichika Cr.
McConnell Lakes
McConnell Cr.
Ingenika R.
Thutadé L.
McCONNELL RANGE
Thutadé Cr.
0 5 10 15
Scale in statute miles

Samuel Black

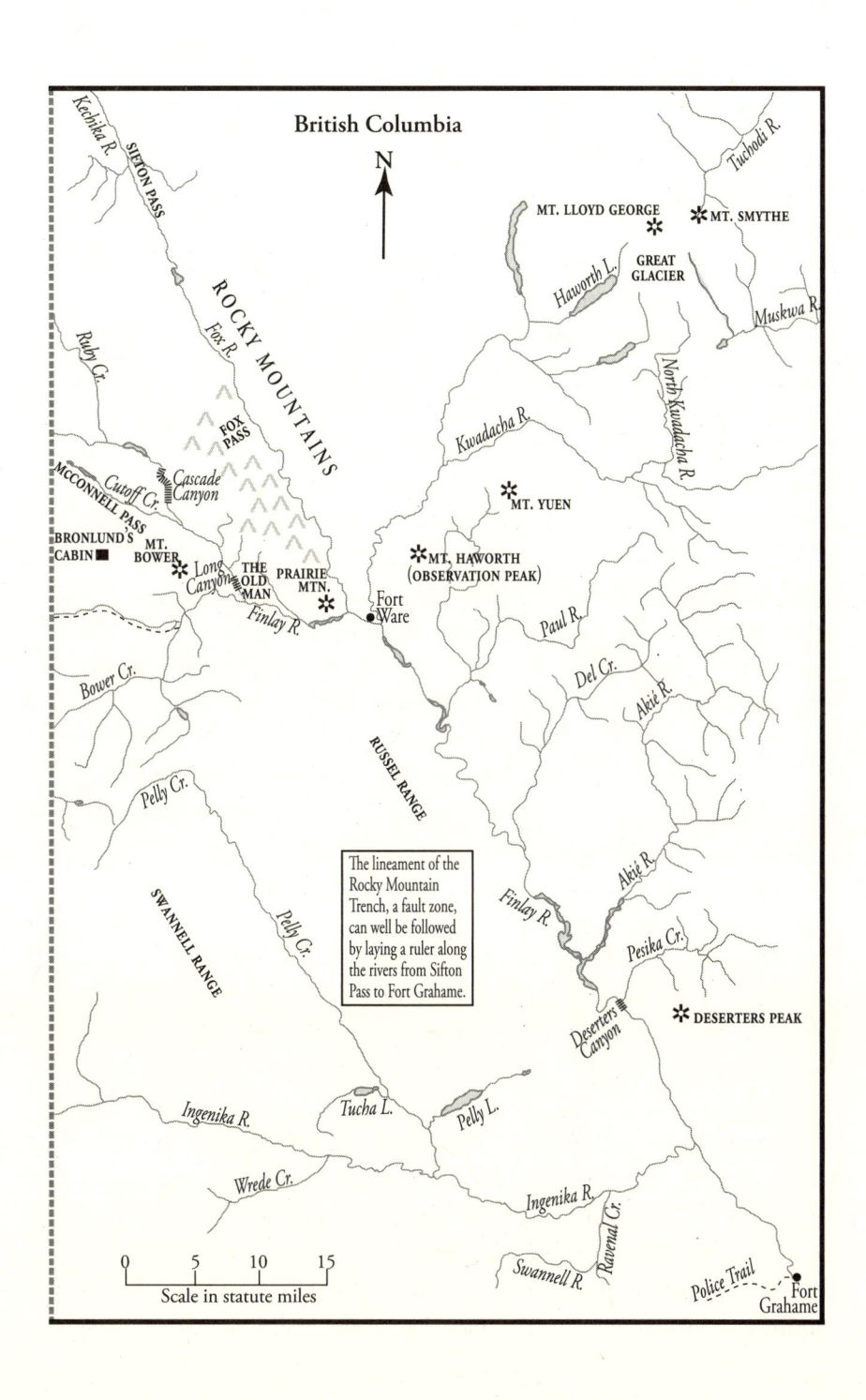

British Columbia

The lineament of the Rocky Mountain Trench, a fault zone, can well be followed by laying a ruler along the rivers from Sifton Pass to Fort Grahame.

Scale in statute miles: 0, 5, 10, 15

them as far away as possible from the council table at York Factory on the shore of Hudson's Bay. That was easy: they could be given assignments "beyond the Mountain." There, west of the Rockies, lay the two districts of New Caledonia and the Columbia, formerly the preserve of the Northwesters. To the north and to the south there were practically no limits to these territories: there were only the Russian posts in the far northwest, and in the south no settlement till the Spanish lands were reached—nothing to contend with but a great emptiness, still well stocked with beaver, known only to the Indians, and penetrated only in the south by the first wandering parties of the American mountain men. This was the ideal outlet for the energies of these inconvenient but, at the same time, daring and capable men, and it was not long before the two chief traders found themselves leaders of expeditions that were a thousand miles apart and headed in opposite directions: Ogden on horseback into the tawny, almost desert country that is now Idaho and Utah, and Black by canoe into the green, moss-carpeted forests of the Trench and the wet, storm-swept uplands of the Cassiar ... For him this was fulfillment. Through all his manhood years he had read and absorbed the stories of the great explorers. Now, at last, here was his chance to become the discoverer of new lands, to find the Great River of the West, and perhaps to fall on some fine stretch of gently rolling country, lightly wooded, where the streams were slow and winding and the beaver dams a maze of quiet waters, flanked by groves of aspen poplar and cottonwood and broken only by the round, rough roofs of many beaver houses. The fur hunter's dream ...

The speed of travel of the old-time voyagers on the Finlay and the difficulties they had to contend with varied with the kind of canoe or boat that they used. By "old-time voyagers" I mean all those who ventured up the river before the days of the machine—and of these one can only speak with certainty about the few who have left some written record of their journeys. That last condition eliminates the Indians, since they recorded nothing. In any case, the local Sikannis seldom made use of canoes on the Finlay: they travelled on foot along the river trails, taking to the water mostly by raft, and occasionally by skin boat, when they had to make a crossing or wished to carry the meat of a big animal downstream to camp. They used very small pine-bark canoes, "not biger than cockle shells," on Thutadé and the smaller lakes, and occasionally on the river. As for the Iroquois, judging by a few remarks let fall by Black, they must have travelled light and fast, using some form of bark canoe.

Of the men who wrote of their journeys in diaries, reports and books of travel, Black alone used the birchbark canoe. That was entirely in keeping for an old Northwester. Furthermore, apart from being the only craft available to Black in that spring of 1824, the birchbark canoe had a number of advantages. It could carry a heavy load in shallow water, yet it was light and capable of being portaged. It could be repaired easily without special tools and from materials readily available in the bush. It could go anywhere that a boat could go, and, in the hands of skilled men who knew how to use it, it had taken the Northwesters swiftly across the continent. The canoe that Black used was probably around twenty-five feet in length, four feet or so in beam, and in depth about a couple of feet. To handle this craft he started out with a crew of six, and in addition to the crew there were four other persons: himself; his assistant, Donald Manson; La Prise, a Chipewyan half-breed who was to be the hunter of the party; and La Prise's wife—in all, ten people. There were also a heavy load of provisions, a moderate amount of trade goods, and the personal gear. With all this they were heavily loaded.

The six members of Black's crew were something of a mixed bag, though they did have one thing in common: they were all ex-employees of the North West Company, retained after 1821 by the Hudson's Bay Company. They consisted of bowsman and steersman, and four middlemen whose duty it was to paddle and pole, track and portage, and do what they were told.

In the bow as foreman of the crew was Joseph La Guarde. He was a French-Canadian half-breed, and Black in one of his private notebooks refers to him as "this cunning Iroquois." He was rather a silent man—however, "when once into it he is a capital foreman but a little over cautious, its said he has made a vow not to drown us or perish the Canoe."

The steersman was Antoine Perreault, a man of twenty-six, and again a French-Canadian half-breed. He was hot-tempered: in the spring of 1823 he had attacked and stabbed one of the Company's clerks at Fort Dunvegan on the Peace River. He was rather less energetic when it came to a job of work, and Black wrote of him before they started: " ... it seems he soon gets tired of anything, I dread he is a bad bargain but I cannot help it." Perreault always showed at his best in the dangerous places.

He also hunted: one August evening, in the Cassiar Mountains on the headwaters of the Stikine, they spotted seven or eight mountain sheep, and Perreault, "our best hunter" (for by that time La Prise and his wife had deserted and turned back), went after them. He blazed off a number of shots into the mountainside, but finally got two young rams, which proved to be excellent eating. Next morning he was "a little proud and a little saucy ... and wanted to be indulged in making Marrow Fat for the day and I wanted to get on which was the only small difference between us." They went on.

That brings us to the third on Black's list—Joseph Cournoyer, a twenty-one-year-old French Canadian from Sorel. Black describes him as "a real rough and tumble, he works with hand and foot, tooth and nail at the Line."

Next comes another twenty-one-year-old, Jean Baptiste Tarrangeau, middleman. Precisely what he was seems to be uncertain: they refer to him as a "Native." Black's comment on him is that he would always be led by Perreault, and that, in the hour of danger, those two would probably be the first to save their bacon, whereas La Guarde and Cournoyer could be counted on to stand to the last.

The two remaining middlemen were Jean Marie Bouché, twenty-five, and Louis Ossin, twenty-four. Both were French Canadians. This pair were to desert Black on the very first occasion that sheer cliffs and whitewater confronted them on the Finlay. They got clear away from the expedition, but there was no escape from the long arm of the Hudson's Bay Company. They were variously punished for their breach of contract and then one was sent east and the other west: one to the shores of Hudson's Bay and one to Fort Vancouver on the Columbia. A continent lay in between.

So much for the crew. Black's assistant and second in command was Donald Manson, then about twenty-five and a clerk in the Company's service. He hailed from Thurso in Caithness, Scotland. Black makes little comment on him, saying only of the passing of one dangerous rapid, "I have every reason to be pleased with him for his active assistance." Simpson wrote of Manson in 1832 that he was fit for any duty that demanded strength and activity "but cannot be left to the exercise of his own judgment in any matter requiring head work."

Of these eight men, officers and servants of the Hudson's Bay Company, Black was forty-four and La Guarde thirty-four. The average age of the remaining six was well under twenty-four years. A young party—which was just as well, since they were to make their way by canoe to the very source of one of the wildest of rivers, and from there to proceed on foot northwestward into the inhospitable mountains of the Cassiar—the first White men into a wilderness that few have travelled even today, and which was then a blank on the map without even a name to clothe its nakedness. As Simpson wrote of them afterwards: "they pursued their course as near as possible through perhaps as rugged a country as ever was passed."

That leaves the Chipewyan half-breed and his woman, "La Prise and Wife." La Prise was in the party in the dual capacity of interpreter and hunter. He was none too good a choice for the job, but just then there was nobody else available from the Peace River forts. In the Lake Athabasca country around Chipewyan, La Prise had been a good hunter, but he had had little success in the foothills of the upper Peace River. With unfamiliar game, and in this unfamiliar, crumpled country, he was at a loss; and if they had been obliged to depend on him alone on their journey through the mountains of the Cassiar, the whole outfit would have starved. He had his pride, and his lack of success worried him: this showed itself in an almost chronic state of buck fever and in hasty shooting. Black diagnosed it as "leveling by the muzzle"—which is to say that La Prise was apt to shoot as soon as he had got the bead of the foresight on the animal, letting the hindsight take care of itself. This system rarely produces anything but a noise, and the trip was far advanced when La Prise got his first big animal. This was near a small lake, three days' march north of Thutadé Lake, and it was Black who spotted the bull caribou, "unsuspecting of danger in his solitary Glen." Black's double-barrelled gun was loaded with ball and buckshot, but he was none too sure of himself as a stalker and also wished to encourage the others by giving them an easy shot.

"I therefore creeped back behind the Rise and made the accustomed signal to the hunters."

La Prise and one of the Sikannis made ready. They divested themselves of shoes, leggings and any superfluous clothes; then they made their stalk and, each one being anxious to bag the caribou himself, let fly simultaneously—with the usual result in such circumstances: each one missed. However, La Prise had thought a little ahead of the Sikanni: he had the powder for a second shot in one hand and the ball in his mouth and thus, with a delay of only a few seconds and being no longer bothered by somebody else shooting, he brought down the caribou. His best previous day had been at Thutadé where, having set out in a new pine-bark canoe that he and his wife had made, he returned with a mixed bag consisting of one beaver, four geese and four trout.

If La Prise was not up to the mark as a hunter in the Finlay country, he was even more unsatisfactory as an interpreter. He could scarcely make himself understood by the Beaver Indians of the Peace River or the Sikannis of the Finlay, two tribes whose languages were much akin. So Black added to the party the only Sikanni who would volunteer for the journey, "the Old Slave." This helped with the language problem but also ensured a perpetual row between the two interpreters: "La Prise understands but by halves and the Old Slave is snappish with him."

Both of Black's interpreters were to desert him on the trail, La Prise some ten days ahead of the Old Slave and each of them when the party was on foot in the mountains of the Stikine headwaters. By that time each one had in his heart the Indian fear of getting too far into the territory of strange tribes, and La Prise was in bad shape as well, "knocked up and cast down." The long struggle up the Finlay, everlastingly on the trackline and in and out of the ice-cold water, had worn him out. And now one ankle was sprained and swollen. He was useless, he said, and he asked of Black to be allowed to return. Then one morning he and his wife lingered behind and hit the homeward trail. Not trusting the Sikannis of the Stikine–Finlay divide, they slipped unseen through their country to Thutadé Lake. There they picked up the pine-bark canoe that they had made and fled on down the perilous river, secure in the knowledge that no punishment would follow on this desertion since La Prise was not a regular servant of the Company.

Such was Black's crew, and it was with these eight men and the one woman that he started to cross the Rocky Mountain Portage on May 13, 1824. On May 22 they lined and portaged up the Finlay Rapids and turned into the mouth of Finlay's Branch. There they found the Old Slave's family, and in the late afternoon the Old Slave himself came in from hunting. The final discussions, dear to the heart of the Indian, were got through and the agreement for the journey was confirmed. This took time and patience, and the sun was already low when they started once more upon their way, "now 13 growen persons and 2 children," some walking, the Sikannis handling their own canoes, the rest lining and poling the big canoe up the river. Growing smaller in the sunset light, at last they vanish round the bend, leaving only the sound of the Finlay Rapids, louder now in the cool of the evening, to break the silence.

8

Pete Toy

Time went by and the Indians came and went, but no White man ventured again up the Finlay for close on forty years. Then, in 1861, Bill Cust found gold in the bars some twenty miles up the Parsnip, and in the following year Pete Toy, a Cornish miner with an acute case of itching foot, ran his canoe into this very snye below McDougall's post and took a stroll with a shovel over the big shingle bar that was to become known as Pete Toy's Bar. He sank his prospect holes in the approved fashion, in line across the head of the bar where the current is slack and where the coarser gold would naturally be deposited—and there he struck it: a hundred dollars a day, according to Captain W. F. Butler, who met and spoke with him. However, that trained geologist and hard traveller, R. G. McConnell, coming later, sets Pete's daily winnings at no more than fifty.

Pete Toy staked his bar and built a cabin in the woods alongside of it—probably on or close to the spot where McDougall's post was to stand seventy years later, that being the natural boat landing. There he worked his placer, traded with the Indians and trapped through the winters. He was still there eleven years later when Butler passed by. By that time placer gold had been struck away up the Omineca—on Silver Creek in 1868 by Twelve-Foot Davis and his party, and in 1871 on Manson Creek—and Pete was consequently able to bring in his outfits from Germansen Landing in the new goldfield downstream all the way: down the Omineca and down the Finlay, instead of by the long haul from distant Quesnel on the Fraser River. Also, in 1864 Cust and his partner, Carey, had established a trading post at the head of the Rocky Mountain Portage, nearly a hundred miles down the Peace. Seventy-five miles upstream to Germansen, or a hundred miles down to Cust and Carey's: there were rapids and canyons in either direction but, none the less, civilization was creeping in on Pete Toy.

By the time Haworth came in 1916, legend had gathered around the Cornish miner. He was a giant of a man—which may well be true, for when Butler first saw him he was carrying "a huge load" over the Black Canyon portage on the Omineca. And he was a rich man, having washed out 70,000 dollars' worth of gold from the famous bar. Pete met his death by drowning in Little Canyon on the Omineca—a bad place, a sharp double bend in the river with the current driving hard on two points of gneiss in echelon. And where had he cached the gold? To this day the story persists of a buried hoard ...

9

Butler

Contemporaneous with Pete Toy was the brief but adventurous visit to the Finlay of Captain W. F. Butler—captain in the British Army, on half pay and on long leave. Here was a soldier of an unusual kind—a soldier who was able to think. Where so many of his brother officers were practically inarticulate, this ability in Butler was backed with a lively gift of expression both in speech and in writing. "His wording was inclined to make stupidity writhe," writes Sir Shane Leslie, "and this was never helpful to a military career."[4] His reports had a sting to them, and, what was even worse, events usually proved him to be right. It is in his autobiography, published a year after his death in 1910, that Butler comments on "the entire absence of the thinking faculty in nine out of ten of the higher-grade officers" that he had known. Elsewhere he has a few observations to make on "the mental congestion of the official mind." With an acute perception and a keen comprehension, he was moved always by a strong sense of pity for the victim of injustice, be it Irish peasant or North American Indian, Boer or Zulu. If there was any one thing in particular that could move him to wrath it was the blockish obstructionism of the petty official with his red tape. He was years ahead of his time and whole ages ahead of the average officer of his day. He towered above the latter, both physically and intellectually. This was a bird of a very strange plumage to find on the Finlay in 1873 …

Butler was born in 1838 at Ballyslateen, County Tipperary, Catholic and Irish of the Irish. At the age of twenty he was gazetted ensign in the 69th Regiment. Service followed in Burma, India, the Channel Islands and Ireland—and then in 1867 the 69th was ordered to Canada. This opened up a whole new world for Butler and he made the most of it, meeting with strange, wild characters; finding on the shores of Lake Erie a veteran officer of the 69th who had fought at Quatre-Bras and Waterloo; getting as far west as Fort Kearney on the Platte River in what was then the Territory of Nebraska. There Butler and a brother officer of the 69th arrived at sunrise in a United States Army mule wagon, to be greeted by the commandant with a large bowl of hot Bourbon whisky egg-flip, which, their genial host assured them, was very effective against Platte fever. Breakfast followed; and then the two British officers, promoted suddenly, each one, to the rank of colonel, rode out with their hosts on a buffalo hunt, armed with the short Spencer carbine, the weapon of the United States cavalry. Buffalo covered the tawny grass of the prairie clear to the horizon, stampeding as the seven or eight riders went in hot pursuit, firing from the saddle. This, to a young man, was romance—and there and then a seed was sown in Butler's fertile brain, a seed that was to germinate and grow into those two classics of Canadian wilderness travel, *The Great Lone Land* and *The Wild North Land*.

The autumn days passed all too quickly at Fort Kearney—days of hard riding and hunting over the open prairie, nights of good cheer and good stories—and it was with the liveliest memories of the still-wild West, and of American hospitality there, that Butler returned to Canada and the regiment. Nearly two years went by—and then he went on leave to England on some private business, to Paris in the last days of her glory (the year was 1869), to Ireland to be with his father in his last illness. In 1870 he returned to Canada to take part in the Red River expedition under Colonel Garnet Wolseley. The occasion was the First Riel Rebellion—and when order had been restored at Fort Garry and the troops had departed, Butler remained behind. He had been requested by the lieutenant-governor of Manitoba to make a journey from the Red River to the Rockies and back, passing through the fur-trading forts of the Saskatchewan and compiling a report on the condition of the Indians in that vast territory. Leave had been granted for the purpose and he left Fort Garry on October 24, 1870, returning on February 20, 1871, with his mission completed. He had become a hardened winter traveller. He had journeyed on foot and on horseback, by Red River cart and by dogsled, and every hazard of northern travel had been successfully overcome. And again, as at Fort Kearney, it was the lonely beauty of the prairie lands and the splendid sweep of the prairie rivers that had appealed to him. All through his life he would treasure a vision of the clean, unsullied emptiness of the North American plains as they lay waiting for the multitudes that were so soon to come.

The 69th had, in the meantime, been sent to Bermuda. But Butler's leave had not yet expired, so he hastened to London and then—determined, as always, to see with his own eyes—somehow contrived to get himself into ruined and burning Paris in the last and most dangerous days of the Commune, when Frenchmen were shooting Frenchmen, and the common enemy, the Prussians, "smoked and laughed, leaning lazily on the ramparts of St. Denis."

At the end of 1871 his leave expired and he went to the depot of the regiment at Chatham, there to write *The Great Lone Land*, his account of that winter journey to the Saskatchewan. There, at Chatham, a discouraged mood came upon him. He felt that there was no future for him in the army of that time—and there came, flooding back, memories of his trails and camps in the far West: visions of the distant peaks of the Rockies cutting into the golden afterglow of the sunset, and of the faint wrinkle of the winter trail running on and on over the darkening snow. There was room for a man in that country ... And, furthermore, he had just made a clear 1,000 pounds on an oil-land speculation in Upper Canada. Now was the time to use it.

Once more, in April of 1872, he applied for leave. Not, perhaps, without subtlety, he gave as his forwarding address Carlton House on the North Saskatchewan River. No objections were raised at the War Office to the application, and Butler had two theories regarding this: firstly that the name of the Hudson's Bay Company's fort had, in the mind of the clerk who dealt with the request, some vague association with Carlton House in London, the residence of the Duke of Cambridge, the commander-in-chief—or, alternatively, that the head of the department involved, possessing a wider geographical knowledge than did his subordinate, had approved the application, muttering to himself as he did so: "Far off—but not nearly far enough."

Butler set out without any fixed plans. All he wanted to do was to go beyond where he had been before, "and the 'beyond' that lay to the north of the Saskatchewan valley was a very big place." There was room enough in it even for him. He left Red River in October of 1872 and did not reach Quesnel in British Columbia until June of 1873—a good eight-months' trip, even without taking into account the getting to Red River from Boston, or, in the West, the hundreds of miles that separate Quesnel from Victoria. Looking back on it all afterwards, he decided that he had had "sport, travel and adventure" in a wilderness through which the only way of passing had been by cayuse and canoe, snowshoe and dogsled. And with that he was content ...

He came up the Peace from Fort Chipewyan on snowshoes, taking to horses at Fort St. John as the river ice rotted with the coming of spring. At Hudson's Hope—which was then on the south side of the partly open river—he completed his party for the passage of the Rockies. With him already was William Kalder, a Scots-Indian half-breed who had accompanied him from Dunvegan, "a very demon" when there was fast work to be done, and furiously impatient with any who were slow or clumsy ... Then there was Jacques Pardonnet, met with at Hudson's Hope, prospector and trapper. Jacques was French, hailing from Belfort in Lorraine, a mere five foot two inches in height but a giant in strength and skill. It would be in his canoe that they would travel, a large cottonwood dugout, a heavy, lumbering affair that Jacques had hollowed out with his own hands some years previously—a clumsy, and therefore a dangerous, craft when it came to poling upstream under overhanging masses of piled-up ice. Jacques was appointed captain and steersman, and it was to his knowledge and skill that the party was to owe its safe passage through the Gap ... The fourth member of the crew was an English prospector, also recruited at Hudson's Hope. This proved to be something of an error: this miner was awkward and slow—and it's quickness that counts on a river. Butler's estimate of the man is best indicated by the fact that he never refers to him by name, but only as "A__." The fellow was not unwilling like Warburton Pike's "John," but he was slow-thinking and slow-moving. On the journey it was all Butler could do to prevent the active and exasperated Kalder from laying violent hands on A__ every time the latter made some slip or wrong movement, thereby causing the canoe to lose dangerously won distance round some ice-cliff or point of rock. A sort of cold-war peace was with difficulty maintained.

The armoury of the four voyageurs was unique. Crossing over the still half-frozen Peace to the little post of Hudson's Hope, A__ gave an initial display of his dexterity by upsetting a small ratting canoe with Butler and himself in it into the deep ice water. Nothing else was in the canoe but Butler's revolver and his gun, a double-barrel, breech-loading smooth-bore. In went the firearms, together with their owner, who was trapped under the thwarts and almost went under the ice, but who eventually got to shore, "numbed, water-logged and frozen." The weapons were at the bottom of the river—but in the morning they anchored a couple of canoes out in the current and patiently dragged for the gun with a fish hook spliced into the end of a long pole. The gun was in a leather case: at long last they snagged this with the hook and gingerly drew the gun to the surface, not much the worse for its night in the Peace River. The revolver was never seen again.

For Kalder, Butler bought a flintlock trade gun, a weapon which, after shooting it at a mark, and after hammering the barrel, first on one side and then on the other, "he declared to be a good beaver gun." It could be relied upon to go off about one shot in three.

A__ possessed a double-barrel, percussion-cap smooth-bore. One barrel was out of action and he had no percussion-caps for the other barrel. Undaunted by these deficiencies, he had worked out a system that involved the use of wax vestas. However, the striking of the match (as for an old-time harquebus) was rather apt to alarm, or at least alert, the living target—bird or beast. Then, by the time the gun had decided to go off, the target had, more often than not, already made up *its* mind and gone off first.

Jacques had the most extraordinary gun of the lot. "She" would shoot plumb, he maintained, though there was no denying she was a bit apt to spit. Otherwise she had only one fault—she operated as if on a delayed-action fuse: you could stand there, holding that gun tightly pressed in to cheek and shoulder and well and truly aimed—and it might be two minutes, or it might be even three, from the pressing of the trigger before she fired. Her owner frankly admitted she was tiring to aim—and from the game she demanded a degree of patience that few animals possess. Sometimes this gun even went off in the canoe after all the shooting was over, so they always laid her pointing out over the stern where, if the restless fit did happen to take her, she could blast off into the river, damaging nothing but Jacques Pardonnet's paddle.

So it was, with Butler's half-drowned gun and these three "maimed and mutilated weapons," and in Jacques' cottonwood dugout, that the four men left the west end of the Rocky Mountain Portage and began to force their way upstream. That was on May 1, 1873. They arrived at the Forks on May 9 and turned up the Finlay, camping that night on Pete Toy's Bar. On May 11 they turned into the Omineca. Some eight or nine miles up that river lies the gateway to the Black Canyon—but the story of their struggle to ascend between those gleaming walls of micaschist must await its proper time and place. From the canyon they go on upstream, to Germansen and the mining camps of the Omineca, and so out of the Finlay story.

Birds of passage …

10

Selwyn

Two years went by from the time of Butler's flying visit—and then, in 1875, there appeared at the Forks no less a personage than A. R. C. Selwyn, director of the Geological Survey of Canada. Selwyn was English, from the county of Somerset; and with him, as botanist to the expedition, was Professor John Macoun, a native of County Down in Ireland. As a young man Macoun had come out to Canada to farm, and it was in the course of farming that he had taught himself the rudiments of geology and botany. Now fully trained, he was distinguished in his own field of research both for his knowledge and for the clarity and readability of his reports.

Selwyn and Macoun and their party left Quesnel on June 5, travelling with horses. With them they brought a light-framed, canvas-covered boat, flat-bottomed and square at both ends—a sort of collapsible punt, about eighteen feet by five, which could easily be taken to pieces and packed on one horse. This forerunner of the collapsible canoe they named the *Nechacco*—and, as may be imagined from her awkward shape, she proved to be a lot more handy on a downstream run than when poling or tracking upriver.

The outfit went, with horses and pack train, by way of Fort St. James to McLeod's Lake Fort. There they managed to pick up a light boat made out of pine boards and one very poor dugout canoe, thus completing the flotilla. Soon after starting downstream, unskilled hands upset the dugout canoe in the Parsnip, thereby losing a large part of the expedition's supplies—and from that day onward rifles and fishing tackle played a major role in the stocking of the larder. All other hazards were successfully dealt with and, on July 10, 1875, the party made camp on the south shore of the Peace at the foot of the high, but still nameless, mountain that was to become Mount Selwyn.

One prime objective of the expedition was the finding and examining of a strange mountain—a mountain of a shape so fantastic that it almost went beyond belief. But still, one never knew: at the bottom of the mystery lay a book—Butler's second book of Canadian travel, *The Wild North Land*—and Butler was not a man who would write with intent to mislead. It might be well to go and see.

In this same month of July, 1875, the author of that book was far away in South Africa, travelling by Cape cart across the plains of the Orange Free State and marvelling at the splendid herds of wild game that covered the veldt. He had completed his long winter journey of 1872–73 by getting out to Victoria. From there he went on to San Francisco, and so across the States to Ottawa, where he arrived at the end of August. There he got wind of an expedition that was being prepared in England for the Gold Coast under the command of a man he greatly admired both as a soldier and an organizer, Major-General Sir Garnet Wolseley—the man who, as Colonel Wolseley, had been the leader of the successful Red River expedition. Butler leapt at this chance of action. He warmed up the Atlantic cable and then rushed, as fast as steam could take him, across the ocean to England. During the crossing, and also in the latter stages of his land journey, he somehow found time to write, with furious energy, the greater part of a book describing his adventures in the North.

He missed Wolseley and his staff by only eight hours, but followed at the end of September on an old, fever-ridden tub, the *Benin*. It was a sudden and dramatic change: from the ice-strewn Gap of the Peace and from the clean wild rivers of the North, straight to the steamy Bight of Benin and to Cape Coast Castle and the White Man's Grave. Butler did, indeed, call to mind the old sailor's song:

Remember, remember the Bight of Benin,
Few come out though many go in ...

—but what young man in wartime ever believes that death or disease will lay their clammy hands on *him*?

Butler landed at Cape Coast Castle on October 22, 1873. Already in the grip of the fever, he crossed the Prah River into Ashanti on

January 15, 1874. He succeeded in the operations that had been assigned to him, was mentioned in dispatches, and eventually got back to Cape Coast Castle in mid-February absolutely rotten with fever, "the wreck of a wreck." He barely got to England alive. He lay in a hospital there for two months, was personally visited by Queen Victoria, was promoted to the rank of major and made a Companion of the Bath. But not till he had managed, with feeble aim, to shoot a snipe in some bog in the wilds of Kerry did he feel his feet firmly set on the road to recovery.

In the meantime the manuscript describing his second winter journey in Canada had become a book, *The Wild North Land*. He had written the preface to it in September, 1873, before he left England for Ashanti—but the proofreading and final production had, owing to almost a full year of travel, war and fever, inevitably been in the hands of the publishers.

It is the illustrations to that book, fifteen in number, that are of interest here. Some are most realistic, based quite certainly on Butler's notes and sketches. Others, such as the one of the upset canoe at Hudson's Hope, are obviously drawn, as to background, from photographs taken by Charles Horetzky in 1872 when on his pathfinding expedition for the Canadian Pacific Railway. At least two different illustrators have taken part in the production; and in places one of them—the author being absent in Ashanti or delirious on a bed of fever—has really felt free to let himself go. And in no pictures more so than in those of the Black Canyon of the Omineca and of the tremendous conical peak at the western end of the Peace River Gap—which was the artist's conception of the mountain that has so impressed Butler. Nothing that could add drama to these two scenes has been omitted. The Black Canyon is a place of terror, with twisted, menacing trees—trees such as Rackham might have drawn—clinging to the streaming rocks; while the vast pinnacle of a mountain, sharp as a spearhead and glowing in the sunset light, makes peaks such as the Matterhorn or Mount Assinniboine look, in comparison, like holes in the ground. No geologist, certainly no director of the Geological Survey, could resist going to have a look at this incredible tower of rock, this remnant of a vanished volcano—or whatever else it might have been. In fact, Selwyn in his report frankly admits to a certain curiosity: "At each turn of the river," he writes, "we expected that the remarkable conical mountain depicted in *The Wild*

This extraordinary artistic conception of Mount Selwyn appeared in Butler's The Wild North Land.

North Land, page 271, would break upon our vision. In this, however, we were destined to be disappointed ... "[5]

So much, then, for the call of the wild as heard by a London illustrator in Queen Victoria's day. Meanwhile Butler, thousands of miles away in Africa, was still speeding gaily across the veldt in his Cape cart towards Bloemfontein and Kimberley, all unwitting of the stir he was causing on the Peace. And, towering above Selwyn's camp on the shore of that river, there still remained the mountain to be climbed.

They got at it on the morning of July 11. They went a little way along the riverbank from camp and then started up a goat trail that they had reconnoitred the evening before. In places the trail was much overgrown and they had to shove their way upwards through the bush, sweating prodigiously in the windless heat. Here and there, in the damp hollows, they ran into patches of devil's club, flourishing like the powers of evil with its poisonous spines and its great leaves up to fourteen inches in diameter. It caused them, Macoun says, much pain and inconvenience. Altogether they had about 5,600 feet to go to get to the summit and for over 4,000 feet of that climb they were in the bush, ramming their way through the tangle of the trees.

For a great part of the distance they could hear the rush of a torrent close to them and below, and when they were about 3,000 feet above the river Macoun asked the others to halt for a spell while he went down into the bed of the stream to see what he could see. Nobody was sorry to lie down and rest and smoke, and Macoun disappeared into the coulee, sliding down, swinging from bush to bush.

In about twenty minutes he was back, delighted with himself. Down below, in the green canyon of the stream, he had found just what he hoped to find—a great number of alpine and subalpine plants, growing and flowering close together in a remarkably small area. The ones he valued were safe in his collecting boxes, and now he was more eager to get on than ever: he had observed that a number of these plants were growing about 2,000 feet below their proper zone, the seeds having been carried down to the lower level by the spring runoff. He knew, now, that there must be something up above that was well worth climbing for.

Timberline was about 6,000 feet and the party emerged gratefully from the trees onto the open slopes. The members of the crew who were taking part in the climb were all volunteers. They were carrying various pieces of equipment for Selwyn and Macoun—and here, for the first time, they got a clear view of the mountain. At the sight of what lay before them one of the men felt his already waning enthusiasm oozing out through the bottom of his boots. No more mountaineering for him, he said. It was impossible to get to the top, anyway: he would wait for them here and it wouldn't be long before they were back. And, with that, he wished the others bon voyage and made himself comfortable on the soft alpine turf to await their return.

They came to patches of snow—and even those who were familiar with high country were amazed, all over again, at the swift growth of the alpines the moment the snow cover had melted away. Out of the still-flattened, wintry grass came the flowers, racing up towards the sun. Macoun found a small ranunculus. "Four yards from the snow the petals had already fallen, and between that and the snow the plant was in all stages of growth, from those just springing out of the soil to the fading flower."

Five hundred feet below the summit Macoun found his Eldorado, a complete carpet of flowers, a shimmering mass of mingled colour. It was impossible to walk without crushing these small and lovely things. They hugged the gravel and the patches of turf, seeking shelter from the winds; even the asters, large among alpines, crouched in that magic carpet on short, dwarfed stems of no more than two inches.

But they still had to reach the summit of the mountain. On they went, scuffling up the last five hundred feet, Macoun with the rest, tearing himself away from what he would always remember, all through his life, as the most perfect of nature's gardens. Quite suddenly the slope ended and they found themselves walking easily across the level floor of the summit, a rock platform "with a little parapet in front on which we stood, overlooking the river, as we gazed upon the wondrous scene." The day had grown no cooler: it was eighty-two degrees in the shade on the mountain peak. A blue, sultry heat haze hung over the cut through the Rockies, reaching out into the foothill country to the eastward. In the west, over the Trench, it was clearer and cooler. Macoun went over to a drift of snow and bathed his head and face in it. For a few minutes he sat on the parapet, entranced with the marvellous view. Then he

This view of Mount Selwyn is from the Peace River, looking downstream.

remembered his flowers and resolutely turned his back on the great valley, laid out like a map at his feet, to busy himself with the flora of the peak. And long before Selwyn had finished taking his angles and making his geological notes, Macoun was gone—back down the first five hundred feet to his enchanted garden.

The men who remained with Selwyn on the summit had the world at their feet. Below, in the mile-deep Gap, they could see the brown ribbon of the Peace. It lay there like a painted river on a huge relief map, calm and apparently motionless, and from it there came no sound. Nine miles away to the westward the last reach of the Finlay showed, just visible over the foothills of the mountain—but except for a few westerly bends, the Parsnip was hidden from view by the intervening ridges. Far in the west, thirty sunlit miles away across the Trench, the line of the Wolverines reared up, blue-shadowed now in the afternoon light. And to the north and the east and the south lay the stony summits of the Rockies, parted only by the escaping river.

Searching carefully with a good glass, a man who knows where to look can see from that peak the bright walls of micaschist that guard the entrance to the Black Canyon of the Omineca. But those cliffs were twenty-five miles away and there were no maps of the Finlay country in 1875. Those shining rocks that mark the end of the Butler Range would have looked, to Selwyn's party, like any of a hundred cliffs that rose above the varied greens of the forest. So the men just sat there, resting and smoking, pointing and wondering, while the shadows crept round and lengthened a little. And at last they saw Selwyn shutting up his notebooks, and knew that it was time to go ...

Dragging the reluctant Macoun away from his flowers, they made their way down the mountain. It was far into the evening before they trudged heavily into camp, exhausted. And it was not till supper had had its benign effect on tired minds and bodies that Macoun came out with his proposal: the mountain they had climbed, he said—bush, devil's club, flowers, rock and snow—should bear the name of Selwyn, as a memorial to that day.

II

R. G. McConnell

Sixteen more years passed. At intervals some lone trapper or prospector would penetrate into the Finlay country. He would blaze and cut his unrecorded trails—and then move on to fresh fields and pastures new, while the relentless growth of the subarctic forest closed in again behind him.

In 1891 a British Columbia government party under N. B. Gauvreau carried a track-survey some fifty miles up the Finlay as far as the Hudson's Bay Company's post of Fort Grahame,[6] and the first outlines of a map began to appear. The men climbed a few of the mountains near the post and gazed wonderingly at the white and shining slopes of a range that formed the western wall of the Trench almost fifty miles upstream from where they sat. A faint weather haze lay over the big valley and the far horizon was hidden from them. But those distant scarps gleamed provokingly under the summer sun—too low for snow, but just as white and clean. Where were they? And what could they be?

On their way up to Fort Grahame, Gauvreau's party had ascended the Omineca almost as far as the Osilinka Forks. They said the river was impracticable for canoes at that stage of water and in the time at their disposal—and so, perhaps, it may have been. But the man who came after Gauvreau was a harder man to stop.

In 1893 Selwyn, the director, decided it was time the Geological Survey of Canada took a look at the Finlay country, and to it he sent, on reconnaissance, that skilled northern traveller and explorer, R. G. McConnell. He could scarcely have picked a better man. McConnell was born in 1857, a native of Chatham, Canada East. He took his bachelor's degree at McGill University in 1879 and joined the staff of the Geological Survey in 1880. He was a man of medium height, lightly built and active as a cat: it was almost as if nature had designed him on purpose for the trail.

Some ten years before the Klondike rush opened up the North, McConnell made one of the longest explorations ever undertaken by the Geological Survey. He left Ottawa in company with G. M. Dawson in April, 1887, and in May the two of them, with their crew, set out for the Interior from Wrangell, Alaska, heading up the Stikine River. They parted company at the end of June at the Lower Post on the Liard—McConnell to descend through the dangerous canyons of that river, and then to make a prodigious loop north of the Arctic Circle to the Yukon. It was September of 1888 before he crossed the Chilkoot Pass and once more set eyes on the Pacific—at Lynn Canal, the starting-point-to-be of the Klondike trail of '98. An eighteen-months' journey: even Butler or Warburton Pike would have been satisfied with that.

McConnell travelled efficiently and fast and covered a great deal of territory in a season's work. So much territory, in fact, that I have heard a former colleague of his say that some of his observations on the geological features of his journeys could not be other than superficial. Nevertheless, the speed of his passage by canoe did not prevent him from observing that the Rocky Mountain system ended at the Liard, nor from making a map of that river that is the best available, even today. Nor did anything in his reports prevent him from becoming deputy minister of the federal department of mines from 1914 to 1921, in which latter year he retired. He died aged eighty-five in 1942.

Quesnel was McConnell's base for his Finlay expedition, and he was held there till June 9, 1893, owing to the scarcity of competent canoemen. He started up the Fraser on that date with a crew of four: two Indians, one half-breed and one White man. It took them, with two Peterborough canoes, exactly two weeks to get up to Giscome Portage; and the party moved fast over the portage trail to Summit Lake. They left from there on June 26. The Crooked River was not yet named, but McConnell's report may well have christened it: "We followed," he wrote, "a chain of small lakes connected by small, crooked, and at times exceedingly swift streams down to Fort McLeod." That was the old "McLeod's Lake Fort," and they got there on June 28.

There they were held up for a week. The bulk of their supplies had left Quesnel by pack train to go by way of Stuart Lake, and the outfit had been delayed on the trail by flooded rivers. The advance party used the extra time to build themselves a canvas-covered canoe, and it was in the three canoes, quite heavily loaded, that on July 6 they started down McLeod Lake River. On July 7 they arrived at the Forks of the Peace.

Leaving the bulk of the outfit at the Forks, McConnell made a swift trip down the Peace and back. With him, as assistant and topographer, was H. Y. Russel: gradually the map of the country was taking shape—this time with the rock exposures marked along the riverbanks in the various colours appropriate to their different geological ages. A hundred years had gone by since Mackenzie's day, and no longer was this the unknown land.

Returning to the Forks, they picked up their stuff and poled up the Finlay to the mouth of the Omineca. There, in a place that was safe from sudden floods, they built a cache in which they placed the bulk of their stores. And from that as a base they tackled the Omineca, travelling light. Their first day brought them to the gateway of the Black Canyon and, as did Butler twenty years before them, they looked anxiously at its sheer walls of gneiss and micaschist. The canyon is half a mile long and from one to two hundred feet wide. Its walls are almost vertical and rise to over one hundred and fifty feet. "At low water," McConnell wrote, "the navigation is reported easy. In flood time the swollen stream is partly dammed back and its effort to force a way through the narrow channel is attended with the production of such whirlpools and billows that its passage with large boats is exceedingly difficult and with small boats is impossible."

This was medium-high water—and navigation of the canyon was still impossible. They set to and cut out a portage trail on the north side, passing above the cliffs and over the tail end of the Butler Range, through which the canyon is driven. From the head of the portage they went on—on above the Tchutetzeca, where the river was nothing but a series of rapids, where the six men could average only five miles a day—on again above Little Canyon, where Pete Toy was drowned—and still onwards, lining up the rapids for another ten miles till quiet water was reached and they could travel with ease. And by that time, they had hauled their Peterborough canoes up a hill of water that was four hundred and twenty-five feet high—a slope of twelve feet to the mile.

They came to Germansen Landing, and from there they went on foot to Manson Creek, and on to Silver Creek—where the gold had first been struck by Twelve-Foot Davis and Ezra Evans twenty-five years before. And all this time McConnell and Russel were noting down the population and the yield of this half-abandoned mining camp, the nature of the forest growth and the height and bearings of the mountains, the dip and strike of the rocks and the lay of the land. And when all was seen and recorded they shoved off again down the river, undoing in one mad rush the long days of upstream toil. They came again to the cache at the mouth of the Omineca, and there they reloaded the canoes and turned up the Finlay. The date was August 5, 1893. It had been a strenuous month, but a still more strenuous six weeks lay ahead of them.

12

Inspector J. D. Moodie

The next articulate and literate visitors to the Finlay appeared on the scene some four years later. These were a different sort of men: they were neither sportsmen nor fur traders, geologists nor trappers: they were men under authority, men with a high tradition, and they came only because the Finlay and the great furrow of the Trench, for so many years the road to nowhere, had suddenly become a potential highway to the Klondike.

Through the winter months of 1896 to 1897 strange rumours had been seeping out of the North—rumours of an incredibly rich strike on a tributary of the Yukon, a salmon river with a name nobody had ever heard of and which was not to be found on any map. This sounded like the usual story, only with a new name; and people shrugged and thought no more of it. Yet the rumours were strangely persistent—and the shrugging came to a sudden end on July 17, 1897, when the *Portland* steamed into Seattle harbour with two tons of gold on board. *That* was something tangible—and the sheer magnificence of "two tons of gold" struck first a spark and then a flame in a bored, credulous and depression-ridden continent. North America went mad and the madness spread beyond the seas. The world and his wife made plans to hit for the golden river. Obstacles vanished in a wave of unreasoning optimism, and various "all-Canadian" routes to the new Eldorado were vigorously promoted by the various outfitting points that hoped to cash in on the rush. Among these routes was the line of the Trench: it led northwestwards and that, just then, was full justification for any route, however impracticable.

Foreseeing trouble as a flood of greenhorn, nondescript gold seekers surged through the lonely valleys of the mountains, raising hell with the game and the country and clashing with the Indians, the Canadian government decided to investigate the possibilities for a trail from the Peace River country to Yukon waters. The creeks on the chosen trail would eventually be bridged and the muskegs corduroyed, and refuge cabins would be built at suitable intervals. This job was handed to the North West Mounted Police, and Inspector J. D. Moodie was sent out with a party of four constables to locate and blaze the trail.

Moodie left Edmonton on September 4, 1897, and reached Fort St. John on the Peace River with winter setting in. He left Fort St. John on December 2 with dogs and horses, battling his way up the Halfway River through deepening snow, hoping to find at the headwaters a pass through the Rockies that would lead towards Fort Grahame. The men saw sheep in the high country but could not get near them. They killed and ate caribou and moose—and the going got tougher as the trail climbed. But they found their pass: they called it Laurier Pass, and on that summit they spent Christmas Day, laying over two nights to rest the men and let the horses feed on the open grazing of that little meadow from which the wind had swept the snow.

On December 26 they had to give up using horses. They killed seven and half-dried and froze the meat for dog feed, sending the rest of the horse bunch back to Fort St. John. Then through deadfall and around small canyons they made their way down the west slope of the main range into the headwaters of the Ospika. On New Year's Eve the half-breed Iroquois hunter attached to the party, Napoleon Thomas, celebrated by shooting two cow moose, and the camp ate well. But the Ospika was taking them too far to the south, out of their course, and another range still lay between them and the Finlay, barring the way to the west. They climbed it and slid down the western side into the Trench—men, dog teams and toboggans—and they reached the frozen Finlay somewhere near Collins' Flat, which is below Fort Grahame. That was on January 16, and on that day they had to feed the dogs some of their precious bacon. Napoleon's two moose were finished, right down to the last marrow bone.

They were now in rather a fix: they had not the faintest idea whether they were upstream or downstream from Fort Grahame. So they tried it downstream until the distant mountains drew closer and changed their shapes, and Napoleon recognized them and swore by all he held sacred that they were the mountains by the Forks. Whereupon they smartly reversed their direction, setting a course northwestward for Fort Grahame over their own well-broken trail.

They arrived there on January 18, and their arrival was well timed: trouble was threatening. The Sikannis resented the sudden influx of Whites who shot their game, treated them like dirt, trampled on their rights, and were not averse, in some cases, from robbing a cache—the unforgivable sin. These Indians, according to Moodie, were a miserable lot, utterly unreliable and with morals of the lowest, but none the less prone to anger and very vindictive. And now they were ready to fight—not without good reason. "We may as well die by the White men's bullets," they said, "as die of starvation."

The detachment wintered at Fort Grahame and their presence prevented an outbreak. But it was an uneasy winter for all concerned—the police, the Klondikers, the Sikannis and the little Hudson's Bay Company outpost under its manager, William Fox. Supplies were low and the moose of the district were becoming shot out. Somehow the people made it through, but when spring came the North West Mounted Police detachment was practically cleaned out of supplies, and Fort Grahame was cleaned out too. Leaving on April 1, Moodie and three constables made the long trip to Stuart's Lake, only to find that there also the cupboard was bare. They were forced to go on to Quesnel, and it was early July of 1898 before they returned by river with their load to Fort Grahame. Two constables were then sent back to bring up various equipment that the detachment had cached on the Ospika on the winter journey. Civilization, however, had now reached the wilderness of the Finlay, and, in accordance with the new morality, a portion of the property had been stolen.

Moodie finally left Fort Grahame on July 15, heading up the Finlay. About forty miles above the fort and a few miles below the Akiéka[7] the detachment rafted across the Finlay in order to take advantage of the wider flats on the west side and to avoid the powerful streams that come down from the Rockies. Later on there was a sort of a ferry there. The crossing place became known as Barge Camp, and at least until 1908 an old scow lay there, drawn up high and dry above flood level, relic of the Klondike rush.

The detachment went on up the right bank of the Finlay until they were above the mouth of the fast and silty Kwadacha River that flows down from Haworth Lake and the glaciers of the Rockies. Then they recrossed the Finlay—now without the milky flood of the Kwadacha and clear as crystal—and held straight on up the Trench, saying goodbye to the Finlay at the foot of Prairie Mountain. They followed the east bank of the little Tochieca, now known as Fox River, after the post manager of Fort Grahame. Forty-odd miles up the Tochieca brought them to Sifton Pass[8] with its small prairie of good grazing and its far view up and down the Trench—and that was the end of the Finlay country: the rivers beyond the pass ran northwestward to the Liard.

They travelled on down the Kechika, coming to a drier country with good hard grass and sound going, a country where a horse can eat his fill and grow fat. But they had no time to linger on that good horse feed: summer was already on its way. They followed the Trench till the mountains fell back from it and sank lower into the earth—and there was no more Trench, and even the Rockies were coming to an end. Then they turned west, up Samuel Black's river, the Turnagain—and another eighty miles saw them to Sylvester's Landing on the Dease. From there they followed the old trails of the fur traders—and they ended by running down the Pelly by canoe, racing against the oncoming winter. Surmounting the dangers of mush ice and unknown rapids, they came at last to the mouth of the Pelly, and so to the Yukon. It was October 24 and the rivers were choked with running ice. Somehow Moodie and his men got across the Yukon and fell into the warmth and welcome of the North West Mounted Police post of Fort Selkirk. It was one year and seven weeks since they had left Edmonton.

There was no fanfare of trumpets. They had simply carried out their orders and blazed a trail.

13

The Police Trail

There matters rested for several years. Moodie, in his report, gave it as his opinion that the trail he had blazed would never be used, in view of the shorter and quicker route to the Yukon by way of Skagway and the Chilkoot Pass. Then the White Pass and Yukon Railway to Whitehorse eliminated the Chilkoot, and the Yukon Telegraph Line was completed by way of Telegraph Creek and Hazelton to Quesnel: one way and another it was becoming senseless to build an expensive trail over a route that no right-minded man would ever follow.

And yet that is exactly what was done—and long after the first fine fury of the Klondike rush had subsided. Years, even, after Dawson City had watched a large part of its population push off down the Yukon River, headed for the golden beaches of Nome.

Once more the job was handed to the now-Royal North West Mounted Police; and on March 17, 1905, Superintendent C. Constantine, Inspector J. Richards, six non-commissioned officers, twenty-two constables, two special constables and sixty horses set out from Fort Saskatchewan near Edmonton. The plan was to cut out and fix up the 750 miles from Fort St. John to Yukon water at Teslin Lake, *not* following Moodie's trail, but going westward from Fort Grahame to Bear Lake and from there to the Yukon Telegraph Trail north of Hazelton. This was the trail that was to receive the full treatment—bridges, corduroys and rest cabins. It would also be a trail that would run transversely to the lay of the country, crossing all the available mountain ranges instead of accommodating itself to them in the valleys. Its highest passes would be blocked with snow well into the average July. It would hardly ever be used. It could benefit nobody except, conceivably, a few Hudson's Bay Company posts. Slowly, unseen by any but a few Indians or some lone prospector, it would fall into decay and the bush would take back its own. It was an incredible scheme. In its utter disregard of geographical facts, it somewhat resembles the Cassiar Central Railway lunacy—and, like the CCR, it was probably a brainwave on the part of the minister of the interior, Clifford Sifton. Yet, once more, it was an order.

The winter of 1905 saw the main body still east of the Rockies; but an advance party under Corporal McLeod, thrown back from Laurier Pass by deep and drifted snow, got around through the Peace River Gap to the Finlay and to Fort Grahame, where they wintered. They arrived just in time. The Sikannis were again in want and feeling that somebody owed them a living. McLeod was able to advance rations to them on condition that they got out to their hunting grounds—and so a raid on the Hudson's Bay Company post was averted.

On August 17, 1906, Fox noted in his journal the arrival of the police pack train with their first load. Two days later he went down to the police camp, about two miles down the river, and had dinner there. A second load came in that evening, and the last load of supplies on the evening of the twentieth. And on August 23 the completed trail reached Fort Grahame, 208 measured miles from Fort St. John.

With a regretful glance from Constantine at Moodie's better line of travel, the trail cutters crossed the Finlay and vanished from Fox's view into the mountains, heading west for Bear Lake. Autumn now was touching the Finlay country with its golden fingers. The mornings saw the whiteness of frost in the hollows. The days were calm and sunny and the nights were laden with dew. And sometimes it rained. But, rain or shine, it made no difference to the men: they were on the job—and they were wet. They were soaked to the skin on wet days, and they were no less soaked when the sun shone. The tall grass and the pea vine, the willows and the fireweed, all dripping with dew, soon had a man drenched as though a cloud had burst above his sweating head. And still the axes swung, the saws played their homely tune, and the trail crawled forward—over summits, past small lakes, alongside new rivers. There were few axe cuts among the men and no sickness. The whole detachment must have been as hard as nails. Only on one occasion did a constable, sodden and dripping with dew, and being obliged through lack of a horse to wade several times across a strong, deep stream on a bridging operation, request of Inspector Richards permission to return to camp for dry clothes. Permission was refused. The constable was put on a charge "for making a frivolous complaint." The trail went forward.

That was 1906. The year 1907 saw the end. The Police Trail reached the Yukon Telegraph Trail at a point four miles north of Fourth Cabin, which was 104 miles north of Hazelton. This point was 377 measured miles by the Police Trail from Fort St. John—and it was 272 miles due west of Fort St. John. Not a mile of northerly distance had been gained; it was still about 170 miles as the crow flies by the Telegraph Trail to the Stikine River and to Telegraph Creek; and the worst of the Telegraph Trail still lay ahead—a frightful trail, known in the rush of '98 as the Ashcroft Trail and guaranteed to take the heart out of man and beast.

The police offered to carry their made trail on to the Stikine, provided the British Columbia government would co-operate. Not unreasonably, the provincial government "did not see their way to assist," and the project was discontinued.

For perhaps a score of years there could be seen on the maps a dotted red line running through Laurier Pass, indicating the existence of a trail.

Even the red line has gone from the maps of today, and the head of the Ospika is once more a trackless wilderness out of which, quite recently, a party of hunters travelling with a pack train had difficulty in finding their way eastward across the Rockies.

14

Fleet Robertson

A year went by, and then on August 19, 1908, a canoe heading downstream swung around Pete Toy's Bar, at the foot of which we have been standing. In it were the provincial mineralogist of British Columbia, W. Fleet Robertson, three other men and eight hundred pounds of personal gear and equipment.

Unlike most of the other explorers and travellers, Robertson had never fought his way up the Finlay against the summer flood: he had come in by the back door, as it were, to the headwaters of the Ingenika by pack train from Hazelton. The reasons for his trip were twofold: the discovery of gold on the upper Ingenika and on its tributary, McConnell Creek—and Robertson's custom of spending every season in the field. He thoroughly enjoyed these long wilderness journeys, and here, readymade for the season of 1908, was one that took him into new country.

The gold on McConnell Creek did not amount to very much, though on the Ingenika itself three prospectors were making at least a good grubstake: they finally took out seventy ounces of gold. Two of these men were Jack Starke ("the Black Pirate") and Jack Stanier, with whom I met and travelled, twenty years later, on the Liard and South Nahanni rivers in the Northwest Territories. To see, unexpectedly, those names in Robertson's lively and readable report brought back a surge of memories: for Stanier, the frightful (though, at the same time, hilarious) adventures and misadventures of the Liard Coal Company Limited, a hapless mining project of 1927—and for Starke, a vision of him standing at the tiller of his scow, unshaven, blackavised, a black pipe in his mouth, and, on his head, that old black hat on which there was never so much as standing room for one more mosquito. And his eyes set, staring straight ahead, watching every swirl on the heaving flood of the Nahanni ...

But to return to Fleet Robertson, whom we left camped by the diggings on McConnell Creek—only a low pass and twenty-odd miles of rough going lay between him and Thutadé Lake at the head of the Finlay. He went that way with his men and his horses, and on July 25 the party reached the lower end of Thutadé. The following day they moved down the last of the lake and the first few miles of the Finlay, to make camp below the Falls, perhaps with an eye to the fishing. In this they were not disappointed: a couple of hours there with one fly rod was more than enough to supply the six men. There were trout from ten to fifteen inches and grayling from twelve to twenty inches; the latter they found the best eating, though not the best sport: a couple of hard-pulling runs, and that was all.

The Finlay, from the lake to the Falls, runs a swift course through a four-mile canyon. Robertson estimated the Falls to be about fifty feet in height. A rock buttress in the centre of the drop divides the falling water into twin cascades—and below the Falls the river is very dangerous, being for miles streaked with rapids and strewn with boulders. Even so, it was apparently no barrier to a determined or a reckless man. "On the afternoon of the twenty-sixth a wild-looking Swede suddenly appeared in camp; he was soaking wet and led an equally wet horse, having swum the river to beg some horseshoe nails without which he could not proceed. After his horse had been reshod he tried four times to swim the horse back across the river, failing each time and nearly drowning when the horse, displaying more sense than the rider, refused to enter the water again. The pair were kept at the camp all night, and in the morning the man made a raft, recrossed the river, drifting downstream half a mile in so doing, secured his baggage and partner (also a Swede), built another raft away up near the Falls, and after almost capsizing twice, managed to get across again; an example of how men of inexperience may disappear in that north country." These two Swedes had been prospecting on the west side of the Finlay for about twenty miles below the Falls, but had so far had no luck.

From that good fishing camp Robertson's party moved slowly down the right bank of the river for about twenty-five miles, finding the going bad and the horse feed poor. To follow the river the whole way round the big bend and into the Trench was evidently a hopeless proposition with horses; and it was decided to turn up Delta Creek and search for a route that would cut across the bend and lead to navigable water on the Finlay below the canyons and the cascades, and to country with which two of the party were familiar.

So they took that road, hoping to find a pass, and the second of August saw them camped seven miles up Delta Creek with the mountain barrier still ahead of them and still unknown. There, in those mountains of the bend, we shall meet them again, searching for a way, lowering their horses over giant steps in the rock, cutting their trail through the tangled alpine forest …

15

Swannell on the Mesilinka

Early in 1913, five years after Fleet Robertson's journey, a young British Columbia land surveyor received his instructions for the coming season. These came in the form of a letter from the surveyor general—and to describe this letter merely as complimentary would be an understatement. "I have much pleasure," the letter ran, "in informing you that your work of last year meets with the approbation of the Department, and in view of the success you obtained in these operations it would appear to be hardly necessary to give you definite instructions.

"You will continue your rough triangulation to the North and East. There is one matter, however ... It is neither necessary or possible in a triangulation such as you are making to obtain results of extreme accuracy, your work being in the nature of an Exploratory Triangulation. Such being the case I must impress upon you the necessity of covering a large area of country rather than looking for refinement in the point of accuracy." Pointing out that only one other surveyor in the whole huge province was engaged in exploratory work, the surveyor general twice again emphasized that what he wanted was "a preliminary knowledge of a large section of country rather than a comparatively correct Triangulation of a limited area." He then flung in the final bouquet: "I leave the arrangement of the season's operations entirely in your hands."

To a strong, active and intelligent man in his thirties, at the peak of his strength and powers, the contents of that letter must have been sweeter than honey. It conferred upon him the freedom of the lakes around Fort St. James, of the Driftwood River country and the tangle of rivers that forms the Omineca. From Takla Lake in the west all the way to Fort Grahame and the Rockies in the east his triangulation would link mountain peak with mountain peak in a network of cross-bearings, and the trail of his party would be marked on the map by the record of their names—even by the names of the dogs that accompanied them. And by this survey a base would be provided at Fort Grahame for the greater adventure of the 1914 season, when the triangulation would be carried on up the Finlay by canoe, past Fox River, round the big bend to the Fishing Lakes—even beyond.

The man to whom all this was entrusted was F. C. Swannell. A native of Hamilton, Ontario, he came west in 1897 and joined the surveys branch of the British Columbia lands department in 1898. His diaries, illustrated with his photographs, are kept in a beautiful surveyor's script which remains unchanged even today, when he can look back across fifty-three years to his exploration of the Finlay. Being a historian, he has omitted no event of the past that can add interest to those diaries. Having the gift of tongues (after his retirement he added Swedish to his spoken languages simply in order to go round the Horn on a Swedish windjammer) he was well equipped to cope with the Chinook jargon and with the Indian languages, or with the French-Canadian patois of the half-breeds. Being endowed with itching feet—that happy affliction which prevents a man, even though burdened with many years, from turning slowly but surely into a cabbage—he is even now, at the time of writing and himself in his eighties, travelling beyond the seas.

As assistant to Swannell came George Vancouver Copley, a native of Vancouver Island, now living in New Westminster. Here was a lightly built man, quick and hardy, good on a mountain and ideal for a tough canoe trip. Furthermore, Copley had a knowledge of botany—a science decidedly with its uses in completing the report of an exploratory survey.

Next we have Jim Alexander, the son of a Hudson's Bay Company factor at Fort St. James and a Carrier Indian mother. Alexander (who died in 1941) was tall and handsome and very strong. He was the canoeman of the outfit and when they were on the water he was captain of the ship: raft, bateau or canoe—whichever it might be. When they travelled with horses they had, in him, a competent packer. He was a friend of the priest-historian, Father A. G. Morice, and helped him on many a long winter evening at Fort St. James with his *Dictionary of the Carrier Language*. He had a strong desire to see the Fishing Lakes on the Finlay, of which he had often heard. In fact he was determined to see them, and that determination drove him on to surmount every obstacle in the river—rapid, cascade or portage. Frank Swannell still says: "Had it not been for Jim Alexander we could never have made it."

The survey party was completed by the cook, Nep Yuen, sometimes known as Jim Young or Jim Nep, a stocky, well-made Chinaman of medium height from Hong Kong. Nep Yuen had come to Canada to work on the construction of the Canadian Pacific Railway, so by 1913 he must have been into his forties. He was competent in his job, and nobody seems to have grumbled about his cooking or been poisoned by it. He worked in well with the outfit, doing his share on the portage or on the trail. He was the fisherman of the party, as his game record shows, but, though he fancied himself at shooting, he was less handy with a rifle. Swannell came back to camp one day to find Nep Yuen in a shocking temper. Using Swannell's rifle he had taken four carefully aimed shots at a lynx across the Ingenika—not at that point the widest of rivers. And nothing, it seemed, had gone anywhere near the lynx. Obviously, according to Nep Yuen, the rifle was no damn good, and he was very annoyed with the rifle's owner. Somewhat puzzled, Swannell examined the offending weapon. The sights were set at nine hundred yards.

Nep Yuen was a Chinaman of character, and two hard and often dangerous trips made him into a friend. The last time Swannell saw him was when he came home one afternoon to his house in Victoria to find Nep Yuen there before him, deep in converse with Mrs. Swannell. Nep's eyes brightened when he saw Frank. "Missie Swannell," he said, "now Flank come you catchee one dipper cold water while I pour dlinks." Wherewith, he produced a bottle of Scotch and poured out four fingers for himself and two for his former chief, saying as he did so to Mrs. Swannell, "That all lite for Flank. He no got stlong head."

This took place at the time of the civil wars in China, and, when questioned as to what line of business was engaging his attention at the moment, Nep Yuen gave the Swannells to understand that he was involved in smuggling arms into his native country. When asked, "For which side?" he gaily replied, "For both sides ... "—which, of course, is sound business, splitting, as it undoubtedly does, the chances of total loss to the vendor. The only trouble is, it requires more skill than does a straight sale to one single client.

They never heard again from Nep Yuen ...

Those three men, with Swannell, were the core of the 1913 party— and in 1914 the four of them, by themselves, would make the great river trip round the big bend of the Finlay, following in the footsteps of Samuel Black.

They started out, in 1913, from Fort St. James on June 1, and for most of that summer they worked on the lakes and rivers northwest of Stuart Lake, occasionally crossing and recrossing the Omineca divide. With them, but as foresters only and not surveyors, were Victor Kastberg and Axel Gold—the latter a Jack London name, if ever there was one. Various packers and horse wranglers, with their pack trains, moved with the party or made rendezvous with them as the work demanded.

On August 19 the whole outfit, men and horses, crossed the divide into the Omineca country. Extending the triangulation as they went, they crossed Boulder Pass from the headwaters of the Omineca to the headwaters of the Mesilinka, the Stranger River, on September 1. They were now on the Police Trail, on the trail that Constantine's men had cut out less than seven years before. Enthusiasm among the police for their futile task may have been waning by the time they reached Mile 280 west from Fort St. John (Swannell found the marker at his Camp 59 of the 1913 season), but forest growth and forest fires, snowstorms, whirlwinds and gales had all lent a helping hand to obliterate the road. "Trail exceptionally execrable," is Swannell's furious comment in the *Diary*—and again, on September 1, "It took horses 4 hours to go 3 miles and Bob nearly kills himself."

Camp 61 saw them at Tutizzi (Long-water) Lake, every man having carried his own dunnage over the horrible trail, and dog Dick the big tent. Since we shall meet these people again and again up the Finlay, let me here explain that in the *Diary*, to distinguish the names of the animals from those of men, dogs always receive their proper style and title—dog Caesar, dog Dick, and so forth—and horses are often designated as above: "Bob."

This camp was a bit over fifty miles from Fort Grahame. The trail along Tutizzi Lake was so badly fallen in that they built a large raft and poled the bulk of the gear down the seven-mile lake on it, while the horses travelled light. The outlet stream proved to be too shallow and rapid for rafting, so they had to abandon that raft and cut trail downstream till they once more reached what a dyed-in-the-wool optimist might call navigable water. Five days later, from Camp 64, Swannell, Copley, Alexander and dog Dick embarked, with a heavy load, on a second raft to run the Mesilinka. They found the river *very* swift and badly obstructed by driftpiles—dangerous piled-up jams of dead and uprooted trees. Careering downstream, steering their heavy craft by means of long pike-poles, they crashed into one driftpile, sheered out and spun end for end three times, being swept in the process under a low sweeper—that is, under a long spar or fallen tree projecting horizontally from the bank or from a driftpile. The sweeper just cleared the load, but the three men had to jump over it as the raft drove beneath. They all cleared it, landing on the raft again, and no man dropped his pole—a neat piece of work. Dog Dick, however, standing on the load, failed to get this jumping idea and was swept overboard into the river. "He made for shore and will have no more rafting, thereby showing sound common sense." That day they travelled seventeen miles.

In the morning they climbed a mountain to take sights back and forward. Then they shoved out once more into the Mesilinka with their raft and its ton of load. They could see in the distance the Butler Range. Where the Mesilinka impinged on that mountain slope and swung away southeastward along its flank, there, they knew, the Police Trail would leave the river and head through a low place in the range for Fort Grahame.

The going was much the same as the day before: fast water and shallow riffles, bad driftpiles and boulders. Swannell had a narrow escape in one of these places. A huge driftpile came in sight which, they could see, blocked the river completely. The Mesilinka was fast there: nothing could stop them from piling into the great barrier of drift and uprooted trees, but as they swept down towards it, close to shore, they managed to hurl most of the load up into the bush. Orders were then given for each man to grab a bundle and jump to the logjam the moment the raft struck. It hit with a crash, and Alexander and Copley jumped clear. Swannell, however, got one foot caught between the poles of the raft floor—and the raft itself began to stand on end, sliding up onto the driftpile in front while the rear end, where Swannell was trapped, was being driven under by the current. Alexander and Copley each caught an arm and pulled. Something had to give—and just as Swannell was being drawn down under the jam his boot came free and they got him clear.

They were not quite down to the Butler Range, but no matter—that was enough of rafting on the Mesilinka. They packed all the stuff up the bank and stacked it where the horses would pass. Then they walked back over what had been, so few years ago, the Police Trail, cutting and clearing for the pack train as they went. Eventually the sound of axes and men's voices could be heard from upriver, and the slam of horses' hoofs on down timber. That was the pack train approaching. They camped that night near to where the outfit was stacked by the trail. The sound of that camp, as evening drew on, was the rush of the Mesilinka through the big driftpile in which their raft was now inextricably jammed ... From that camp, starting in the morning, Swannell and Copley walked the twenty-two miles in to Fort Grahame, being ferried over the Finlay by the Hudson's Bay Company post manager, Ross. The pack train came in one day behind them, on the afternoon of September 16.

Early on the morning of the seventeenth they chose with care a large cottonwood and felled it. A section well over twenty feet in length was sawn out of the best part of the tree, and this they rolled over and over while Jim Alexander considered it. Finally they bedded it and pegged it steady. Alexander marked it, and then they got at it.

What they wanted from this cottonwood was a dugout canoe, no heavier than need be but strong enough and seaworthy enough to carry four men with their supplies, camp equipment and survey instruments safely through whatever might await them on the big bend of the Finlay, where they planned to use the canoe in the 1914 season.

They needed an adze—and there was no adze at Fort Grahame; neither was there any forge. And there were no blacksmith's tools. They soon fixed that. Alexander and Copley, aided by Nep Yuen and Rossetti, a Sicilian who had come in with the pack train, built a glowing, orange-red fire of cottonwood bark. With that as a forge they beat out the tools they needed from any odd bits of metal they could lay hands on, using rocks or anything handy as anvils, and ordinary hammers or the heads of axes as blacksmith hammers. The adze they made from a "Hudson's Bay" axe—a type of axe with the normal width of blade, but with the body of the axe drawn inwards and upwards behind the cutting edge, tomahawk fashion, to a smaller head. This axe they heated in the fire. Then they picked it out with their home-made tongs and carefully turned the blade over till it was at right angles to the head. Reheating it from time to time, they shaped the blade into something of a curve, drew it out fine, retempered and sharpened it, and finally fitted a haft. That settled the adze problem.

For two solid days they chopped and chipped with the improvised adze and their axes—and the chip pile grew and the green log began to resemble a canoe. Ross helped, and Jim Alexander did the shaping of the outside of the hull. At last they got a long, narrow trough, with the walls and floor sufficiently fined down. This they filled with water while nearby, in their fire, they heated big, round river stones. These stones, gingerly handled with green poles flattened at the ends into makeshift shovels, were lowered, hissing and spitting, into the water in the canoe, raising it slowly to boiling point. While the water heated and steamed under a covering of green spruce branches, and while the wood of the canoe became softer and more pliable, they cut thwarts—seven or eight of them in varying lengths: longer ones for the body of the canoe, shorter towards bow and stern. Then came the ticklish part of the job: they had somehow to stretch into the shape of a canoe the narrow, parallel-sided trough they had made; yet if they stretched it too far it would split and all the work would be to do again. But under Alexander's guidance all went well. The hot water was tipped out, the walls were spread apart and the thwarts were set in place; then the shrinking, drying cottonwood closed in upon them, holding them as if in a vise. Some more fining down with the axes and some more shaping of the hull—and a canoe

It took two days for Swannell's crew, using tools they fashioned on the site, to transform a cottonwood tree into this dugout canoe in September 1913 at Fort Grahame. Jim Alexander is in the foreground, with axe. Standing in the chip pile is the Hudson's Bay Company post manager Ross. (Photo courtesy of F. C. Swannell.)

lay before them, riding steady on a vast bed of sweetly smelling chips. A bit heavy, perhaps, and the lines of her would not quite be those of Peterborough or Chestnut—but, none the less, indubitably a canoe.

On September 19, two days from the felling of the cottonwood, Copley, Nep Yuen and Rossetti left with the horses for the Omineca country. On the twentieth, Swannell and Alexander put a few finishing touches to the canoe and hewed out a set of paddles. And on the following afternoon they started down the Finlay.

Here, for about a couple of weeks, till the survey starts again, the *Diary* records little beyond the day's travel—and at the time of this writing the diarist is far out of reach, not available for questioning. Fifty-four years make a wide gap for memory to bridge, and there seems to be some doubt as to what followed with regard to the canoe—not a matter of no importance, since it has considerable bearing on the course of the exploration of the following year.

Copley remembers that the two foresters, Kastberg and Axel Gold—rarely mentioned in the *Diary*, and here mentioned not at all—were taken down to the settlement at Finlay Forks in the cottonwood canoe. There they must have been dropped, to make their own way out of the country down the Peace, or to go out in somebody's boat by way of the Parsnip and McLeod Lake. We hear no more of them. They vanish.

At the Forks, Swannell and Alexander took "Sunday"—which, on survey, may be any day in the week that is convenient—visiting at the old settlement at the meeting of the rivers. For fun, and to see how the canoe would take it, they ran the Finlay Rapids. They found that the big waves at the foot of the race came too close together for a long and heavy canoe to ride clean over them: they dived through the last wave and swamped, half filling the canoe with water and getting soaked. That was a valuable bit of knowledge gained—and they made no further scientific experiments till they reached the Black Canyon.

From the Forks they poled a canoe back up the Finlay and up the Omineca to the canyon. There they left this canoe while they walked on through the bush towards the Mesilinka to make contact with Copley and the pack train. Memory has it that the canoe they left at the foot of the Black Canyon was the new cottonwood dugout. Yet photographs taken in the canyon seem to show that they were using a large and almost new Peterborough. And there would seem to be another man with them—a stranger to the outfit. That would be reasonable enough since, no matter which canoe they used, they would want somebody with them to take it back to the Forks. As to the strange canoe—if anybody did offer to lend them a nice, light Peterborough for that upstream trip, one can bank on it that they promptly accepted. That may have been what happened, and perhaps the owner came along with them to run the canoe back again to the settlement.

Swannell and Alexander found Copley and Rossetti cutting trail towards them for the horses, so they turned and cut trail with them back towards the Omineca. They reached the river, and there, in the very low water of October 5—and purely in the spirit of scientific investigation—the two voyageurs brought the canoe with pole and line up through the canyon and up the steep chute at its head. It was just over forty years since Butler had struggled his way up the Black Canyon against the May flood, and this place was already becoming historic, as history is rated in a very new country. Swannell, the historian, had studied Butler's book, *The Wild North Land*—and now, having thoroughly examined the scene of the action, he could visualize the whole exciting adventure perfectly, from rock to rock. He was content.

They ran the empty canoe down again—but this time without incident—and in some mysterious, unremembered way it departed for the Forks. That was the end of river travel for the season. From there the survey party travelled with the horses, passing over the Wolverines in the first snow, headed for Fort St. James and "the outside." The cottonwood canoe was to be sent up to McLeod Lake to await them in the spring. Everything was ready and their big year on the Finlay now lay ahead of them. Only the winter ice stood in between.

16

Haworth

The year 1916 came and in the course of that August a strange kind of canoe, carrying a strange, new type of man, came slipping down the little riffles of the Crooked River. The man was Paul Leland Haworth, an American professor of history. With him, as guide and canoeman, was Joe Lavoie, a French Canadian from Quebec who—as was usual on the borderland between civilization and the bush—had been everything by turns and nothing long: lumberjack, fire warden, prospector, trapper, and now homesteader at Finlay Forks. Haworth was travelling for his own pleasure and also because he hoped to get into unmapped country up the Kwadacha River where, report had it, there were mountains of great height carrying extensive glaciers. This would be a non-professional exploration, since Haworth was no surveyor, nor was he able to establish his position by means of observations.

As to the canoe—Haworth, who had been assured that he could have his pick on arrival in Edmonton, found when he got there that he had no choice whatsoever: he had to make do with what he could get. This proved to be a seventeen-foot Chestnut "Pleasure Model" canoe fitted with sponsons—that is, with air chambers along the gunwales so designed that the canoe, with an average load in it, would float even when swamped and full of water. Disadvantages are that the sponsons can be a bit awkward in paddling or poling and they add to the weight. This canoe was thirty-five inches in beam, twelve inches deep, and weighed seventy pounds.

Haworth has left an account of that summer's journey in his book, *On the Headwaters of Peace River*. It has been described as "an outstanding book of travel and exploration" and, more critically, as "a useful and informative non-technical record of his journey." After rereading that book, I am left with the feeling that relations could have been better between Haworth and his guide: one senses an undercurrent of friction. It seems that Lavoie was a lot better man on the river than he was when packing in the mountains. He was certainly much happier when on the water and I doubt whether his heart was ever in the land journey—and that's putting it mildly. Yet I can remember Roy McDougall saying, years afterwards: "Joe Lavoie was a good man on a river or in the bush." But weariness, shortage of food, lack of contact between two men of such different backgrounds—all these things must have played their part in creating a feeling of unease which the reader cannot but sense. One also has the impression that either Lavoie knew little about real mountain country, or else that he was overruled—for the two travellers climbed, with very heavy packs, a number of high ridges, only to find that they had gone over an obstacle instead of going around it by a much easier route. Yet Haworth persisted, and in the end, and on a later trip, he was rewarded by a sight of the lakes at the foot of the glaciers he had tried so hard to reach.

Haworth gives us one particularly interesting bit of information. A provincial election, he writes, was pending in that summer of 1916, and the Conservative candidate had gone down the Parsnip and the Peace a month or so ahead of our two voyageurs, touting in person for the few available votes. He had travelled in considerable luxury with a large and variegated stock of firewater, and the motive power had been "a detachable motor or 'kicker.'" This was the dawn of the outboard on the Finlay. It was no more than two years since Swannell and his devoted three had rounded the big bend in a cottonwood dugout—yet here was the borderline. From this time onwards the machine takes over and the technique of the rivermen changes. Haworth was the last to voyage up the Finlay in the old way and to leave some record of his journey. One must salute that trip as a tremendous physical effort, made by a man coming straight from his professorial chair, unhardened by previous training, into a tough country. One look at the photograph of Haworth on the summit of Observation Peak, weighed down with the most colossal pack, and you wonder how he ever managed it at all.

Well—there they go, Joe Lavoie poling the canoe around the edge of Pete Toy's Bar, Haworth cutting across it on foot with the little .32 in the crook of his arm, ready for anything that flies or runs. They go silently, except for the clink and click of the shod pole on the stones of the riverbed—and they will be among the last to do so since, very soon, the whine of the outboard will be breaking the age-old silence of Finlay's River. They grow smaller in the harsh glare of noonday, their dwindling figures distorted by the mirage, until they vanish round the bend in the wake of the Iroquois and of Samuel Black, and of all that pageant of travel-hardened men—the old-time travellers on this dangerous river. And with their going comes the ending of an age ...

PART THREE

To the Headwaters

17

Deserters Canyon

For the visitor, time passes pleasantly at a northern trading post. We spent three whole days at Finlay Forks as guests of the McDougalls, and much of that time was passed in listening to stories of the river told by men who travelled it. Tales of desperate trips frogging boats up the Parsnip and the Crooked in the late fall, with the water on the drop and ice forming in the eddies; tales of the trapline and of unprovoked attacks by the unpredictable grizzly bear; tales of freeze-up and breakup and of hazardous flights on the mail plane—coming down through a low ceiling of cloud to find, unexpectedly, the river littered with running ice or forest trees. An old prospector, Mort Teare, whose cabin lay a little north of the trading post, would speak of the side-streams of the Finlay, where almost anything might lie hid—even, it was said, tin. He had seen good rock brought down from one of those rivers by an Indian whose hunting country it was. That Indian was dead now and his family either knew nothing or wouldn't speak—but a man ought to get back into that country and put in a couple of seasons. Who could say what he might not find? Listening to him, I would wonder all over again why anybody was ever mad enough to tie himself down to a few trimmed and parcelled acres, when the freedom of the mountains was his for the taking. It was old Mort who, seeing the rough canoe pole that I had cut on Summit Lake, lent me one of his own—a slim, straight spruce pole, light, polished and shod. A pole that would slip down to the river floor with little resistance to the current, yet strong enough to take the hardest shove. "You can let me have it back," he said "when you come down the river. That tree of yours'll do all right for running down the Peace."

Or one could go and have a yarn with Ed Strandberg. He was usually to be found in the machine shop, doing some delicate job on an outboard or neat piece of carpentry. He made his home at the post, trapping out from there in the wintertime. It was Ed who asked Alan if there wasn't something he could make for him that he would like to take home with him. And Alan said, "A model kicker like the one on your boat. One that'll really run." I said, "Steady on—that's quite an order!" But none the less Ed made him one, all to scale and powered with the innards of an old alarm clock—a lovely job of work. For years to come it would be called upon to drive a model riverboat to and fro across a sheltered inlet of the sea.

West across the clearing from the store lay the radio station and a small, neat house occupied by the operator, Chalmers, and his wife. And downstream at the foot of the snye was the camping place of the Sikannis. One way and another there was a great deal of social visiting—and in the evenings, bridge or cribbage. And several times a day we were summoned to the kitchen of the trading post, where a long lunch counter had been built by Ed Strandberg specially to Marge McDougall's design. Five hungry mouths would line up there with unfailing regularity: Roy, little Margie McDougall, a grandchild, Ed, Alan and myself. Twice, in an effort not to "ride the grub line" quite so hard, Alan and I made lunches from our own outfit and slipped away with the canoe to the head of Pete Toy's Bar. There were some old prospect holes there and we dug in them with a borrowed shovel, panning the dirt by the water's edge. The results were always the same: a heavy tailing of black magnetite sand, spattered with tiny "rubies"—the name they had for garnets on the Finlay—and a colour or two of gold.

On August 5, in the middle of the morning, the sound of an engine was heard from downriver. All hands promptly lined the bank, eyes right and downstream. Soon there appeared a long, open riverboat with two men in it, nosing its way towards us on the edge of the shore eddies, close in to the overhanging trees. The boat slipped into the still water of the snye, the engine was cut, and the men stepped ashore and tied up.

That made two more for the famous lunch counter at noonday. The men were Art van Somer and Ludwig Smaaslet—Art whose home was up at Fort Ware, and Ludwig who had had, till that summer, the trapline on Bower Creek at the start of the big bend of the Finlay. Both men were dark-haired, clean-shaven, sunburnt and smiling. Art ran the engine and was captain of the ship. He was the smaller man. Ludwig was built to a larger scale—taller, and broader across the shoulders. Art said little on first acquaintance: Ludwig talked more easily. They both moved quietly and without hurrying, but there was nothing slow about them, especially when danger threatened.

That morning soon went. The two rivermen unloaded freight for the trading post while Alan and I packed and carried our outfit to the landing in the snye. Then our stuff was passed aboard and stowed away beneath the heavy tarpaulins. The canoe was lifted out of the water and laid upside down in the riverboat on top of the load. A comfortable seat was fixed up just aft of the forward thwart for Ludwig, Alan and myself: the seat and backrest were made by laying sacks of sugar crossways to the run of the boat, the sacks in question being nice, handy little pokes containing, each one, a hundred and ninety-six pounds of sugar—guaranteed, at that weight, to stay where they were put. Out of our own outfit we kept handy two small tarps and the large canoe tarp so that, if it blew with a cold wind or came on to rain, we would have something to lay over our knees or drape over the heads and shoulders of all three of us. As we sat low on our sugar sacks the big tarp, if we used it, would not obstruct Art's view from the stern, where he sat at the wheel. Finally, full of Marge McDougall's good midday dinner, we arranged ourselves. I laid a small packsack, containing two cameras and a field glass, between us on the seat. Ludwig made certain that a heavy, six-foot paddle lay handy, took a last look around to see that nothing had been forgotten and loosed the mooring lines. Art already had the engine running gently, warming up. He now backed us easily down the snye, shot the engine into a forward speed and nosed out into the river. The current caught us with a swirl and a rush; the sound of the engine changed from a mutter to a steady thrum; the boat shuddered and began to force its way against the stream. We gained speed, and on our left Pete Toy's Bar went sliding by—and soon, even in the brilliant light of this perfect summer's day, the little group of waving figures at the landing was hidden from us, lost in the mirage that was dancing insanely on the sun-warmed waste of stones ...

This boat was forty-five feet in length and up to six feet, or a bit over, in beam. She was powered by a 65-horsepower Gray Marine inboard engine, and she was painted grey with a red trim. Well up in the bow and on the outside, about where the "eyes" would be painted on an old-time Indian canoe, there was a red circle on the grey and, inside the circle, the silhouette of a wild goose in flight. That was to be found on all Dick Corless' riverboats—you might call it the mark of the Corless Line. It was to him as a well-known cattle brand is to its rancher-owner.

In the stern, and well over on the port side, sat Art at the wheel. He had a good clear view along that side, and the upturned canoe on top of the load cannot have been much in his way, for he never mentioned it. No words ever passed between the two men during the day's run: they seemed to know exactly what to do in any emergency—and anyway Art, sitting almost on top of the engine, was deaf even to shouted speech from where we sat. One could gain his attention by bellowing at him, but the rest was by signs. For us, sitting almost forty feet forward of the engine, life was most pleasant. We could converse without yelling at each other, and in Ludwig, who knew all the gossip of the Finlay and all the many stories of the rivers that flowed into it, we had a wonderful guide.

Islands, wooded with tall spruce and cottonwoods; wide-open shingle bars, gay with dwarf fireweed, and with millions of tiny willow seedlings trying to gain a foothold; fast water sliding strong and deep beneath high cutbanks where the river and the spruce forest meet in never-ending battle—and where the river always wins; snyes winding away into the bush behind big islands, the home of waterfowl; old channels of the river, blocked at the head with drift cemented solid with sand and gravel—and vast driftpiles, sometimes extending along the shore for as much as half a mile, built up with the wreckage of the forest, the cuttings of the beaver and the rare plank from some wrecked boat or from some trapper's cabin that has been cut into the river by the flood—all these things go to make a wild river. Gazing at them, one could imagine how the Rhine or Danube or winding, beaver-haunted

Seine must have looked in the days when Paris was still nothing but a stockaded wooden fort, built for safety by the savage Parisii on their lonely island.

In a few miles from McDougall's post we came to the mouth of the Omineca, obscured by a screen of islands. It came into the silty Finlay from the west, clear and sparkling in the afternoon sunshine, and I looked up it, towards its mountains, with the glass. Somewhere up there lay the Black Canyon, which I was determined to see on my way down in September. Another mile or two went by, and the Ospika entered the Finlay from the northeast. All the way from the Rockies and from Laurier Pass that water had come—and I asked Ludwig about the Police Trail, which I had seen on the older maps. "Gone," he said. "All gone. No horse could travel it now. The bush has taken over—and God knows what they made it for, anyway."

Above the Ospika comes the "Deadwater"—twelve miles or so of river where the current, except in flood time, is no more than two miles an hour. For ages the silt, which is easily carried by the fast water, has been dropped here, building up good alluvial soil. This supports a dense jungle of bush: the trees crowd against one another and the willows lean out over the water, seeking for light and air. They make it practically impossible to land and camp without a major clearing operation; in fact the whole stretch resembles the slow, calm reaches of the Crooked River, only on a much larger scale. Over much of this quiet water there is no poling bottom, and in the days before the coming of the machine many a hard slugging match with the Finlay has been fought out here, the crews paddling furiously and the bowman hauling up on the willow branches. Being slack here, the current does not have the surplus energy required to break down and destroy, and to cut new channels. The river is narrow, comparatively straight and in one channel—an absolute gift for a boat or canoe with power.

With the Deadwater well behind, we came to what was known as the Picket Fence—vanished now, swept away by floods and running ice. Ludwig told us about it as we approached —though, owing to the mirage, it was hard to see just how it lay until we were close upon it. Here, several years previously and at the tail end of the flood, the Finlay had built up an enormous driftpile clean across the channel.

Then, when breakup came next spring, it had piled up against this barrier thousands of tons of ice. Something had to give way—and that something had to be the driftpile. However, while the main mass of it was swept away downstream, the bank on the west side, on our left, was walled off from the river by a tremendous agglomeration of drift that appeared to be jammed solid, as though it would be there forever. This reached well out into the channel—and on the east side the river shallowed to a wide-open point of shingle, above which it swung to the right and disappeared in the direction of some low mountains near Fort Grahame. It was in this constricted channel between the shingle bar and the vast driftpile on the western shore that the Picket Fence lay in wait for the unwary or unlucky traveller.

By now we were almost into it. Ludwig jumped up, seized his outsize paddle and ran forward, to kneel down in the very bow of the boat with the paddle held crossways in front of him. From there he could scan the water ahead of us. This was his invariable "alert" station, and he called out as he jumped for it, "I do not like this place. I do *not* like this place *at all*."

It *was* rather like a fence. Where the mass of drift had once blocked the river there now ran a well-staggered assortment of sweepers in midstream across the channel—dead spars of trees, stripped by the ice of bark and branches, firmly anchored by their roots to the bottom and all pointing downriver. A bad-looking lot of snags, foaming at the base and quivering as the river drove against them—and the trouble was that there were more of their kind hidden just below the surface. We might run up on one of those, or ram it through the bottom of the boat—yet one had to have speed to get through this mess at all. Ludwig was signalling to Art, now—with his hand—a fraction this way or that, avoiding some danger that we couldn't see. They never spoke and Ludwig never took his eyes off the water to see if Art was watching him. There was no need to look—he *knew*.

Slowly the boat made its way through the Picket Fence and gained the open water. Still Ludwig remained, kneeling in the bow, tense and alert. We were not out of danger yet: should the engine choke and quit, or even hesitate and lose power, we could easily be swept backwards, and perhaps broadside on, into that palisade of dead trees that ran across the river. Not till we were well clear and round the point of the bar did Ludwig return to his seat beside us.

Towards evening we pulled in to the west bank and tied up below a trapper's cabin. Art had the key and we put a fire in the stove and made supper there. Thunderheads were climbing up into the sky above the Rockies, and the mosquitoes, sensing rain, were beginning to bother. It was nice to see them raging up and down on the outside of the screen door where they could do us no harm.

This cabin, during one of the wartime winters, had been the scene of a tragedy. Two young and well-liked Germans had trapped out from here. They minded their own business and kept out of trouble, and they were left without restraint to carry on in their own quiet, industrious way. Nobody bothered them.

For some reason—and it may have been through listening to incessant war talk among the White men—a too-smart, crackbrained Indian decided that he could do these fellows in, take their fur and get away with it. He waited for them at dusk on a cold winter evening when they were both out on the trapline in different directions. No doubt he lit the fire in the stove—just as we had done—and made himself warm and comfortable. Then he took his rifle, put on his snowshoes

His big paddle in front of him, Ludwig kneels in the bow watching for snags and sweepers.

and set off down the river trail. He met the first partner coming home with his day's catch; coming home pleased, probably, to think that *his* partner was home before him and had the cabin nicely warmed and supper started—for he would have seen the woodsmoke drifting out over the frozen river. The Indian raised his rifle and shot him through the hip. Then he turned and left him, twisting and moaning, to bleed and freeze to death in the snow.

The Indian returned to the cabin to wait for the other German from upriver. In due course he appeared and greeted the Indian, who told him that his partner had had an accident with his rifle and was in trouble away down the river trail. That, in the second German's mind, would account for the single shot which, in the silence and the intense cold, he would have heard. Dumping his pack, he turned and snowshoed down the slope towards the river ice, his mind no doubt a-whirl and with but one coherent thought—how, in this godforsaken, frozen wilderness, he could do anything for his friend if the accident should prove to have been serious. But he never reached the river trail, for the Indian shot him in the back, killing him instantly ... The scene is a sombre one: the flash of the rifle splitting through the winter twilight; the dark figure lying motionless in the snow; the Indian standing for a moment, stock-still, regarding his handiwork. Then one can see him turning away and going back into the warm cabin, and soon the lantern would be lighted ...

The story was told to us at suppertime in that same cabin. The Indian, it seems, stole the dead men's fur and took what he needed of their outfit. But in that empty country there can be no concealment for a murderer who is also a thief. Such a man might be safe in a big city, but not in wintertime in the wilderness, where every movement leaves a trace, and where every man and his possessions are known, discussed and valued. Suspicion soon fell on the Indian and he was taken outside for trial. There the appalling details were brought to light—and in spite of all the efforts of defence counsel and the benefit of every reasonable doubt, the Indian was found guilty and hanged.

Leaving that haunted cabin, we travelled on until late in the evening, making camp on Collins' Flat on the east bank of the Finlay. This was the original site of Fort Grahame—or rather, the spot where the original effort to establish Fort Grahame bogged down in the late fall of 1888. There are two versions of this. One has it that Collins, who was to be post manager, had got this far up the river when his men quit and left him stranded. The other and more likely story, as told to Swannell by Jim Alexander, is that Collins and his men were stopped here by ice. In either case a house was built, known as Collins' House, and trade was carried on there through that winter. By the time we arrived, sixty years later, the Finlay had taken Collins' House and scattered the fragments of it in many a far driftpile, and the only sign of human habitation was an old campground of the Sikannis.

However, we were not too interested in the history of the place just then—we had other things to worry about. Thunder was muttering to itself in the Rockies, the dew was starting to fall, the mosquitoes were on the warpath and the thrum of the nighthawk was sounding from the upper air. Under these conditions and at this late hour speed is what counts—and a hidden watcher would have seen four bug tents suddenly erupt on Collins' Flat and four harried humans hurl themselves into their welcoming shelter. He would have noted a brief period of active scuffling, during which the mosquito-screen walls of the tents were carefully tucked in between eiderdown and groundsheet, and the few enterprising mosquitoes that had entered the tents were hunted down and killed. And then a more leisurely scuffling, indicating that boots and various items of clothing were being arranged as comfortably as possible to deputize for pillows. And then silence. High above the shadowy valley and catching the last slanting rays of the sun, the nighthawks still dropped with thrumming note upon their prey—but on Collins' Flat, as on a thousand other lonely flats by a thousand lonely rivers of the North, the camp was sleeping ...

No rain fell and breakfast was at six on a cool, lovely morning. And at seven we hit the river and thrust hard against fast water towards Fort Grahame, where we arrived a bit before noon. The little cluster of white buildings could be seen from a long way downstream. It looked forlorn and lifeless against its background of tall spruce and low mountains; no smoke came from its chimneys and nobody came to the landing to wave us in. It had been abandoned by the Hudson's Bay Company only two months previously, in June of that year, and its sixty-year history was now at an end. Store and warehouse, post manager's house and Indian cabins—they had seen the Klondikers come and go, and the whole procession of men that came after them: police, geologists, surveyors and traders. And very soon the buildings themselves would be on their way, headed for the driftpiles, for the Finlay was cutting into the flat with every flood and already it was close.

We lunched there and unloaded seven hundred pounds of freight, which we stacked away and locked up in the old storehouse. Then we went on, through a warm, cloudy afternoon and far into the evening, to camp in a trapper's cabin two miles below Deserters Canyon. It was another bad evening for mosquitoes, and we cooked and ate and slept inside. Alan spread his eiderdown on the floor in a corner and made himself comfortable there—and just about the time he was nicely bedded down for the night Ludwig produced a gory tale of a suicide that had taken place in that cabin. "And that was where they found him," he wound up, "over there in that very corner where Alan's lying. Blood all over the floor—a hell of a mess!" I rather wondered how that one would go; but Alan, already sleepy, merely looked around him with added interest, saying not a word. Then he turned over, pulled the eiderdown over his head and was seen no more till breakfast time. It had been a long day.

I asked whose cabin it was that we were in, and Art said, "Hamburger Joe's."

"But he must have more of a name than just that?"

"Oh, sure—yes. It's Joe Berghammer that's our host for the night."

So it was for Joe Berghammer that we fixed up a note of thanks, leaving it in a glass jar on the table where the mice couldn't get at it. Just a few words to tell him who'd been in his cabin and when.

In the dark cabin we overslept and it was well after seven in the morning before we hit the Finlay. Soon after we started, the river narrowed and the boat had to force its way between two points of rock. The current was strong, one could see the power of it where the water broke against the rocks of the shoreline—and Ludwig was on his knees in the bow with his big paddle in front of him. Slowly we passed between the capes and then the river opened out into a great eddying pool. Ahead and on the left, gleaming in the early morning sunlight, one could see a high, golden cliff and, at the foot of it, an angry surge of whitewater. Rocks appeared and disappeared in the narrow passage as the waves rose and fell, but the water of the big pool was quiet. This was the entrance to Deserters Canyon. Here the Rockies come very close and Deserters Peak has flung a spur of sandstone and conglomerate out into the valley. Through this spur the Finlay has cut a canyon half a mile in length, narrowing in places to a hundred feet. The drop in that half mile is considerable, and at high water a roaring torrent surges through the cleft. We had come at a medium stage of water, and even at that it looked as though we would have quite enough on our hands. In flood time the eddy where the river emerges from the canyon mouth must be extremely powerful, and in the course of ages it has scooped out the big pool and cut down the alluvial slope on the west side of the Finlay into a splendid beach of shingle and fine sand. Towards this Art turned the riverboat and we ran gently ashore.

Besides the four of us and our personal outfits, the boat was carrying about two and a half tons of mixed freight for Fort Ware. According to Art we hadn't a hope of making it through with that much on board, so we unloaded a ton or so, rolling drums of gas and oil down on to the beach and throwing off some of those handy little sacks of sugar. During this operation Ludwig, bending down, gave a sudden exclamation of pain and straightened up with difficulty. "My back," he said. "Something's happened to my back. It's shot and I can't lift anything. God, but it's painful!" He was worried: a strong man suddenly put out of action for no visible reason and not knowing what had hit him. He had never had anything like this in his life—but I had, twenty times and more. I did my best to reassure him. I promised that I would make big medicine for him when we got to camp, and told him also that he'd better lay off lifting and heaving. Art and I would shift the stuff.

Soon we had things fixed and the load on board trimmed and snugged down. Then we went at it. Gaining speed we shot across the eddies of the big pool, then swung round the foot of the high cliff into the torrent that issued from the canyon mouth. The bow raised a little as we hit the fast water—and it stayed raised. Huge rocks, wave-washed or almost submerged, went by. The noise of the water and the din of the engine at full speed made speech futile—but nobody cared: it was too exciting for mere words. Ludwig was at his usual alert position, occasionally signalling, and Art was edging the boat up the eastern shore, taking advantage of the eddies. We were still gaining—but ahead of us there was a definite step where the water came surging over a submerged reef and fell a good two feet. We had to make this step close in to shore, where we could gather some speed from the eddy. Racing in the upstream current straight towards the step, Art set the boat at it and swung the stern out of the eddy and into the stream. One could feel the boat heave and rise and start to climb—and then slow down and hang, nosing a little this way and a little that way, searching for a weak place in the current but not finding one. And there we hung, nose in air, about a third of the way over the step, with the water flying past and the boat shuddering under the strain.

The high cliffs in Deserters Canyon are all on the west side of the river. We were over on the east side, and the shoreline there is low and of solid rock covered with huge blocks of loose rock that have tumbled down from above. The thick green spruce forest clothes that inhospitable shore right down to highwater mark, and now that timber came in handy. Our water speed was great; but when I lined up a couple of trees on the bank and watched them carefully, they moved not at all. We were making not one inch of headway. I turned round and looked at Art and slowly shook my head—and he shook his. The thing was hopeless.

And now what's he going to do? I wondered. Can he back down and turn round in all this turmoil of water? Or do we go down stern first? Or what?

With a masterly touch on the wheel Art backed away from the step, easing the engine. Then, picking his place, he swung the boat end-for-end in among the waves and the rocks and the whirling eddies. When the boat was still swinging he gave her full speed, and we rushed down the canyon, past the isolated rocks and the churning "holes" in the water, and close under the tall Gibraltar cliff, giving a wide berth to the Devil's Thumb, a fearsome wave-washed rock in the centre of the river at the canyon mouth. Then, with the engine barely turning we slid easily across the calm lagoon, to run up with a gentle crunch of shingle on the shelving beach. Art cut the engine and a blessed silence fell on the party—broken first by Alan, who had remained unruffled throughout the uproar of our attack on the canyon. "End of Act One," he said—and that was a true word.

Art took his hat off and mopped his brow. "I've been through that canyon a lot of times," he said, "but it never gets to be monotonous. Every time I tackle it I wonder what's going to happen *this* time—and I'm always glad when I get out the other end. And here we are—out the wrong end and back where we started. Now—I'll tell you what we'll do. We'll throw off another ton or so and then see if we can't make it in three trips with about seventeen hundred a time. Let's go."

So once more we heaved and slid and stacked—and then tarped up the dump on the beach, eased the boat off the shingle and climbed aboard again. Away we went across the pool and round the sandstone cape, riding much higher in the water than before and pushing less river. We shot up in the eddy and hit the overfall at the first step at a much greater speed—and this time we climbed up and went on. There was half a mile of this sort of thing with some wild water on the way and some stiff waves at the head of the canyon, but Art saw us safely past every hazard and in due course we felt the bow grinding onto the rocky beach at the head of the portage. Art mopped his forehead again (it was the mental strain, and not any physical effort, that had fetched the sweat out) and we set to work to empty the boat. We cleaned everything out, including Ludwig and Alan. "We'll leave them here," Art said, turning to me. "Ludwig's no use with that lumbago or whatever it is, and Alan's too young to heave on these heavy sacks and drums. With them two out, that'll be about three hundred gained—and if you'll come with me and help, we can handle everything between us."

As far as I was concerned, Deserters Canyon was the best thing yet on the whole journey; and as for making four more trips through it with Art—why, I'd have paid good money to be allowed to do just that. "Yes," I said, rather inadequately. "I'll come with you." And I slung the camera sack into the boat, clambered in myself, grabbed Ludwig's big paddle and went forward and knelt down in the bow. Having observed the drill, I knew that was my action station. The others shoved the boat out into the current and away we went.

This view looks towards the Gibraltar Rock in Deserters Canyon.

That was the best part of all—running down light, slapping over the waves, and with a grandstand seat for it right in the nose of the boat. It was a bit rough using a camera with the boat behaving like a bucking horse, but I managed to get some pictures on the second trip. There was one in particular that I wanted—a place where we just shaved past a sunken reef that had the whole force of the Finlay cascading over it, making on the downstream side a boiling hole in the water well below the general level of the river. Had we ever lost power and got into that, it would have done us a bit of no good in very short order. But I got my picture, with Art in it at the wheel, and with the hole about ten feet away on his left hand.

The pile on the beach divided neatly into two loads of seventeen hundred pounds apiece. When we got to the upper end of the portage with the first lot, we found our two partners crouched with the gold pan by a little eddy, panning the river gravel. When we arrived with the second jag we found them building a fireplace. They had collected a pile of driftwood and they wondered audibly why we had not had sense enough to bring the grub box up with an earlier load. So did we, when we came to think of it. After loading the last sack down at the foot of the portage, I had done some figuring with a stick in the sand. Figures are not my long suit, but after rechecking with Art it seemed that, in order to get two and a half tons through Deserters Canyon, we would have actually moved by hand, including ship-to-shore and shore-to-ship, approximately seven tons. Understandably we were hungry. Now, while we reloaded, let somebody else boil up the mulligan and make the tea.

After we had eaten Art wanted to do some tinkering with the engine, so I seized the opportunity to walk back over the portage. The trail climbed sharply and then levelled off, running through small spruce growing in a carpet of moss and low-bush cranberries. I got my

Seeming quite unperturbed by the danger, Art van Somer steers around the boiling "hole in the water" in Deserters Canyon.

pictures—some of them from points of rock where, in 1824, Samuel Black and the Old Slave must have stood, just as I did, looking down into the canyon. The two of them, the officer of the Company and the Sikanni interpreter, had left the party negotiating with difficulty the fast water at the twin capes below the big pool, and had walked ahead to size up this new obstacle, this unknown canyon. They, too, climbed down the cliffs to get to better vantage points—and finally Black decided that most of the load would have to be portaged, but that the big canoe could be taken up light, with a few "pieces" in it, by means of some skilled work with the line and with the poles fending against the cliffs and the rocks. That is, it could be taken up through the canyon to the last "cape"—the rock point that creates the big waves at the upper end. There they would somehow have to land and make a short carry—and then they would be through.

That was in late May, when the Finlay was roaring through the canyon almost in full flood—a tremendous force of water, far more than we had had to tackle. Yet Black was satisfied that the thing could be done, and he turned and walked with the Indian back towards the portage beach by the big pool. There, from the top of the hill, he could see his men assembled, and the big canoe and the little Sikanni canoes drawn up on shore.

But when he came closer he found that his bowsman, La Guarde, and his steersman, Antoine Perreault, were missing. They, too, had gone ahead to examine the canyon and somewhere, in the bush or on the cliffs, Black had missed them. Now there was nothing for it but to sit down and wait.

Eventually the two men appeared, coming down the slope towards the pool. They shook their heads when Black questioned them: "They say," he wrote, "tho they might go up in the Canoe they think it a risque and want to make the Portage." So they portaged ... Now the amazing thing about this is the hardihood of those men. They did not regard this turbulent canyon as an impossibility—as it has been regarded ever since. They merely *thought it was a risk*! Having made five trips myself through Deserters Canyon on an August morning and having marvelled at the force of the August water, the thought that these old Northwesters should calmly consider the possibility of making that passage in a birchbark canoe, and with the Finlay almost into the June flood, leaves me filled with awe and with admiration for the confidence of men skilled in their craft. No wonder it was the North West Company that opened the river roads across Canada from sea to sea ...

I took my last picture from the head of the portage hill, looking down on the big pool with the gently circling eddies, and on the twin capes below the pool. Then I ran back over the portage trail and scrambled down to the shore, to find Art replacing the last bits and pieces and almost ready to go. Soon we were once more on the river. Within a few miles we passed the old Barge Camp and ferry crossing of the Klondikers—but the old scow was there no longer. We wound slowly round enormous bends and came to the mouth of the Akié. Five or six miles away to the southwest lay the snow-white mountains that Gauvreau and his men had seen and wondered at in 1891 from near Fort Grahame. Big Buffalo Mountain and Little Buffalo Mountain, Ludwig called them—and as to their shining whiteness, R. G. McConnell took the romance out of that in 1893. He went to have a look, and he found those glistening slopes to be simply bare rock—"a fine-grained, whitish, compact limestone." And with that cold-blooded pronouncement, away into limbo went all dreams of mountains of massive, gold-bearing quartz and of a veritable Eldorado only awaiting the magician's touch.

Camp that night was at Del Creek on the east side of the Finlay. Only three bug tents sprang up on that occasion: we planted Ludwig with his ailing back in Del Miller's cabin and I took charge of the case. Plenty of hot drinks, I said—tea, soup, anything he fancied. And a couple of aspirins, a good rub with capsicum ointment and a large pink slab of thermogene wool on top of the capsicum. There were plenty of blankets and I put a bit of a fire in the stove. It was a perfect summer night, warm and dry—Ludwig must have been practically on fire, himself. In fact, as I was shutting the cabin door, I did hear a plaintive voice saying something about being hotter than hell. But the mumbo-jumbo worked. Exactly what it was that I did for him in a doctorial way I do not know, but he was ever so much better in the morning.

Leaving Ludwig to tough it out in the shack, I rolled into my bug tent and tucked in the side curtains. Twilight still lingered in the northwest. I used it to write up my diary for the day and I included the various stories that I had heard about the deserters who had given Deserters Canyon its name. I also compared them with the few notes I had made before I left home. Black's *Report* was not to be published for another six years—and in the meantime we simple denizens of New Caledonia still thought the explorer's name was Finlay. It was not—as I have already mentioned—and as for the stories of the deserters current on the river, they were mostly pure legend.

What really happened was that Black's expedition arrived at the beach at the foot of the portage a little before sunset on May 27, 1824. As we have seen, they looked the situation over and finally decided to play it safe and to portage. There was no sign of any portage trail ever having been cut, and Black concluded from this that the Iroquois hunters must have either gone up at extreme low water, lifting over the points of rock, or else wiggled through the bush, carrying their little canoes, in much the same way as a Sikanni would do—without cutting a twig. This was not the way the Company did things: they hoped to find a fur country up here, and a well cut-out trail would be a necessity. Black set the men to sharpening their axes. Camp was made. "The Old Slave set the Lines here and took 3 Fine Trout." The evening shadows reached out over the portage bay ...

In the morning Black was disgusted to find that two of the party had deserted—the middlemen, Bouché and Ossin. They had been on the first watch and, instead of calling their relief, had decamped in the night in one of the small canoes. They had gone off well equipped for a long journey: they had taken both Company and private property— five pounds of tobacco, a two-gallon keg of spirits, moccasins, their guns, pouches and powder horns, ammunition, a bag of pemmican and much other stuff. To add insult to injury they had taken "Mr. Manson's Pot Crook"; and if there's any one thing that's sure to make a man mad, it's the theft of some insignificant object of that description— insignificant, that is, to others but treasured by its owner: in this case a cunningly whittled piece of birch or willow that had been used so long by Manson that it had become a mascot, irreplaceable.

Black had his finger on the trouble: "Bouché is the Rascal," he wrote, "and debauched the other who is also a worthless scamp but a simple devil and thinks to get to his wife at Fort Chipwean." The immediate reason, he well knew, was "the Roaring of the Rapid through the Chasm before us and the steep Hill to carry up the Canoe and Baggage and prelude to further Toil and harder duty." The two deserters had been on watch as twilight came on, and in the last gleams of day, fast water always looks worse than it really is. Then, as night falls, the sound of water increases. That was no place for the faint-hearted, standing guard in the short northern darkness, listening to the thunderous surge that issued from that canyon mouth. Always a doubtful couple, they had finally lost heart and hit the trail.

Black gathered the men around him. He spoke of the base conduct of the pair that had fled and said he expected better things from the rest of them. If there was any plot to put an end to this voyage of discovery, they could let him know now. He personally was going on, alone with the Sikannis if need be. He meant to get a sight of the country, come what might—and the first duty of them all was "to prove the practical Navigation of this River."

The men backed him up. They said they were as much surprised as he was at the desertion. La Prise volunteered to take the place of one of the deserters as middleman—and without more ado they all fell on the portage trail with their axes, and the sound of a furious cutting was heard from among the trees. Even the Old Slave took up his axe to assist ... By about four in the afternoon they were over the portage with the whole outfit and once more on their way. "Made about 4-5 Miles and encamped late," Black wrote in his notebook. And in two days' time he was already referring back to "deserters' Portage"—the name that place has borne since then ...

R. G. McConnell, coming almost seventy years later, scarcely mentions Deserters Canyon as an obstacle. He knew pretty well what lay ahead of him there and he had no intention of trying to line his light Peterborough canoes through that wild water: he simply made the portage—which was an easy one compared with those he had carried over on the Liard, back in 1887. He had set out from his cache at the mouth of the Omineca on August 5, 1893. He had travelled with his usual speed as far as Fort Grahame, which he reached on August 8. But from there he took thirteen days to get to the mouth of the Kwadacha, making camp not far from the site of Fort Ware, which was not then established. The greater part of those thirteen days he spent, not in travelling, but in clambering over the rock exposures along the river, or in climbing the mountains that lay back some distance from it. From these excursions, together with his photographs and samples, he was able, when writing his report in the fall, to build at least the skeleton of the geology of the Finlay country ...

A few details of Haworth's passage of the canyon were also written into my notebook, and I looked to see how he had fared. It was on an afternoon of late August that he and Joe Lavoie stepped ashore on the shingle beach at the foot of Deserters Portage, and by the time dusk was falling they had carried most of the loads across. In the intervals between trips Haworth had tried the big pool for fish, but had caught only a two-pound Dolly Varden. However, he had caught several fine Arctic grayling earlier in the day at a creek mouth where they had eaten lunch; and now Lavoie was cleaning these for supper down by the water's edge. This, if there are any big Dollies anywhere near, will always bring them in to clean up on the heads and guts—and, sure enough, when Haworth walked down to the canoe for something, there was a tremendous splash in the shallows and a big fish darted away into the deep water.

Haworth went and got the .32 and stood there quietly, waiting. The fish came again, a big dark shape nosing silently into the shallows. Haworth fired and hit him hard, and thought he had got him. He lost no time in going after him; but the fish, at the very last moment, came to life again and slipped away into the depths of the pool. After that, Haworth took once more to his rod and soon caught a splendid Dolly Varden weighing around eight pounds.

They slept that night at opposite ends of the portage in order to protect the outfit from any animal marauders—Haworth at the upper end with the portaged stuff, and Lavoie on the beach by the pool with the grub box and cooking outfit. When Haworth walked over the following morning, all set for breakfast, he found that Lavoie had caught another fish just as big as his of the evening. Not to be outdone, he took his rod and soon got into a *really* big fish, one that gave him a battle royal, and which he would have lost at the last moment had not Lavoie grabbed the fish in the shallows just as the line broke. This again proved to be a Dolly, the biggest of the three, and the odd thing was that he was the fish Haworth had shot the night before. The bullet wound was four inches in length, yet it had not impaired the fighting power of the fish or even spoilt his appetite. The fact is, *nothing* will deter an unsophisticated Dolly Varden, and I have even seen one monster hauled ashore simply because he had his teeth sunk into the rear end of another Dolly that was caught on a night-line—the first fish being either unwilling or unable to let go of the second.

Haworth and Lavoie had the canoe and the remainder of their stuff over the portage by noon of that day, and then they went on, slowly and with difficulty against the increasing current, reaching the Kwadacha on the thirteenth day after leaving the Forks, "thanks to good luck and Joe's skill as a river-man." The first leg of Haworth's journey was over.

18

Swannell on the Ingenika

That camp at Del Creek was the last camp with the riverboat, and on the following afternoon we came to Ware. We had started later than usual, owing to Ludwig being still partly out of action, and on the way we had picked up from the west bank a Beaver Indian with his family and the meat of a moose he had killed. Then we had stopped for lunch at Art's cabin. It stood on the edge of a fairly recent burn, one of the first we had seen in the green valley of the Trench.

"Did somebody let a fire get away?" I queried. "Or was it lightning?"

"Neither one," Art said. "It was caused by one of those Jap fire balloons in 1942, an awful dry year around here."

That was the year the Japanese started sending up balloons bearing various nasty devices designed to spread fire or disease. These things would circle the earth on the high westerly air currents until North America lay beneath them, at which point, the enemy hoped, their timing mechanism would function and down they would come. I was on the Buffalo Head Ranch in the southwestern foothills at that time and we were advised of these balloons. We were warned not to pick up any strange objects that we might find in out-of-the-way places, and we were asked to report any sightings. Then, as if to aid the enemy, something went sadly wrong with the climate that summer. Normal conditions were reversed: the North, including the Nahanni country, experienced an unnaturally dry season, while on the Buffalo Head a veritable deluge descended, particularly, it seemed, when the hay was cured, windrowed and ready to stack—rains that turned small beaver streams, ankle deep, into raging brown torrents, impassable for a man on a strong horse. Thus, with the rainfall rearranged, any area of the vast wilderness of the North that happened to receive a functioning fire bomb was free to burn, there being no equipment and no men to fight the flames, and no rain to put them out. One balloon fell east of the Buffalo Head and did no harm. Several fell in the Nahanni country and did no good. Mostly they must have come down in the sea or in the stony places of the mountains where they were harmless—or else, falling where they could do some damage, their mechanisms failed to function. Eventually the Japs decided the game was not worth the candle and gave this up in favour of more predictable and less chancy warfare.

Wild raspberries had sprung up in the blackened acres of the wartime burn, lovely fruit, large and delicious. We fell on them till we could eat no more, and then we went on. A mile or so below Ware the Kwadacha rushes into the Finlay in a milky flood, carrying a heavy load of silt from the glaciers of the Rockies. Above this river the Finlay is crystal clear—and as we pressed on through this lovely water we could plainly see the white buildings of the post shining in the afternoon sunlight against their background of tall green spruce. On our right a high gravel cutbank was tapering off, sloping down to the little flat on which Ware stands. Straight ahead rose Prairie Mountain with its open slopes of dry, hard grass, tawny against the deep blue of the sky. Already one could see the course of the Finlay swinging to the left of the mountain to embark upon its climb through the barrier ranges of the big bend. In the northwest lay the valley of the Fox River, continuing in the Trench—but that was hidden from us by the fast-approaching trees ... And now we were coming in and there were people at the landing, waiting to welcome us.

The Hudson's Bay Company's long-established habit of adding the prefix "Fort" to the names of its establishments can be misleading. Time was when the Company's posts were built four-square with stockades and bastions, and with buildings loopholed for defence against marauding Cree or Assiniboine, Blackfoot or Nez Perce. Those days have long since gone, though one can still see traces of the fortified rectangle at some of the older posts such as Fort Simpson, Chipewyan or Norway House. The more recent establishments are simply trading posts, sometimes dignified by the title of Fort. Such was Grahame and such was Ware—a scattering of cabins, mostly Indian, and the neat buildings of the Bay, white with red roofs, up a slight slope from the landing. We were welcomed by the post manager, Mr. Pattie, who kindly gave Alan and myself the Company's bunkhouse to camp and sleep in. Art and Ludwig took care of themselves. They were at home at Ware.

We took possession of the place and looked it over. The last inmates, we thought, had been poor housekeepers, so we went up to the Bay house and borrowed a broom from Mrs. Pattie—being requested to bring it back when we had done with it and to bring ourselves as well, to a cup of tea. Soon we had the bunkhouse civilized and then we proceeded once more up the hill, to find that the promised cup of tea included all manner of cakes and cookies; and upon them we browsed till we could browse no more, so good do these things taste after bannock and moose mulligan. Gratefully we waddled down the hill again, wondering what would be best to have for supper—or whether we even needed any supper after tea with the Patties.

Late that evening the desire to wander came on me. I am an inveterate twilight prowler. I love that last hour of day, especially in the North; and when all is done and the rest of the camp is sleeping, I am usually to be found afoot, enjoying the shifting, sinuous pattern of the river, watching the fading light of the sunset on the stony summits of the hills—trying to fix the scene in my memory so that, in years to come, I can say: "Yes—I remember that camp. That was the one in the big spruce at the foot of the rapid ... " And I can go on from there, for the whole picture will come back to me and I can hear again the rustle of the hurrying water, and I can smell once more the warm scent of spruce or pine or juniper that still lingers in the woods, last sweet exhalation of that summer's day ...

And now the fit had taken me again, and the sign was right: all was serene in the bunkhouse, and Alan, not yet thirteen, had hit the hay and was dead to the world. Now was the time to hit the trail.

I thought I would go to the mouth of Fox River and back, about two miles each way. I took the river trail—the road of the Sikanni hunters, which, if you followed it far enough and rafted twice across the Finlay, cut through the mountains of the big bend and went on to Caribou Hide and the headwaters of the Stikine. Horses were used on this trail, so it was easy to follow—still, it was later than I had thought, and by the time I reached a rock point with a big eddy below it, dusk was already falling. I had left too late for Fox River and this was my turning point. But there seemed to be a good place in the eddy for beaching a canoe, and before going back to Ware I simply had to go down to the water's edge and have a look at it.

There had once been a camp on the little flat by the eddy. There were old, cut-off stumps standing in the moss—they were rotten now, one could kick them over easily. And there was an oval-shaped hollow; I stirred it with my foot and a few fragments of charcoal emerged from beneath their covering of green: a campfire must once have burned there for several days. And there was a blaze on an old spruce—and a bit of rusty wire looped round the spike of a broken branch of that same tree. I poked around, thoroughly interested now and wondering why anybody would have camped here in the bush for so long when Fort Ware was only a mile and a half downriver.

But Fort Ware did not exist when that camp was made.[9] That was Swannell's Camp No. 62 of the 1914 season, and after thirty-five years and two great wars had gone by, some restless impulse had led me to that very spot. My casual record of events and his beautifully kept journal coincided absolutely when we came to compare them. Besides, Swannell also remembered the rock point and the eddy …

His journey to that remote spot had not been entirely without incident. In 1914, Quesnel was no longer the best base for the Finlay country. The Grand Trunk Pacific was, at least in theory, running out of Prince Rupert to Fort Fraser and Prince George, so it was to Prince Rupert that Swannell, Copley and Nep Yuen came in late April, by sea through the Inland Passage. They left immediately for Rose Lake, which at that moment, owing to floods, frost coming out of the ground and a general collapse of the railroad system, was the end of steel. The track was appalling, the trains travelled only in daylight, and the Bulkley River was in flood, lapping at the grade. However, the cars were derailed only twice and not one of our three men was hurt—the only fly in the ointment being that their baggage and all the survey equipment had been unloaded at Smithers. Copley was sent back to pick it up, and Swannell and Nep Yuen got horses and rode on over a muddy trail to Burns Lake. The railroad grade was soggy and impassable.

They tried it by boat down Burns Lake next morning but were stopped by ice. So they abandoned the boat and walked on in the rain till they could get saddle horses—but that was no go, for things got worse and the horses couldn't make it through the yielding mud. They then met two men poling a push-car along the flooded track, so they boarded it and poled back to Burns Lake, arriving at eleven P.M. In the morning they tried it again, this time with wagon and horses. The wagon road was flooded and the corduroy was either rotten or had floated out, so they tried to get around the floods on the railroad grade. This proved to be an error, for the horses, floundering along the waterlogged grade, carried away about twenty feet of the embankment and slid down with it into the river, the leading team being nearly drowned. No teamster could venture more for them than that, and Swannell decided that wagon transport had had a fair enough trial. They returned, as before, to Burns Lake.

There followed two days of waiting, enlivened by the news of a train wreck down the line in which Copley and the outfit had participated. Cars had rolled off the track, falling down on to pine stumps or into the river. A number of people were seriously hurt, but Copley was not among the injured. He and the train engineer built a big fire with new ties alongside the track and kept the spirits of the passengers up by swapping yarns all through the night. Towards dawn the engineer told a thrilling story of a boxcar that wrecked a whole train. The passengers were held spellbound. The scene around the fire must have been like the one in Owen Wister's book, *The Virginian*, in which the Virginian tells the story of Delmonico and the frogs.

Next morning a boxcar train lurched up to the scene of the wreck to take the stranded passengers out—but so well and with such dramatic force had the engineer told his tale that, to a man, they refused to board it. The train departed sulkily. After an interval of some duration the engine returned with a string of flatcars in tow, and to these the passengers consented to entrust themselves and their belongings—though, perhaps, without any too great confidence ...

Having arranged for a pack train to meet Copley when he should arrive with the outfit, and leaving Nep Yuen at Burns Lake to come with the horses, Swannell walked on through a country that was beginning to be short of food owing to the breakdown of railway communications. He arrived at Fort St. James on the eleventh day of May. Copley rode in alone on the evening of the twelfth. On the afternoon of the thirteenth two more riders appeared, the packer and Nep Yuen, with five pack horses. The men all camped in the old schoolhouse. From now onwards they would have to cope only with the reasonably predictable hazards of the bush and of wild rivers. The more irritating, because man-made, chaos attendant on the intrusion of a haywire railroad into the ordered life of the frontier now lay behind them.

Various small survey jobs were completed around Fort St. James and then the whole outfit, with the same pack train and the same packer, Carroll, moved on towards Fort McLeod. Progress was slow: the Salmon River was high and the packs had to be rafted across while the horses swam; and right at McLeod Lake one horse almost drowned at the mouth of the McLeod River. It was May 22 when the party finally camped by the Hudson's Bay Company's post at the north end of the lake, within a stone's throw of the site of Simon Fraser's fort of 1805.

No time was lost. On the following morning, Nep Yuen, with two McLeod Lake Indians as crew, started down the Pack River in a Hudson's Bay Company canoe with thirteen hundred pounds of outfit, and with instructions to build a cache for the stuff at the mouth of the Ingenika River, above Fort Grahame. The rest of that day and all of the following day Swannell spent taking observations for time and latitude, working out his observations, making up accounts, checking the outfit and negotiating for a canoe. For the cottonwood dugout which they had made so carefully at Fort Grahame in the previous autumn was not there to meet them. They had last seen it departing from the Black Canyon of the Omineca—or else they had last seen it at the Forks (it will be remembered that memories differ on this point) and they had expected to find it waiting for them here at McLeod Lake. *Now* where the devil had it got to?

Nobody knew.

At Cascade Canyon, portaging the long, heavy cottonwood dugout canoe proves a challenge for Swannell and his crew. (Photo courtesy of F. C. Swannell.)

Luckily they were able to buy a cottonwood dugout of exactly the same type, "larger than the one we made in 1913," Copley writes, "but poor-shaped." This canoe can be plainly seen in the photograph of the portage at Cascade Canyon on the Finlay: it is long and obviously heavy: it has six main thwarts and a noticeable bulge on the port side. The stern is somewhat over to the port side of the centre line. They could see that it would be a canoe with a mind of its own, one that would need knowing—but it would have to do.

In the afternoon of May 25 Jim Alexander arrived, on foot and pretty well played out. He had walked the sixty miles from Fort St. James, somehow getting himself over the rivers—and now he was mad as well as tired: at the crossing of the McLeod River, less than half a mile from the post, the McLeod Lakers had held him up for fifty cents before they would ferry him over by canoe. With him the party was complete. On the morning of May 26, the canoe being very heavily laden, Swannell, Copley and Alexander left McLeod's Lake Fort for the Finlay. Accompanying them were dog Dick of 1913 fame and a nameless stray they had recently adopted, later to be known as dog Caesar. Two days' travel saw them to the Forks, where they made canoe poles and nailed a strip along the gunwale of the canoe for extra strength and freeboard, having in view their heavy load. Then they started upstream.

It took them three hard days to get to Collins' Flat, where they met Ross from Fort Grahame on his way out in a big, clumsy boat with the year's accounts and the Company's fur. The weather was mostly cold and squally, and the Finlay was high. All the way up through the twelve miles of slack water they had had to paddle furiously and without stopping, there being no tracking beach and no poling bottom even for the sixteen-foot poles. Jim Alexander had fortunately devised one further aid to navigation: into the end of one pole he had spliced and bound a large iron hook. With this he could reach ahead from the bow and hook onto any projecting log of a driftpile and so, with his great strength, haul the canoe up while the others shoved with their poles on any bit of the driftpile that they could reach—and while, perhaps, somebody who had crawled ahead through the jungle pulled on a line that he had floated back to the canoe, tied to a piece of drift. These places were dangerous with the frothing water driving into and through them, and the men always felt easier as they drew slowly away from them, upriver. But on they went, paddling, poling and lining, hooking themselves up on the logs, hauling themselves up by the willow branches—no holds barred. The morning they passed Collins' Flat it took them five hours to go three miles.

On June 2 they reached Fort Grahame, to find sixty Sikannis camped there awaiting the Catholic priest. From the Indians they acquired a new expression: Hudson's Bay honey. This proved, on investigation, to be a mixture of syrup and bacon grease. There have been times in my life when I would have been only too glad to eat this revolting mixture—though fortunately not many. Shortly before reaching the post they had caught up with Nep Yuen. He had had a hard time making his two Siwashes work, and he aptly described one of the pair in particular as "Number one *hyiu cultus*"—which, when rendered out of Chinook and into English, means "Absolutely no damn good."

Two full days were spent at Fort Grahame—chopping out and measuring a baseline, observations for latitude and longitude, calculating, overhauling the outfit. Then the whole party, with the two canoes and the two Indians, moved up the Finlay to the mouth of the Ingenika River, the big western tributary twenty river miles above Fort Grahame, the Finlay being for the greater part of that distance a maze of islands and up to two miles across. On arrival, the two Indians were paid off and departed in the Hudson's Bay Company's canoe for McLeod Lake. Now the little survey party was on its own at last, and, as Haworth would undoubtedly have expressed it, "beyond the last outpost of civilization."

They got their cache built and the bulk of the outfit stacked away in it. Then, on June 11, they started up the Ingenika, taking with them only the bare necessities, travelling as light as possible. The river was approaching full flood and rising every day with the frequent rains, but in spite of that they made camp on the second night twenty miles up from the Finlay at the mouth of a large fork that was later named Swannell River. To conserve their supplies they were now living as far as possible off the country, and Copley had started his seasonal war on the rabbit population. It was at this camp that Nep Yuen promised them labbit pie for supper, and the others pretended not to understand.

"Labbit?" they queried. "Never heard of it. What's labbit?"

"You no savvy labbit?" came the quick reply. "All samee pussycat no more tail!"

It was here that Nep Yuen missed the lynx with Swannell's .303 Lee-Enfield carbine—here, too, that Jim Alexander varied the menu with a couple of beaver. They ate pretty well everything that crossed their path and a careful game record was kept in tabulated form from about mid-June to the end of August. From it I have extracted the main items:

	F.C.S.	JIM	COPLEY	YUEN
Willow Grouse	8	5	25	1
Rabbits	26	29	100	5
Fool Hens	15	11	52	18
Blue Grouse	2		1	
Moose	1	1		
Goat	2			
Duck	1			
Rainbow Trout	2			25
Silver Trout	1	2		2
Sapi*		2		45
Beaver		3		
Geese		6		
Porcupine		1		

*The Finlay River name for Dolly Varden.

A footnote follows the Game Register: "Nep Yuen," it runs, "has picked 13 quarts of black currants and cranberries."

In view of the fact that most of their time was taken up with arduous canoe travel or with survey work—packing survey instruments through the bush and up mountains, taking observations, calculating, plotting—and seeing that Copley was so busy with his botanical collection—tabulating, preparing specimens for pressing and so forth—that he had no time even to keep a diary, that bag of game is not to be despised. And for the seven weeks or so that it covered it made a most welcome addition to the larder for four active and hungry men.

By June 22 they were fifty carefully surveyed and measured miles up the Ingenika, following the windings of the river. R. G. McConnell, himself a hard traveller by canoe, had ascended only thirty miles in 1893. That, according to him, was the limit of navigable water, and above that the Ingenika was simply a succession of rapids.

A day-to-day account of the Ingenika exploration would be wearisome. You must imagine the work of the survey going on all the time, even on the days of hard and dangerous travel. And in the evenings, until daylight fails, Swannell will be busy with his calculations and his field notebooks—Copley helping him or working on his botanical specimens. They work after the wind has dropped and right through the hour of the mosquito. They carry on till they can no longer see the small neat figures or the detailed sketch plan of some intricate bend of the river with its islands, its confining mountains and its tributary streams. The fire smoke wreathes and eddies around camp, keeping the mosquitoes more or less at bay; the homely clatter of pots and pans indicates that Nep Yuen is on the job, making ready for the morrow's breakfast. Jim Alexander is not idle: he is sharpening the axes, splicing a line, replacing a broken pole with a slim, sixteen-foot, fire-killed stick from the bush. Finally he mends a hole in his torn pants ...

Sometimes they would spend several days in a camp, moving only when the work was completed up to and beyond that point. Then they would go on. And the further upstream they went the worse the river became. The gradient was increasing, and now, when they ran into a scattering of islands, the channels between were often blocked with a tangle of drift. And when that happened they would have to get into the river or climb on to the driftpiles and cut a way through. They poled on, up to an old cabin and cache on the north bank, and there the river trail ended: beyond that it was nothing but a trapping blaze. The cabin had been built by a prospector-trapper by the name of Wrede. He had vanished up the Ingenika in 1896, leaving word at Fort Grahame that he would be back in about five months. He never came: he must have stayed in to trap and hunt and prospect through another season. Then, in the spring of '98, his body was found at his main camp: he had cut himself badly with an axe—and he must have been a long time a-dying, for a pair of home-made crutches was found lying near him ... It was on June 24 that they came on that old cabin—and even Jim Alexander knew nothing of its story. That was unearthed by Swannell when they came down the Finlay in October. Browsing around for references to the Klondikers in the old post journals of Bear's Lake Outpost—which was to become Fort Grahame—he found the entries about Wrede: the date of his departure, and then, two years later, the story of his lonely death up the Ingenika ...

From the old cabin, leaving Nep Yuen to guard camp and to fish or hunt for fool hens, Swannell, Copley and Alexander and the two dogs, all five carrying packs, set out for a three-day sashay up the strong creek that flowed into the Ingenika from the southwest on the opposite shore. They practically fought their way up that creek, travelling on side hills that had been burnt, perhaps in '98—now a criss-cross of down timber with a dense jungle of willow and alder poking up through the deadfall, and with second-growth spruce making its appearance. By climbing they were able to get some sights to the main features of the country, and on the third day they "packed back to Main Camp, arriving completely played out at 8.0 P.M. Heavy rain all night." That was the creek they afterwards named Wrede Creek.

Three days later the four men and the two dogs, all packed, left the base camp, crossed a summit on the north side of the Ingenika and made camp by a lake[10] thirteen miles back from the river. No sooner was camp set up than a moose appeared on the meadow at the head of the lake. Swannell and Alexander executed a brilliant stalk, crawling from bush to bush in the meadow. At a pre-concerted signal they fired simultaneously and both bullets struck the moose behind the shoulder, dropping him stone dead. Then the two hunters went back and helped to move camp up to the moose.

The next day was July 1. Swannell and Copley climbed Espee Mountain that day and set up a station on the summit. Before leaving camp they helped the other two to cut away all the best of the moose meat. Then they attended to the education of dog Caesar, a stubborn thief who would eat anything in camp that was left lying around, even for a moment. The only time so far that anybody had got ahead of Caesar had been when Alexander shot a coyote pup—on a Sunday, the record states, so the day may have had something to do with it, like planting roses only in the dark of the moon, and so forth. Alexander skinned out a hind quarter of coyote and fixed it up carefully, as with any other meat. Then he left it within reach of Caesar, who sneaked up and started in to bolt it as usual. The people watched with interest. Sure enough, the expected happened: long before the dog got to the end of his cannibalistic meal he dropped the coyote meat and vomited all he had eaten of it, having suddenly realized that this was all in the family and that he was making a meal of a near relation.

That made him think twice for a while about grabbing every bit of meat in sight; and now his owners intended to complete the cure. They tied him for the day to the moose carcass, on a long line so that he could reach the little stream that came winding through the meadow and past camp. There they left him happily gorging himself—with more meat and more water than any dog has ever seen, and all his own.

Alexander and Nep Yuen built a rack and set to work smoking the moose meat. Swannell and Copley, accompanied by dog Dick, went to their survey work on the mountain. At about 3,000 feet above camp they came upon eighteen mountain goat quietly feeding; otherwise the day was uneventful and visibility was good. When they returned to camp in the evening they found a bloated caricature of a dog, distended and abject, stretched flat out on the grass as far as it could get from the moose carcass. That was dog Caesar and, as far as meat was concerned, he'd had it: he never stole again.

Two days later they returned to their camp by the river, dogs and men loaded with smoke-dried moose meat. And in the morning they went on. All the old obstacles confronted them—only more of them now, and tougher and closer together. There was one rapid in particular: with all four men straining at the pole they almost got up it, but at the last moment somebody's pole slipped and they were swept backwards out of control and almost swamped. The mountains were closing in on them here—high rugged peaks, timbered right down to the river. They made Camp 35 at the foot of these green mountains and there they stayed for one whole day. It was a Sunday anyway, the fifth day of July: "In camp. Computing Triangulation."

This camp was sixty-five miles up from the Finlay. On the Monday morning they cruised upriver through the bush and came on an old placer camp and burnt cache at the foot of a ditch. On one of the cache uprights there was a blaze with the writing on it almost illegible. "June 20/1899," it ran. "Please do not molest this cache. Jas. Malzer." Other signatures could not be deciphered. This was a better spot than the one they were camped in, so they moved the whole outfit one mile upstream to it, negotiating a bad logjam and rapid en route and again almost swamping the canoe. They spent four nights in this camp.

From here Swannell and Copley twice climbed what they christened Bad Luck Mountain. The summit was 3,700 feet above camp, or 6,200 feet above sea level. On the first occasion they left camp at five A.M.

The weather turned bad: halfway up, a freezing rain fell on them while the mists drove through the valleys below on a wind that had nothing of July in it. And above them everything was blotted out by a whirl of snow. They climbed on in snow and sleet, but there was no visibility from the summit and they could get no sights at all. Hoping that it might clear, they dropped down a little and found some shelter beneath an overhanging slab of rock. They were sodden and chilled and they built a fire with heather there—but it was no good: they were frozen out with chattering teeth and fingers numbed. They were forced to go down to timberline on the north side of the mountain where they could make a good fire and thaw themselves out. There they waited patiently, enduring hours of mist and rain and climbing up once more to the summit. By four P.M. it was hopeless and they started straight down for camp—by a hair-raising route, which included a long descent in a chimney that finally petered out, sending them scuffling all the way back up it till they could get out again and try the open face. In the midst of all this Copley was not so drowned and frozen that he was unable to observe and record: "an acre of snow-white *Epilobium angustifolium*[11] surrounded by a rim of half-white and half-pink, merging into the common colours."

The following day was frightful—rain and mist driving up the Ingenika valley, wisps of vapour rising from the dripping forest. "In camp all day. No observations to be had." It was at one of these places far up from the Finlay that Nep Yuen and Copley went to work and washed out about two dollars and fifty cents in fine gold right from the grass roots on the bar below camp. However, "when we came back to camp we found we had lost Nep Yuen's $2.50 pocket knife—hence profit nil."

A second assault on Bad Luck Mountain, while not all that could be desired, was away ahead of the earlier effort. The two mountaineers reached the summit in two and a half hours from camp, the last 2,000 feet being up an interminable rock slide. On the way up they spotted eight goat feeding along the ledges; they shot two of them, but one fell and lodged among the crags where they couldn't get to it. Snow squalls greeted them on the summit and their spirits sank to zero as the neighbouring mountains vanished into the smother. But they waited, doing their best to keep warm—and the storm moved on and the sky cleared, and at last they were able to make their triangulation ties. Then, burdened with the survey instruments and a hundred pounds of goat meat, they slid and crashed down Bad Luck Mountain for the last time—trying a new route which gave them only 1,200 feet of rock slide, but confined them between high crags in an ever-narrowing couloir from which, till the last moment, they could see no way of escape.

From this camp they moved only twice more upstream—one move of six miles, and then one more of about a mile, which brought them up to the foot of a bad rapid. One good look at that was enough: they had come to the end of the road. So, on Day 75 of the trip, they made Camp 38 on the right bank of the Ingenika on a flat by the mouth of a small stream. The drop of the river in the last few days' travel had run up to forty-six feet to the mile. Ten feet to the mile gives strong, fast water. Forty-six means practically a cataract—nothing but rapids and driftpiles.

By river they were seventy-eight miles up from the Finlay and it had taken them sixty-three hours of actual travel to reach Camp 38. They might have thought that they had come further by water than men had ever been, had they not observed, on the day of the six-mile move, the wreck of a large, clinker-built boat high and dry on top of a logjam. They clambered up to it and examined it: it had been there a long time and it had been made when nails were a luxury on the headwaters of the Peace. It had been put together entirely with wooden pins; there was not a nail in its construction. "One wondered as to the fate of the crew and how long ago it was."

This highest camp was deep in the mountains. Craggy bluffs rose from the flat, and snowslides came right down to the river. They spent three nights and two full days here. Copley and Swannell carried the survey instruments to the summits of two mountains, one 4,000 feet above the river and the other 3,200 feet. That day it was warm, but on the peaks a cold wind was blowing and the sky was heavy with cloud. On the remaining day they cruised on foot up the Ingenika, finding the river barred to all craft by a canyon only two miles above camp. The canyon was a hundred yards long, narrowing to eight yards at the lower end. Through this the shrunken Ingenika roared with a drop of fifteen feet—and over this frothing race the two men passed on a bridge of trees, to find, on the left bank, an old burnt cabin and cache.

Could that have been the place where Starke and Stanier got their gold? For at the furthest point of that day's walk the men were no more than fourteen miles from the mouth of McConnell Creek, to which Fleet Robertson had come in 1908 with pack horses from Hazelton. Had Swannell and Copley only had the days to spare, it would have been an easy matter for them to pack on to Thutadé Lake, the source of the Finlay and distant by trail only some forty miles. But their assignment was to carry the survey the whole way by river—to Thutadé if they could get there, but otherwise as far as possible—and from Camp 38 to the head of the Finlay by canoe was over two hundred miles. On bad rivers that was a long way and it was already the middle of July. It was time to turn and run for the Finlay.

They made it in two days, a total of fourteen hours on the river. "The worst place was above Camp 35, which we were foolish to run." Camp 35 was the moose camp, and the bad place was a fast S-bend with a shingle bar, an island, a huge driftpile, and a logjam across one channel—all strategically arranged to promote disaster. A plan of this hazard, neatly drawn in blue and red ink, is in the margin of the *Diary*; and how they ever got around that double bend only God knows. Swannell still shakes his head when he thinks of it.

Another dangerous place was where, on the way up, they had cut a narrow gap in a driftpile that blocked the whole river. They knew that it was impossible to let the canoe down on the poles at this spot: the river had scoured out under the drift to such an extent that they couldn't touch bottom. So they were forced to spend an hour here going only a few feet—letting down inch by inch on the line. One mistake and they would have been jammed crossways to the current, work and instruments lost and perhaps somebody drowned. That and similar places fetched their average speed down and they finally had to settle for just under six miles an hour. From the canyon to the mouth of the Ingenika was a drop of five hundred and forty-five feet. On a river the clearest way to visualize the gradient is as a hill of water. Slowly and laboriously the canoeman climbs that hill, poling, lining and frogging—but he surely comes down it on the run!

Swannell's party had to negotiate hazards such as these driftpiles on the Ingenika. It was a tricky, delicate process and one mistake could have been disastrous. (Photo courtesy of F. C. Swannell.)

There followed, for Swannell, four days of intensive work on the map of the Ingenika. The mosquitoes were at their worst; sometimes it rained; always the fire smoke came drifting in under the wet canvas. But always the careful, meticulous work went on:

"Day 79. Camp 40. Ingenika Mouth. In camp figuring out triangulation, Copley tying in Mountain Peaks."

"Day 80. Self in camp plotting up map."

"Day 81. I remain working on the map. Heavy rain ... "

"Day 82. Plotting map. Showery day. A beautiful double rainbow in the evening. Rain at night. The men get back from Deserters' Canyon."

Swannell had been alone through those last days. Alexander, Copley and Nep Yuen had taken the bulk of the outfit by canoe up to the beach at the foot of Deserters Portage and cached it there. Now, as soon as the Ingenika maps and journal were complete, they would be able to travel light up to the canyon.

Camp was moved across the Finlay to the east bank, and from there Swannell and Copley made a quick trip on foot to Fort Grahame. There were a few things the party was short of and, more important, the Ingenika map and records could be left at the post, safe from the hazards of the upper Finlay.

The distance was eighteen miles, and the two men came in to Fort Grahame early in the morning after camping in the bush a few miles upriver. They were surprised to find a bunch of Sikannis hanging around—but no sign of Ross, who had not yet returned from his trip out with the fur. A sickness had broken out among the Sikannis; nobody was hunting, and now they had lost heart and were starving. Five were already dead. Yet they could plainly see, through the windows of the padlocked store, food and all they needed piled in plenty on the shelves.

On the trip Swannell had been reading Butler's *The Wild North Land*, and now he was once again impressed by the innate honesty of the Indian before he has been corrupted by the White man's ways. He was reminded particularly of Butler's story of the Moose-that-Walks,[12] the Beaver Indian who found himself in a situation somewhat similar to that of these Sikannis: through a rent in the parchment window of the Company's store at Hudson's Hope the Moose could see all that he needed for the beaver hunt; yet because the factor was away at Fort St. John he was unwilling to go in and help himself, even though he had the furs to pay for all he took.

But here at Fort Grahame men were dying. To the amazement of the Sikannis, Swannell broke the sacred lock and served out rations to them, chalking them up to their accounts. Then, while Copley brewed up a concoction of wild strawberry leaves and maple syrup to cure those who were suffering from dysentery, largely brought on by starvation, Swannell attended to his own wantages—to use Samuel Black's expressive word—clothing, needles, stuff for Nep Yuen's grub box, a new pair of pants for Jim Alexander. And when all was done and the Ingenika material was left in safety, he sealed the door and hit the trail. Carrying fifty-pound packs, he and Copley made it back to camp in eight hours ...

Early in the morning of July 24 they drew the dugout up on the beach at Deserters Canyon. With the heavy rains of the last few days the river had been rising, so that a bad cascade and a "terrible whirlpool" had formed at the entrance to the canyon. And on the beach were the tracks of two mountain goats. From the signs it seemed that they had tried to swim across—perhaps to get back on to their home range around Deserters Peak—and only one had made it. The other had probably been drawn into the whirlpool and sucked under—which might account for the dead goat that they had seen the evening before, floating past their camp two miles below the canyon.

They got the load across the portage that day, and then, around four P.M., a downpour started that continued through the night and into the following morning. But there was no time to wait for fine weather: soused by the rain and with every tree a dripping fountain, they tackled the portaging of the big canoe. This was achieved by sheer brute strength—sliding the canoe along on skids that were lifted and carried forward, to be laid again—and also by rigging up in suitable places a "Spanish windlass." This was a rigging that functioned on the capstan principle. A strong log was placed crossways against two trees, and was held there, about waist-high, by a couple of saplings spiked vertically to the tree trunks. To one projecting end of the horizontal log was attached a short, strong pole to act as a two-man power lever, one man turning at each end. From the log to the canoe—stern or bow as the situation demanded—ran a stout line. All was then in readiness. And, when the skids were laid and the two men began to turn on the lever, the rope would be taken up by the horizontal log acting as a revolving drum, and the canoe would have no option but to move forward. That was the theory as laid down by Jim Alexander—and that was how it worked in practice. But it took them most of the day to portage that heavy canoe, even over a reasonably good trail. Quite obviously, where Black, in the canyons of the big bend, had been able to take to the cliff edge or the mountainside with his birchbark canoe, Swannell, with his dugout, would somehow have to go right up the riverbed or not go at all.

The rain continued and snow came low down on Deserters Peak. The river in the narrows at the head of the canyon rose six feet in four days; in the big pool at the foot of the portage it rose four feet. The Finlay, penned in between the canyon walls and heard from the silence of the woods, sounded with a booming note like the roar of distant drums. Large spruce and cottonwood, torn by the river from some far-off cutbank, would vanish at the head of the canyon, sucked down by the swirls, not to reappear for several hundred yards. No canoe, the men were certain, could run Deserters Canyon at this stage of water. And no Northwester, master of rivercraft, was there to prove them wrong.

In all they were ten days camped on and near the portage. Swannell sketched, mapped and photographed the canyon. He cruised down the Finlay, finding excellent land, while Copley and Alexander went exploring westward, coming on a string of small lakes which, from their colour, they named the Emerald Lakes. They packed a camp out there from which to extend the survey—and at that camp they made a sad mistake. To guard the outfit they left dog Dick tied there through the whole of one long day. Loneliness beset the hound, the sun was hot, the steamy heat after the rains brought out an amazing crop of young and vicious mosquitoes—and, in his struggles to get loose, Dick upset his supply of water. He must have gone crazy, for he not only tore up the mosquito tents but dug a hole and buried them as well. When the men came home that evening and let Dick loose, he rushed into the lake and swam to the far side, where he remained until morning. In camp a horrible night ensued as the men, their protection destroyed, found their slumbers disrupted by what Samuel Black so aptly calls "the importunate Bizz of the Musquattoe."

The men left Deserters Canyon on the third of August. For the next couple of weeks they moved steadily on upriver with little in the way of incident to break the normal routine of travel and survey work. On August 5, Swannell recorded in the *Diary*: "Noticed first leaves turning yellow." What he did not know, and so was unable to record, was that this was the first day of war between England and Germany—a war that would sweep him into its net and take him to France, to the lovely manor house of Teffont in Wiltshire as an ever-remembered guest, and finally to Archangel with its splendid stock of Russian mosquitoes, every bit as ferocious a breed as their cousins of the Finlay.

Frost began to touch the big valley with its autumn colours—red of chokecherry and wild rose, pale gold of poplar and willow, deeper gold of cottonwood. Near Paul's Branch, Nep Yuen hooked a big Dolly Varden, but lost his fish, which went off with hook and cast. Two miles further up the Finlay, on the opposite shore and one hour later, Nep Yuen hooked a big Dolly Varden. This time he got his fish to shore and was delighted to find that it had brought with it the hook and cast it had taken from him lower down. The fish was twenty-four inches in length and weighed five pounds. That night the water froze in the camp kettles.

They camped for three days at the mouth of Paul's Branch, an eastern tributary. Nearby ran the trail of the Klondikers—which was also Moodie's trail. In an old camp of gold-rush days they found what they first thought was a winter grave—the body wrapped up in birchbark and slung between two trees. Investigating gingerly, they found that the "body" was a cache of dynamite. The explosive had lain there for sixteen years of sunshine and storm, enduring temperatures ranging from eighty-odd in the shade to sixty and more below zero. Under such conditions dynamite can become irritable and touchy. Not wishing to disturb its rest, the investigators moved softly on—to find, close by, the skeletons of two pack horses with their saddles lying beside them, one with the name "Sousic" branded into it. Some of the Klondike farers were so green and helpless that they never unsaddled their pack horses or even took the packs off them. Some old experienced packer had shown them how to load a horse and had done it for them—once. And that was that: the packs stayed on till the horses practically rotted under the saddles. That may not have been the case here at Paul's Branch; nevertheless—and significantly—it was no more than five miles beyond this camp that they found another two horses' skeletons lying by the Klondike Trail, again with their packsaddles beside them.

It was Paul's Branch that Swannell and Copley forded with some considerable difficulty on their first morning in that camp. Before entering the swift-flowing stream they removed their pants and socks, replacing their boots on their bare feet. With every step into the water the force of the current whirled more and more sharp grit and small fragments of rock into their boots until the slightest move became an agony. They almost had to give it up—but they persisted and won through to the far shore, where they sat down gratefully and proceeded to wash the grit from feet and shoes. Returning in the evening, and not wishing to suffer again the torments of the Canterbury pilgrims, they cast around for a better place to cross Paul's Branch. They found, one half a mile upstream, a natural bridge of solid rock, a vast improvement on the morning's performance—and one can well imagine the blasphemous silence in which they walked over it ...

On August 21 they passed the mouth of the Kwadacha, and that evening they came to a big eddy sheltered by a point of rock, a little short of Fox River. The day had been perfect, hot and sunny, and to save themselves the trouble of clearing a space in the bush they made camp on the sandy beach of the eddy. As twilight drew on they could see the flicker of hidden lightning from behind the mountains, and they could plainly hear the rumble of thunder coming closer. Then in the night the storm broke over them and down came a torrential rain. And with the first faint greyness of dawn the Finlay began to rise. Soon it was lapping at their beds and then, rain or no rain, they *had* to move, and in a hurry. So it was in the bush above the drowned beach that Nep Yuen lit the breakfast fire that morning. For two days and nights the fire burned in that same spot. Then for thirty-five years the moss crept over the fireplace, and the small cranberries followed the moss. Slowly the charcoal vanished from sight and lay hid, until I came along in the dusk and stirred the green carpet with my heel.

19

Prairie Mountain

Breakfast had been eaten and Alan and I were squaring things away in the Hudson's Bay bunkhouse when Art suddenly appeared in the open doorway. He was just the man we had been hoping to see: he had said something at Del Creek about running the two of us and the outfit up the Finlay to Bower Creek. This was just sheer good nature on Art's part. All his contract called for was to land us intact at Ware, but he had refused to accept any pay for the extra twelve miles or so. "We have the time," he had said, "and it'll save you that much poling and lining."

And now here he was with an even better suggestion. "You said something yesterday about how you'd like to climb Prairie Mountain? Well—Ludwig and I are going to be here until tomorrow with the boat. How would it be if you and Alan fix yourselves a lunch right away and then we'll sling your canoe on board again and run you up to the foot of the mountain? Then you can come down in the canoe in your own time in the evening, and tomorrow we'll take you up to Bower Creek like I said."

This was wonderful—everything was being handed to us on a plate! It seems to be a way they have in the North, and many a time have I, the lonely traveller, been helped and handed on my way like this. Our cup was filled when a second shadow fell across the grass and Pattie looked into the bunkhouse with an invitation to supper...

Soon we were once more on the Finlay and heading upstream. We passed Swannell's old camp, snug below its point of rock—and then, on our right, Fox River came foaming into the Finlay down a chute of shingle. It enters at right angles to the Finlay current, thrusting a ridge of tossing water far out into the main stream and making some intricate eddies against the further shore. The passage of that river mouth is the one difficult bit of navigation for a canoe without power between Ware and the foot of the Long Canyon of the Finlay, a distance of about fifteen miles.

Art landed us close to the foot of Prairie Mountain and we took our canoe, with our stuff in it, from Ludwig and laid it gently on the shingle. Then the two men and the boat with the wild-goose brand on the bow swung out into midstream and raced away towards Ware, straight into the eye of the morning sun and on a dazzling flood of green and silver.

But we, land-bound and earthy for that day, lifted the canoe further up the beach and tied it with a double line to a stout tree. Then we departed, walking inland through the bush towards the mountain, carrying in our one packsack camera and field glasses, map and lunch. We would not find any water on the summit ridge so the tea pail was left tucked into the nose of the canoe, together with tea, sugar, chocolate and two enormous jam sandwiches, to await our return. We hoped no wandering bear or wolverine would happen along and find it.

Prairie Mountain is exactly what it appears to be from the river—a very steep grassy slope with the odd bush or tree, and with a few outcrops of rock which can be easily climbed or bypassed. Haworth, on his ascent, succeeded in getting among some dangerous cliffs, where he was worried lest Joe Lavoie might fall. But it seemed to me that one just walked straight at the mountain and up it at whatever speed the state of one's wind permitted. Alan's long stride seemed to make light of it—but, remembering what it was to be twelve and permanently hungry, I thought we had better eat our lunch when we were about two-thirds of the way up. So we did that—and the oranges that we had bought at Ware served excellently as lubricants to an otherwise dry meal. Then we went on to the top, which is really the southeastern point of the Kechika Ranges. McConnell's aneroid informed him that here, on this spur of the range, he was 2,400 feet above the river.

Clouds had drifted over the country from the northeast and the sun was gone, but in spite of that, and even from this humble height, we could see far. Northwest up the Trench and forty miles distant a low hump of land ran transversely from wall to wall. That was the ridge of Sifton Pass. It marked the head of Fox River, the end of the Finlay drainage; and beyond it, fading away into the haze, were mountains that drained to the Liard. Down the Trench and fifty miles away one could pick out with the glass the distinctive shape of Deserters Peak towering above its fellows. In the southwest and at our feet the Finlay threaded its way between wooded islands, dimly shining under the cloud shadow, glittering as some shaft of sunlight moved slowly across it, to sweep on over the green forest of a wide valley. Beyond the forest the moving pillar of light would slowly climb the stony slopes of the range through which Bower Creek had cut its way to join the Finlay. And then it would be gone ... In the west Bower Mountain broke the view; and in the northwest the country, except for the Trench, was hidden from us by higher ground of the range on which we stood. Even so, we could see enough: fifty miles and more each way, up and down the great valley. And I looked longingly through the glass at the eastern wall of the Trench, beyond Sifton Pass, where at last it merged and became one with the shadows, running on towards the Liard. Sixty miles to that last dim mountain, if it was an inch—and the Liard was still for me the river of romance. "Upon those roads are high adventures won."

But the interesting view was to the northeast. There, behind the lower ranges that bordered the Trench, ran the line of the Rockies. From those high peaks came the Kwadacha and the Akié, both laden with glacial silt; the windings of the former river could be followed for many miles. Among the tangle of high hills between the main fork of the Kwadacha and the Finlay there appeared on the map two familiar names. A high, stony summit six or seven miles up the Kwadacha bore the name Mount Haworth. That was the mountain Haworth had christened Observation Peak, and it ran a little over 6,000 feet above sea level. It raised its head a scant ten miles from where we stood and it almost, though not quite, obscured the view of a mountain that was higher but much further back, somewhere near the source of Paul's Branch. This peak was 7,300 feet above the sea, and its name was Mount Yuen. So, in a country that has little history, the names of the early travellers are not forgotten. Indeed, that of the stocky little Chinaman who planned to run guns to *both* sides is remembered not only here, but also at the headwaters of the Omineca, in Yuen Creek and Yuen Lake, close under the Kettle Glaciers.

Traversing a glass slowly along the main range of the Rockies, one could discern a whiteness held high against the clouded blue of the peaks. That was the Great Glacier, first reported by R. G. McConnell and sketched into his map of 1894 from Indian report and from the sight he got of it from Prairie Mountain. Haworth had read the report and studied the map, and one of his purposes in making his journey was to get back towards the headwaters of the Kwadacha and get a close view of this glacier and of the high mountains that were supposed to exist in that region—"peaks taller than Mount Robson."

Today more is known about that group of mountains. F. S. Smythe and Rex Gibson climbed there in 1947, having flown in from Fort Nelson to land on a five-mile-long lake that has been named Haworth Lake. No peak in that little group can rival Mount Robson—the highest being Mount Smythe, at 9,800 feet. But, seen from Prairie Mountain at a distance of forty miles, and described by the Indian, who is by nature an artist and a dreamer and who will never allow a good story to falter for want of a little adornment, that mass of snow and ice might well seem, to men unversed in the local climatology, to depend for its very existence on mountains of extreme height. And so the story got around, and so those mountains grew, reaching for the sky.

In his attempt to reach them Haworth went at it the hard way. He had with him McConnell's map, which slightly exaggerates a bend of the Kwadacha and overestimates the distance of the glacier from the Finlay, putting it at fifty miles instead of forty. Considering that this map was mainly based on a long-distance view from the top of Prairie Mountain, it gives a very fair picture of the Kwadacha country.

That being so, it's hard to see why Haworth did not do the obvious thing and follow straight up the Kwadacha River. That sort of a trip has its drawbacks: one is occasionally confronted by the frightful debris of a landslide with its tangle of down timber, and frequently one is forced to make a small climb to avoid some steep cutbank or spur of rock. To offset these disadvantages the traveller is often presented with a wide-open stretch of shingle bar up which he can walk as easily as on a city pavement. And rarely does he have to do any serious climbing.

Haworth and Lavoie cached the canoe and outfit on a small island in the Kwadacha, a few hundred yards up from the Finlay. Then, ignoring the parallel-ridge structure of the Rockies, they decided to go straight up the big foothill ridge that lay due east of camp and rose some 3,000 feet above the river. Haworth would be unfamiliar with the nature of these ridges and the valleys that lie between them, and Lavoie gave him no warning. Up they went on a warm, still day, Lavoie carrying sixty pounds and Haworth fifty in a clumsy, monstrous-looking pack contrived out of his dunnage bag and some leather straps. They arrived on top of the ridge in the early afternoon, exhausted and consumed by a raging thirst, to find that their mountain was devoid of springs, and that beyond lay no alpine plateau but only, as might have been expected, another valley. They cruised along the ridge for some distance, and eventually had to drop down a thousand feet on the *western* side in order to get into the timber and to a trickle of sweet, delicious water by which they camped. That was the end of Day One of the expedition, and night found them all of three miles from their starting point, though considerably above it, and with a thousand feet of the same ridge to be climbed for the second time after breakfast in the morning.

To follow their wanderings in detail would be pointless. They milled around like that for the next two days, obsessed with this ridge-climbing idea, only to be driven in the end back to the banks of the Kwadacha, to camp about twelve miles' travel above their cache on the island. Having tramped all that way to get there, over unnecessary ridges, across wet moose meadows, and through a shocking ram-down of brûlé, Haworth estimated that distance as twenty miles.

By this time Haworth was becoming exhausted by the unaccustomed effort of packing, and Lavoie was fed up to the teeth with the whole performance. Meat would have made all the difference to both of them, but, apart from a moose or two out of range and a swimming beaver missed by Lavoie, they saw nothing. The general atmosphere cannot have been too pleasant: Lavoie cursed the country, wished he was back on the Finlay, and said plainly that if Haworth did shoot a head in this muskeg-brûlé mess he, personally, would not take any part in carrying the trophy out. Haworth, meanwhile, had his eye on the packs. They were eating mostly out of Lavoie's pack, and his nightly pillow, which was the sack of flour, was growing visibly smaller. The point was at hand at which Haworth would be carrying more weight than his guide. This was getting to be one of those trips which one can read about with interest, but at the same time be glad one had no part therein.

Haworth managed to get Lavoie forward to one more camp, keeping now to the Kwadacha—as they might have done with advantage in the first place. The next day, after a mile or two of difficult going, they dumped their packs by the river, opposite a thousand-foot limestone cliff, and went on with only rifles and cameras to the Forks of the Kwadacha. This point McConnell had spied—or, rather, had inferred from the lay of the country—from his eagle's aerie on Prairie Mountain, and he had set it on his map as being about thirty miles up from the Finlay. Actually the distance is about twenty miles; but to Haworth, who had walked all the way with an awkward pack and over a needlessly tough trail, it felt more like forty, and he was convinced McConnell had underestimated.

Gazing at the two rivers that met at the Forks, Haworth was convinced that McConnell was still further mistaken. McConnell, on his map, has the North Fork coming down from the Great Glacier—yet here it was, under Haworth's eyes, flowing crystal clear without a trace of glacial silt. The East Fork, on the other hand, came churning down loaded with the grindings of the mountains, white and silty and resembling clam chowder made with milk. Yet there was no sign of any glacier to be seen up the valley of the East Fork—nor, for that matter, any sign of one up the North Fork. To us that is not surprising, since today we can see from the map that the Forks are a full twenty-five miles in an air line from the big icefield, and that mountains lie in between. Joe Lavoie, at this point, threw in his solution of the puzzle: he openly scoffed at the idea of any glacier in this country, and said the siltiness of the East Fork could only be due to the river cutting through banks of fine white clay.

Taking no notice of this, Haworth came to the conclusion that McConnell had been mistaken: either he had located the Great Glacier as being too far to the north, or else there was a second glacier hidden away somewhere from which the main fork of the Kwadacha got its load of silt. The North Fork, presumably, did not reach the big glacier at all.

He was wrong and McConnell was right. The North Fork draws its water in three main heads from the western slope of the Great Glacier, but each of these three streams passes through a long, morainal lake. The smallest of these lakes is four miles long, the largest eight miles—and, as is invariably the case with these glacial lakes of turquoise blue, the silt is dropped as soon as the glacier stream hits the dead water. There, at the head of the lake, the bar forms, pushing slowly forward year by year, filling by degrees the trough ground out of the rock by the vanished river of ice. Beyond the steep edge of the bar the finer silt drifts out into the deep water like a cloud of smoke, slowly sinking into the depths—but still leaving behind a mist of infinitesimally fine particles to give the lake that lovely bird's-egg blue, the delight, on cloudless days, of the mountaineer following some goat trail under the rimrock, or perched thousands of feet aloft upon some rocky pinnacle.

From such a lake the outlet stream issues clear and transparent, with every reef and pebble showing as through glass. Had McConnell made his way to the Forks, the very clearness of the North Fork would probably have led him to deduce the existence of the glacial lakes—which a man unaccustomed to the ways of high mountains would be unable to do.[13] Men were earthbound then and airplanes were still hazardous and chancy things, unable to venture far into wild country. In 1916 the time was still distant when it would be possible to photograph and map from the air the hidden places of the hills; and Haworth in this twentieth century was no more mobile than Samuel Black had been almost a hundred years before him. And even Black had felt the need of a plane. "I wish I had wings to go and see," he wrote in a moment of perplexity, "for in such a country our progress is slow."

Haworth turned back from the Forks of the Kwadacha, making it back to the cache on the island in three days. On the way he turned aside from the river to pass over what he called Observation Peak—the height in the second range of foothills that now bears his name. This summit rises some 3,500 feet above the river and Haworth forced himself to climb it with his last burst of energy. And from that barren, treeless ridge he got his view. It was much the same as the view one has from Prairie Mountain—but the heart of it for Haworth was the Great Glacier, straight into the northeast and just over thirty miles away, dimly shining under the canopy of heavy cloud that blanketed the Trench. This was his first sight of it. Longingly he looked at it—and even Joe Lavoie at last conceded that he was seeing "what makes the Kwadacha white."

The lakes on the North Fork were still hidden from them—nor could they know that the East Fork forked again, sending its northern head around to drain the great icefield from the east, sharing that side with the Muskwa and Tuchodi rivers. The second eastern fork takes its rise in minor, residual glaciers, and nowhere does any lake of any size intervene on this system —hence the milky, silt-laden river. Pondering, without being able to solve, this conundrum of the clear and the discoloured streams, the men moved on down the west side of Observation Peak, searching for a spring by which to make their camp ...

It has been said, and with some truth, that the Rockies are the worst-named mountain system in the world. That night, stretched out luxuriously by the glowing embers of the fire, Haworth, in a fit of wartime enthusiasm, decided to suggest that one further alien name be added to the ill-assorted register: as soon as he got out he would propose to Ottawa that the high mountain he had seen that day, holding the Great Glacier in its lap, should be called Mount Lloyd George. With regrettable haste his suggestion was adopted. Time and the verdict of history have not added to the stature of the little Welsh politician.

Only a few miles away from the mountain of the prime minister of England you can find on the map the name of a traitor who collaborated with the enemy in the Second World War.

What next? After all, we still have lots of nameless mountains, and prime ministers are more plentiful now than they used to be. A good deal cheaper, too ...

One more day brought the two explorers to the cache on the island, where they found everything secure, just as they had left it. In the morning they loaded up and pushed off for the main river, where they turned upstream. They ran into an encampment of Sikannis just below the mouth of Fox River, and they had considerable difficulty in getting through the chute of whitewater that the Fox flings out into the Finlay; nevertheless, they came that afternoon to the foot of Prairie Mountain. There they made camp, cached their canoe and load, and sorted out what they wanted to take for their next overland trek—this time a hunting trip, with a special emphasis on Stone sheep.

Neither of them knew the country and they had no special plan—only that they would go northwestward along the crest of the Prairie Mountain range and hope to see something in the way of game. They disregarded the advice of one of the Sikannis who suggested that they should try the Bower Creek mountains, being certain that he was simply trying to steer them away from his own hunting grounds. Later on Haworth rather wondered about that.

Up they went in the morning, contriving, as we have seen, to find some dangerous cliffs to climb, and midday found them on top, enjoying the splendid view. They made camp early that afternoon a few miles up the range in a wooded ravine and Haworth spent what must have been a delightful evening prowling along the crest of the range ahead. It was alpine country with small meadows of grass and clumps of stunted firs, broken by stretches of rock and gravel. Simply to move over such a country, after a week of shoving like a wounded animal through bush and deadfall, was pleasure enough, to say nothing of the magnificent view from this ridgepole of rock that separated the Fox from the Finlay. I know it would have kept me on foot till the shades of night drove me back to camp, and it took Haworth in much the same way. He found himself "alone with primordial facts and eternal verities."

Well—every man has his own way of expressing his feelings. I once sat with a fellow rancher on a mountaintop in the Alberta Rockies—in late June and with the west wind rustling softly around us. Our horses had been left far below, and silence lay on us except for the quiet whisper of the summer wind. One could almost hear the cloud shadows moving. I broke that silence: "You know—there's something about the mountains that lifts a man out of the ordinary run of life. No branding, no bawling calves, no dust, no sweating horses and swearing men, no—"

"I like the mountains," came a lazy voice from under a battered, wide-brimmed Stetson, "because they're so damned *clean*!"

There you have three men's versions of the sweetness of the timberline country, the nearest thing to heaven that there is on earth. In their very different ways all three have given expression to the same thought ...

Snow fell that night on the little camp in the ravine. Some melted under the sun the next day, but not on the main ridge, which remained white and slippery under a cutting west wind. As they went on, the range became higher and more broken, and towards evening they made camp in an alpine basin on the east or Fox River side of the ridge. They had seen nothing in the way of animal life except marmots—and the tremendous upheavals of rock and earth where grizzlies had been digging these little whistling beasts out of their burrows.

After supper Haworth took the two largest cooking pots and his rifle and set out for the spring to get water. On the way he climbed a low spur of the mountain in order to get a look into the next basin to the northward. Below him, when he topped the rise, he saw the gleaming waters of a little tarn reflecting the sunset sky. And away beyond, on a small patch of green grass close to some snow, something was moving—a creamy white object, square and blocky, deliberate in its gait. Quickly focussing his glass, he found himself gazing at his first mountain goat, *Oreamnos columbiae*, "the finest mountaineer of all time."

Haworth's fatigue fell from him. Down into the shadowy basin he went, dumping his water pots at the tarn and making a swift stalk towards the goat, using as cover an isolated knoll and the scattered clumps of fir. It was unavailing: as he made his stalk the goat quietly grazed away from him, climbing as he went. The best Haworth could do was to get within six hundred yards of the goat, and the light was fast fading. An experienced hunter would have left the goat alone till morning—but impatience and an unfortunate love of making long shots got the upper hand, and Haworth proceeded to lay down a barrage on the goat, four or five shots from the .401.

The goat held on his way in his own leisurely fashion, pausing now and then to look back down into the basin to see what was causing all the din. The last Haworth saw of him he was parading up and down on the top of a thousand-foot ridge, where he had been joined by a nanny and kid. Haworth kept himself hidden, waiting for darkness before beating a retreat. The goats still stood there on the ridge, outlined against the afterglow of the sunset, slowly becoming one with the darkness of night.

Returning belatedly to camp with the water pots but with no trophy of horns, Haworth found that the worst part of all was explaining the uproar in the neighbouring basin to Joe Lavoie.

Lavoie's Cassandra-like predictions that the goats, having been thoroughly disturbed, would now quit the country were not fulfilled. In the morning, when the two travellers passed the mouth of the basin below the tarn, there again was the goat family on the same patch of green grass by the snow. And once again Haworth made his stalk, with the same result: he could creep unseen to within about six hundred yards' range, but no closer. And the goats were climbing as they grazed.

In desperation Haworth left his cover and walked straight towards them over the open turf. Now a goat is not an animal that can be easily stampeded. He is careful and deliberate and will not be hurried in a dangerous place. Furthermore, so secure does he feel after untold generations of mountaineering on inaccessible precipices that he will even stand on some dangerous ledge and regard his pursuer with a look of scorn, thus giving a chance to the rifle bullet against which his agelong immunity from attack has given him no warning instinct. Provided one can get near him he is, therefore, an easy animal to shoot.

Only once have I scared a goat into the clumsy-looking lope that is his top speed. That was on a blazing July afternoon, when I had climbed up out of Alberta onto a narrow ridge of sandstone, which happened to be the main range of the Rockies, the Continental Divide. I looked over the ridge to find myself face to face, at about twenty yards' range, with a splendid old billy goat with horns on him like twin black daggers. His flanks were heaving, for he had climbed thousands of feet out of British Columbia on the sun-blasted western side of the mountain, all the way up a hot, sliding sandstone scree, headed for the green uplands of Three Isle Lake. It was only for a second that we faced each other. Then the goat gave a snort that was more like a sniff and turned and loped away into the depths out of which he had come, crashing recklessly but surely down that precipitous slope of broken stone on which a man would have moved—if he dared to move at all—slowly and delicately, mindful of the sheer drop of thousands of feet below him where the scree tumbled off into the Palliser valley. I was sorry I had headed that goat. He looked so hot and thirsty and he had nothing to fear from me.

Haworth's goat disdained to lope. While the nanny led the kid up the rock ledges, he acted as the rearguard, stopping now and then to watch the two-legged animal below him. The sun was in Haworth's eyes, the range was six hundred yards, and the goats were, he thought, a thousand feet above him. Standing, he raised his rifle and let fly with five or six shots. The echoes of the basin roared. The goats walked on. Sadly Haworth came to the conclusion that he had not enough ammunition to carry on this kind of a Chinese war against the goats of Prairie Mountain.

As they went on, northwestward along the range, the going got more and more difficult. Finally they decided to leave the summit ridge and drop down on the west side to the Finlay at the foot of Long Canyon. They had heard of a trail that ran northwest from there into good sheep country.

They followed a creek down the mountain, camping that night in a deep ravine without a level place on which to sleep. An icy rain fell on them, and continued through the next day, while snow whitened the peaks. At nightfall two "drowned rats" reached the Finlay, they knew not where—and the clouds were low and the rain still poured down. In the morning Haworth made his way upstream, clambering over the screes and the down timber, through the dripping bush, vainly trying for grayling. In half a mile or so he came to a huge outcrop of rock, an island in the narrow, swift-flowing river. That was what Black had named the Old Man, and Swannell the Split Rock. The water roars past it on either side with a steep drop: the main channel, which is on the right bank, is only fifty feet wide in September water; the chute is about thirty feet long, with boulders at the lower end.

This was the landmark Haworth had been given for the trail to the sheep country. Now he knew where he was—a bit over two miles into Long Canyon—and he made his way back to camp and told Lavoie. Camp was in a gloomy spot; the Finlay raced tumultuously between

This view looking down the chute shows the left side of the Old Man, a huge outcrop of rock in the narrow, swift-flowing river. (Photo courtesy of Palmer G. Lewis.)

steep cliffs; the sodden clouds sat down low on the mountains and the rain continued. They waited there till noon and then, with the weather clearing a bit, they got going on the trail up what they came to call Sheep Creek.

Two days later they came in the afternoon to a broad valley running east and west. This was an ancient course of the Finlay which, in some bygone age had cut clean through the Prairie Mountain range, to fall into the Trench where now only the Fox River runs. They came to a trapper's cabin, provisioned, they decided, by pack train from Telegraph Creek. They found some food in the grub box there and they eyed it longingly, for they only had about two days' supplies left, plus a fool hen that Lavoie had shot. But they took nothing and went on.

The following morning they ran into a bear. They were sitting on the edge of a cliff, rather listlessly, wondering whether to go on and chance killing something, or whether to play it safe and head back to the Finlay while there was still a little grub left. Haworth was just about all in. Packing in the mountains had been tough on him: every muscle was protesting and he was wondering how much further he could travel on willpower alone—when suddenly Joe Lavoie spotted the bear. The animal was down below, some four or five hundred yards away and feeding on blueberries. They needed that fat, black bear and they lay there for a long time with their mouths watering, watching him. Owing to the lay of the cliffs and the set of the wind they couldn't get any closer—and Lavoie must have been worrying lest Haworth should get impatient and try to pull off one of his favourite long shots, because he kept urging him to take it easy and keep cool. They were both lying with their rifles at the ready—and, just as Lavoie was dealing out words of wisdom, there was a splitting crack right in their ears and a bullet smacked into the rocks quite close to the bear. That was Lavoie: in his excitement he had inadvertently pressed the trigger of his own rifle while begging Haworth not to shoot too soon. The bewildered bear rushed into a patch of berry bushes and lay hid for a while. Then he emerged on the run, bent on getting away from this place where strange, uncouth noises woke the echoes and disturbed his meals. Both men opened up on him and Haworth killed him with two well-placed shots.

That solved the problem of fuel for the human engine. They fell on that bear and skinned him, and Haworth took the pots and dropped down a thousand feet or so for water. When he got back the steaks were sizzling gently in the pan, and great was the feasting. They had very little else with them except tea and salt and a small quantity of flour, so they ate and ate of the bear meat till they could eat no more. It was late afternoon before they made their next move, burdened now with the extra weight of the bear meat and hide. They went northeastward, angling up the slope of the small range they were on, and the hot September sun was on their backs. They sweated, and it was already evening when they reached the crest and looked over into the deepening shadows of the northeast slope. Not far below them they saw a typical timberline valley with its meadows and scattered clumps of alpine fir. Beyond this shallow depression rose a high range with jagged peaks that were still catching the last rays of the setting sun. And, sweeping gently up to the bare rimrock, they could see grassy, open slopes—country that might hold sheep or caribou, provided it had not been cleaned out by the Sikanni hunters.

Haworth sat down and pulled out his glass. Dusk was coming on, but there was still just light enough to make out a small group of animals about a couple of miles away. Haworth was unable to decide what they were; however, sheep, goat or caribou, it mattered little: the most pressing thing at the moment was to make a snug camp by a streamlet down in one of those clumps of fir and eat some more of that bear meat. The animals, whatever they were, would have to wait till the morning.

They proved, on closer acquaintance, to be *Ovis stonei*, Stone sheep—two ewes, a ram lamb and a young ram. But to the unpractised eye, and in the distance, they were just sheep—and Haworth proceeded to make his stalk without knowing exactly what he was hunting. The stalk was successful and he got to within fifty yards of the little band. His trouble then was that, crawling on his hands and knees, he couldn't see the sheep—there was too much brush in the way. The only thing to do was to stand up and shoot quickly before his sudden appearance caused a panic and got the bunch on the run. So he did that; and down went the first thing that moved—it happened to be a ewe with the short, slender horns of her sex. Haworth finished her off with a second shot and then swung round and got the young ram, who was just starting to run. Frightened and bewildered, the remaining ewe and her lamb took off—but soon returned, perhaps puzzled that their companions were not following. Finally they vanished into the safe crags and corries of the mountain, to be seen no more.

Lavoie came up and the men got to work on the sheep. As trophies the horns of the two dead animals were not worth taking. However, as specimens they had some value, so they took the complete head and hide of the young ram for inspection by the American Biological Survey, and the horns and plate of the ewe. They took also the best of the meat. All this they packed over to their camp among the firs, and there they devoted the next two or three days to drying the meat, scraping the sheep and bear hides, cleaning the skull and eating prodigiously of sheep and bear cooked in every way they could think of—from the frying pan, via the cooking pot, to the forked twig of green willow set in the ground close to the glowing embers.

Even with this rest Haworth was now very tired: the trip had been a hard one and for the time being he had no further wish to hunt. He was fed up with shooting things, and the thought of three animals dead and rotting on the heather was without charm.

Summer by now had gone and golden-fingered autumn was spreading its gaudy colours over the hills. It was time to be going—time to be returning to the Finlay. One long day down the stream by which they were camped brought Haworth and Lavoie back to the east–west valley[14] and to the trapper's cabin. There they planned to rest a day, for they were now weighted down with very heavy loads. And there the hunter's instinct, or whatever one may choose to call it, returned to Haworth.

In the dusk, as they were making camp, a very large moose had dimly shown itself down below in the marshes of the valley. Haworth spent much of his rest day lying up for that moose on a timbered island of hard ground in the muskeg—a frustrating performance because, when the moose did appear towards evening, he was for a long time unable to get a clear sight of it owing to the willows. Fortunately for the moose, when it did emerge into the open it proved to be a cow.

They came again to the river. From their old camp at the lower end of Long Canyon, Haworth estimated that it would be about twenty-three miles down to their canoe and cache at Prairie Mountain, while the going, both he and Lavoie were certain, would be bad. Actually the distance, following the river, was more like fifteen miles, and for most of the way there was a trail of sorts. But they could not know this, and it was not long before the vague idea of making a raft had crystallized into a set purpose.

They were not too well equipped for raft-building. They had a hatchet—a damnable tool when compared with a light axe—and they had eight large spikes that Haworth had been carrying around the country. For ties they had some lengths of twine, their packsack straps, and a roll or two of gauze bandages. Haworth extracted a few more spikes from a cache at the mouth of Sheep Creek and picked up some ancient and unreliable rope that he found lying there. And that was that.

Somehow, with five dry spruce logs and the unpromising materials listed above, they built a raft. Cross-braces were mortised into the five floor logs at each end and spiked there. Haworth spiked on a couple of diagonal braces, and they tied the whole thing together with everything they had, including the bandages, twisted for greater strength. Lavoie made a pair of paddles and they laid on the deck a couple of poles. The load was put aboard wrapped in the silk tent they had been carrying on the trip. Haworth christened the raft *Necessity*, and all was ready to go. The largest sack of dried meat still sat smugly on the bank—behind a rock, probably, keeping out of the sun. They would remember it when they were making camp at Prairie Mountain.

They hit the river in the late afternoon. They poled and swept out into midstream and the current took them. Down through the clear water they could see the stones of the riverbed flying past—and the rocks. If they hit and lodged on a couple of those their raft might well go to pieces and they would be lucky to get away with their lives. So they steered like mad with pole and paddle, and at the same time they laughed for the sheer excitement of it—and Joe Lavoie burst into song. He must have had a Northwester somewhere in his ancestry, for a river was home to him and he was happy there—and doubly so after days of plodding over the hills under a heavy pack. The speed was exhilarating; and for each man a particular paradise was waiting down at Prairie Mountain: Haworth could see in his mind's eye a can of jam, sweet and alluring—and, for Lavoie, a phantom can of pork and beans floated down the river ahead of him, intangible as the Holy Grail.

They got into a strong eddy and *Necessity* spun round and round until they could sweep her out into the stream again. Rocks raced past beneath them but they touched nothing. Waves swept over the load, drenching the raftsmen. The mountains marched by and the shadow of the western ranges, golden-rimmed against the sunset, fell upon the tossing water. Day deepened into dusk—and in the last light *Necessity* grounded with a satisfying scrunch on the bar at the foot of Prairie Mountain. Wet and chilled, Haworth raced for the cache. Thank God, all was as they had left it! Now for that jam—and the can of pork and beans ...

Much of that trip of Haworth's, Alan and I had been able to follow from the rock outcrop where we had been sitting. And now our afternoon was on its way and it was time we made a move towards the river. Getting down Prairie Mountain was not quite so simple as one might expect. Standing on the edge of that very steep open slope, I suddenly realized that it was full of possibilities. If care was taken and all went well, there was nothing to it. If, on the other hand, anybody ever slipped and started rolling, then there was no good reason ever to stop—not until one slammed into an isolated tree or rock and broke every bone in one's body. I made a brief but, I hoped, impressive speech to Alan on the dangers of slippery, sun-baked grass, and then we started.

Here and there on the slope grew a tree or a willow bush, and we made these our stopping places, angling cautiously down and across the hill towards each one—resting beside it, where we had firm support and could plan our next move. I had no line with me, and in such a place it was useless to try to hang on to anybody with a view to giving assistance. All I could do was to set an example of caution, moving carefully and in the lead, leaning back in the steepest places to steady myself with a hand against the hill. Down we went steadily, the whole of McConnell's 1,400 feet—from poplar to willow to wind-twisted fir, and then again to poplar, scuffling around the little outcrops of rock. At last the slope eased off, and I was surely glad to see that boy walking ahead of me into the blessed trees, easy-gaited as on the hill and all in one piece. It was not till then that we realized that each one of us had developed a colossal thirst. A dry lunch except for the oranges—then an hour or two of walking about on top in the sultry warmth of a cloudy day—and finally this descent, concentrating open-mouthed on every move: in a word, we had had it. And now, where was that canoe?

It was exactly where we had left it, and in record time a small fire was flaring and crackling on the shingle. Soon the tea pail—an old lard pail, smoked and blackened by hundreds of campfires—was singing, swaying a little over the flames on a stick of green willow. In went a handful of tea, to be stirred vigorously with a forked twig. Now—off the fire with it and into the river. Let it stand there for half a minute to cool—and get those mugs out of the canoe while you're about it. And where's the sugar? A good heaping spoonful for mine. Lay that chocolate on the rock—we'll finish off on that ...

Never did afternoon tea find a kinder home, and for a while we sat there contentedly with the woodsmoke drifting around us, watching the clear, fast-running river. Then we threw the canoe into the water and departed from that place, full of ambition and well-sugared tea, chocolate and jam sandwich.

In a short burst of spray we shot through the Fox River riffle and swept on down the Finlay, paddling furiously towards Ware. It was getting on for six o'clock, there were still two miles to go, and foremost in our thoughts was our supper engagement with the Patties ...

About noon on the following day the riverboat came upstream from Art's cabin and slid in to shore at the Bay landing, where the canoe was lying. We were ready for it: we loaded the outfit and then laid the canoe back in its old place, upside down, resting on the thwarts. We fixed up a seat, using the eiderdowns and the bug tents—but then Mr. and Mrs. Pattie appeared, plus young David Pattie, who was all of one year old, so we installed them in the place of honour. At the last moment, at least half of the remaining population of Fort Ware clambered aboard: it was a royal send-off and they were all coming to see us up to Bower Creek.

The big boat took the Fox River riffle in its stride. On we went, westward, out of the Trench, past Prairie Mountain, through the islands, past the Seven Mile Pool with the slender spires of its tall spruce reflected deep down in its calm water against the shining summer clouds. Now the mass of Bower Mountain seemed to bar the way, and for the last four miles we thrust straight at it up what my diary calls "a good river"—which, to me, is a river with clear water, good tracking beaches and a poling bottom.

We landed on the point between Bower Creek and the Finlay, at the foot of a snye behind an island. A big cabin stood on the point—a cabin with a large, sheltered porch that faced the south and the sun. A few yards away stood a solid-looking cache—a strongly built log cabin, the size of one small room, set up off the ground on uprights that were eight or nine feet high and tinned around just under the cache platform to prevent inroads by small climbing animals. The log walls of the cache, I noticed, were covered over and made weatherproof with sheets of spruce bark—easily peeled from the parent tree in early summer when the sap is running, good to keep out driving rain or drifting

The slender spires of tall spruce surrounding the Seven Mile Pool are reflected deep down in its calm water.

snow. Heavy padlocks secured both cache and cabin doors. Ludwig gave us the keys to them: this had been the main cabin of his trapline. Now he had sold the line to the Indian Department, and when we had done with them, the buildings would pass into Indian ownership. About a dozen pairs of hands passed our canoe and outfit overboard to us: we laid the canoe on the shingle and splashed ashore with the stuff. Then we said goodbye to Art and Ludwig, and the boat departed. The last we saw of it, away downstream, a riot seemed to have broken out on board. Raven-haired, plum-cheeked children were bounding up and down ...

We made ourselves pretty comfortable in that cabin. We knew that we had just two days there together. Then, on the third day, the August mail plane would come in to Ware, and Alan would go out on it. And that would be that, and I would be poling back up to Bower Creek alone.

Those two days soon went. Rain and low cloud driving down the Finlay valley blanketed the first morning. We made good use of the uncharitable day: we cleaned up and cooked—and then, when every pot was full of some camp delicacy, we ate an early lunch and hit the trail up the Finlay, keeping high above the river, winding through the

Patterson climbs the ladder to Ludwig's solidly built, heavily secured cache eight feet above ground.

dripping trees in a dank Scotch mist. We must have gone about four miles when we came on a large spruce growing on a muskeggy flat—a spruce with a blaze on it and with writing on the blaze. Ludwig had told us how the Finlay River Sikannis often left messages on blazed trees, or simply records of their passing, all written in the English they had learnt at school. And here was one of these, left by some earlier sufferers from the weather:

"Feb. 26. 1949. Rain and snow so we dont make much fun. Massiter."

Neither did we: the mountains were withdrawn, wrapped in cloud and invisible, and nothing moved in the sodden bush except the grey-green streamers of moss, swaying at the touch of the wet, cold wind that came sighing down the valley. A miserable prospect—and we moved on, coming soon to a high, Jack-pine knoll from which we had a splendid view of the Finlay valley narrowing into Long Canyon. From there we went down to the river and made tea—a pleasant interlude by the cheerful fire.

On the second day we walked about eight miles up Bower Creek in sunshine and west wind, finding an excellent fishing pool, full of trout, at the base of a low cliff—and finding also that we had come away

Float planes such as this one were the fastest way to get back to civilization. Alan, seen here, boarded one to reach Vancouver Island in time for school in September.

without our fishing tackle. No matter—home in the evening to plum pudding and bed.

That plum pudding was in the nature of a celebration. It had been carefully hoarded for the last night—and this, we supposed, was it. The following morning we packed Alan's stuff and I wrote a couple of letters and sorted out a camp outfit for my return trip to Bower Creek. Then we loaded the canoe and ran the twelve miles down to Ware. On the way it seemed to me that I caught sight of movement away down in the green depths as we slipped silently over the surface of a lovely pool. We circled in the eddy: and, sure enough, there they were—fish, and big ones. It took a little time, but Alan caught two big grayling and one slightly smaller rainbow. Then we ran on, arriving at the post only a short time before the mail plane, a Beaver, came into view from the south. It alighted on the river, tying up close to the canoe at the Hudson's Bay Company landing.

Out of the plane came two or three people, one of them being the district nurse, Nurse Martin. Some businesslike bags and packages came with her and, with these, she took possession of the bunkhouse. Then it gradually dawned on us why the place was stiff with Indians—Indians who had been summoned in some mysterious way to rendezvous at Ware—Indians from upstream and from downstream, from the Akié, from Fox River, from the bush and from the mountains. Mortality in general, and infant mortality in particular, had been too high on the Finlay and now the whole outfit was going to be inoculated against tuberculosis. With this bunch around, that would be no five-minute job—so we put the fish in the shade in the nose of the canoe, which was riding easily in the cold water, covering them with sprays of green willow. We piled our stuff and tarped it up, thanking God we hadn't come down earlier and got it all spread around the bunkhouse—now become the district clinic. Then we sat ourselves down on the grass to watch the show, talking now and then with two of the older Sikannis, Isaac Seymour and old McCook.

One by one those children and young people were put through the mill in the bunkhouse. There may have been a bit of hesitation at first—but that soon vanished, largely owing to the determination of those who had already had their shots that nobody should escape. They had suffered: now let everybody else be stabbed, scratched or otherwise punctured. Some were dragged up to the shack by the self-appointed press gang, blubbering and protesting, fighting every inch of the way. Others were marched along unresisting, in mute terror—only to emerge, a minute or two later, beaming and ready to hunt down the next victim.

The sun dipped towards the wooded hills beyond the river and the shadows lengthened on the grass. Alan and I began to think of those grayling lying in the canoe. Finally Nurse Martin appeared in the doorway. Somebody was missing from her list: George—she hadn't got George. Fetch him along.

That was easier said than done. George had taken to the bush. The old men laughed. The women talked excitedly. The young acted: they hit for the timber—and they must have had George's mental processes pretty well taped, for presently there came a yell from out of the tall spruce, and the last young Sikanni was hauled out into the open, to be dragged up for execution ...

The plane would not be leaving till the morning—so once more we borrowed Mrs. Pattie's broom, this time to clear the bunkhouse of swabs and cartons and small bottles. Then we set about the two grayling and the trout. Hungry as we were, they were all we could manage—allowing, of course, for the bacon and bannock and butter that went with them, and the tea to wash the whole lot down. Then we slept the sleep of those who have passed their whole day under the sun.

More Indians seemed to be about next morning—Indians we hadn't seen the day before. But nobody else—until, at last, Taylor, the pilot of the plane, emerged from the Bay house and looked approvingly at the blue sky and the sun. He smiled and waved and went down to the landing to check over the Beaver. Then he vanished again, and no more active White life was observed till Nurse Martin came out and walked off towards the little cemetery. She had gone to photograph the small graves there: there were too many of them, and a photographic record would be visible proof to the Indian Agent that it was high time something was done.

The mail plane left at midday and Alan was on it. I watched it race downstream, climb into the air and vanish. Pattie was standing beside me. "That's that for another month," he said. "Now come on up to the house and have a bite with us. Then I'll run you up to Bower Creek. I want to try my new boat on that bit of river. I've never had it up there and now's the time to go."

20

The Explorer

Supper was early and a bit lonely that evening at Ludwig's cabin. The place seemed dead with Alan gone, and I, who had always laughed at the idea of loneliness, found myself missing his cheerful conversation, often livened with a dash of the purposely absurd. The only thing with life in it now was the restless, unsleeping river. The murmur of it filled the warm stillness of the evening—and it was to the river that I went for companionship. I untied the canoe and slid it off its driftwood skids into the water. Then I poled and tracked it upstream to a good eddy that Alan and I had noticed on that wet afternoon walk in the mist. And there I fished till I could see the line no longer, getting only two trout for my trouble—but nice ones: about two and a half pounds apiece. With them on the floor of the canoe I ran down to Bower Creek in the last light, with the water the colour of pale, translucent jade, the reflection from the evening sky. On its rippling surface every swirl and every riffle showed black and sharp as the carving on a jade pendant, the work of a master hand.

The cabin looked snug by candlelight. I lit the stove and made some coffee, unrolled my bed on its tarpaulin, sawed some wood for the morning and wrote up my diary. Outside, groping around in the starlit dark, carrying armfuls of wood towards the shaft of orange light that streamed from the open doorway, one could hear everywhere the noises of flowing water—Bower Creek chattering to itself beyond the cache, and behind the cabin the small riffle at the foot of the snye. That point between the creek and the river is a natural camping place, and I wondered if Finlay had stopped there. At the back of Haworth's book there was a resume of "Finlay's" journey to Thutadé Lake: it had been copied by Dr. J. B. Tyrrell from one of the unsigned fragments of Black's rough draft of his *Report* that had been wrongly attributed to John Finlay. The *Report* itself (Black's final and signed copy) was already on the list for publication, and the archives staff of the Hudson's Bay Company had already got as far as banging the dust of a hundred and twenty-five years off it and making a transcript from Black's fine and sometimes difficult handwriting. But in the West, in 1949, these things were beyond our ken.

Black—whom we last saw getting away from Deserters Canyon— never camped on the Bower Creek point. He passed by there under conditions that were almost arctic, having run into a spell of horrible weather somewhere below the Kwadacha. Though he did not know it, he was making his Finlay River exploration at the low point of a long cold cycle, and the year 1824 was a year—almost *the* year—of extended glaciation and maximum rain and frost. May went out in a deluge of cold rain, and the morning of the first of June was even worse. The Finlay had risen a good deal in the night and was still rising. Cold, gale-force winds from the west drove stinging showers of sleet across the river. Mist rose off the water, mingling with the sleet—and through this smother Black could dimly see "the stout Pines Noding and bending like Willow Wands and the Snow (like in the Middle of Winter) drifting along the lofty Mountains."

It was towards midday when Black's party broke camp below the Kwadacha and got going in this chaos of the elements. They found the current getting stronger and the rising river throwing the drift away from the centre and towards the sides.[15] They crept along, hugging the banks with the canoe, passing the line around the leaning trees, cutting the sweepers out of their way. What with the lopped-off sweepers surging down on them and the drifting trees flung out towards the banks by the river, the heavily loaded birchbark canoe must have been in constant danger.

At last the sun came out and the black storm clouds drifted away towards the Rockies, and they came to the Tochieca or Fox River. "At this Fork," Black wrote, "we had some perplexity in our Councils." The Old Slave was all for taking the way of Fox River and over the pass to the Liard, which he painted as a land abounding in moose and beaver. The main river, he said, cut through high mountains and came from a lake called Thutadé—but he had never been to the lake by way of the big bend and knew that route only from hearsay. And so forth. Having listened, as diplomacy required of him, to the Old Slave, Black pointed up the main Finlay, away from Fox River and the Trench. Thrusting on the poles, hauling on the line, and with disappointment written on all its faces, brown, ruddy and copper-coloured, the expedition moved on. The men could see, through the gap in the west wall of the Trench, a barrier of snow-covered mountains, and they were wondering what lay ahead of them. Perhaps it was as well they couldn't know, for they were indeed taking the hard road: the hill of water that they had to climb to reach Thutadé rose almost a thousand feet from the mouth of the Tochieca.

The Finlay was rising to its June flood, and with the increasing slope the current was becoming always stronger. Negotiating some reefs a short distance above Prairie Mountain, the men broke three of their poles and put ashore to cut new ones, lighting, as they did so, a roaring fire by which they could stand and work, steam and dry out a little. They were clothed in hats of fur; in coats of blanket, moosehide or buckskin; in trousers of tanned hide or of some stout English fabric that had made the journey out to Hudson's Bay. On their feet they wore moosehide moccasins. Each man had devised some sort of protection from the freezing rain—a cape of canvas, it might be, or some wrapping of an animal's hide fastened around the shoulders with laces of tanned moosehide. But, come rain or shine, they were in and out of the river all through the day—on the line, embarking to cross to the further shore, leaping into the water as they landed to catch and hold the canoe from crashing into the rocks. And so they were always wet—trousers flapping clammily against their scarred and battered legs, moccasins limp and slippery ... That evening of the first of June they noticed, when they made camp, that ice was forming on the gunwales of the big canoe.

It was going to take them twelve days to get around the big bend: twelve hard days before they could enjoy a brief respite from the "sound of clashing water" (to quote McConnell) and send their canoe flying across the placid mirror of the Fishing Lakes. That distance by river is about forty-five miles: they would average, therefore, less than four miles a day. For a skilled crew to make only that low mileage is a fair measure of the difficulties to be encountered on the bend of the Finlay.

The two men who have made, with their followers, this dangerous passage were on entirely different missions. Swannell was to come along ninety years later and map and measure, record and name the various hazards in detail. Black passed by, content to describe the rapids and cascades, and to keep a record of the distances travelled and the compass bearings. He bestowed few names: there was the Old Man—which was Swannell's Split Rock and Haworth's "immense, ragged boulder"—and there was Point du Mouton (Sheep Point), and L'Ence [Anse] du Sable (Sandy Bay)—and then the Indian names of lakes and rivers. But for the most part Black was simply concerned with getting on—and so with the temper of his men and the Sikanni followers. He had a long way to go: to the source of the Finlay, and then on foot into the northwest, all new country to the White man. Two of his men had already deserted: two more were yet to leave him. All the vague dreads of the unknown lay on this little party, now reduced to eleven "growen persons and 2 children." If, at times, in my telling of their perilous journey, some anachronisms creep in—if, that is, I use some of Swannell's place names of this century—that will only be to avoid confusion.

Black passed the mouth of Bower Creek on the second of June. His people were battling the weight of the Finlay in semi-flood: hardly any tracking beach was exposed and the men were perpetually clambering over rock points and passing the line—that is, carrying the line ahead with them and then floating it back to the canoe by means of a piece of driftwood. Then they would haul the canoe up on the single line while those on board poled wherever they could find a rock to shove against, and fended their craft off the sharp rocks of the shore.

They were also working the canoe upstream by "catching the eddy." Often on a river the rock points on either side alternate—or there may be points of rock on one shore and points of loose rock or shingle on the other, but not directly opposed. In that case a canoe will travel as far as possible upstream in the eddy below one of these points, gaining speed as it does so. At the last possible moment it swings out into the stream, hits the surge around the sheltering point at a fine angle and then, all hands paddling furiously, makes across the river to catch the tail end of the eddy on the far side, there to repeat the process. These crossings could be difficult and dangerous. If the eddy on the far bank was missed, the canoe might be immediately swept backwards into serious trouble. If it was caught, then the canoe would shoot upstream in the favouring current. Incidentally, no mention is anywhere made of the method of progress of the two Sikanni women and the two children. Reading between the lines, it seems hardly likely that they used their own light canoes, "no biger than cockle shells," in these dangerous waters. They must have made their way on foot through these gloomy gorges, being ferried across in the large canoe when absolutely necessary, perhaps to some evening camp or to help the Old Slave in fishing or the hunt.

On that same day of June 2, they came to the red gates of Long Canyon. The rapids down which Haworth bounced so gaily on the raft *Necessity* gave them trouble. Evening caught them in the middle of a difficult stretch of water and they had to camp on a steep, stony slope with the river rushing below and no level place whereon to sleep. This was not so good: La Guarde was ill and shaking as if with fever; and Cournoyer, climbing ahead, had fallen off one of the rock points into the river, to be hauled ashore, saved only by his death grip on the line. They all needed at least a sound sleep—but they had almost given up hope of that when the "Sikanni Ladies" saved the day. While the men saw to the canoe and the outfit, the two women scrambled up the scree and gathered great quantities of moss. Then, by heaving out a few rocks and levelling the nesting places with moss, everybody somehow slept— La Guarde with a good hot drink of rum inside him, mixed by Black.

Another uncharitable dawn came: the rocks were white with frost and ice was once more forming on the poles. The men dug themselves out of their lairs in the rocks. They launched the canoe, loaded it and started. "The People," Black writes, "[are] not very loquacious, which is very well." This was the old system of travel in the days of the fur trade: break camp and get going; then have breakfast later. It was the custom and it was the way of the voyageur. But no wonder there were some grumpy, silent starts!

Black walked ahead and came to the Old Man, where he could see that a portage would have to be made alongside the main channel on the right bank. He went on for some distance, finding the river better than he had expected, "for, as far as I went, tho' the Rapids are boisterous yet by catching the eddies on each side the Canoe can come up." Then he returned to the Old Man, to find the men already there, packing the outfit over the portage. There they all breakfasted—and there the gloom of the grey, frozen dawn departed and the normal high spirits of the young returned to that young crew. Later on that same day they passed through the Iron Gate, "a dreadful chasm" where the Finlay is no more than thirty feet wide.

It was about two miles above the Old Man that in 1893 R. G. McConnell[16] decided to cache his canoes and proceed on foot. By his reckoning, Long Canyon begins at the island rock. "Twelve miles above Fox River," he wrote, "canoe navigation definitely ends, the river above that point being simply a succession of canyons, riffles and rapids, often narrowing to less than a hundred feet and causing wild rapids."

McConnell, being of the Geological Survey, was in an entirely different position from that of either Black or Swannell. Black had to prove or disprove the Finlay as a possible fur-trade route; Swannell had to survey and map its course: each one, therefore, had to stay with the river. McConnell could go as he pleased, provided he returned with accurate information as to the structure of the country. Faced, therefore, above the Old Man with a river which, when seen from above, was nothing but a creaming ribbon of white—or, as Black puts it with his touch of poesy, "pouring its white foaming torrents through the deep, narrow chasm with great impetuosity, and the swelling surges dancing in great Majesty"—McConnell, himself no mean canoeman, decided that it would be quicker to walk. And he was right. He made the Fishing Lakes in one week from the mouth of the Kwadacha.

I mention McConnell here because he did not follow the river for the whole distance. Bypassing Cascade Canyon, he made use of a valley, now named McConnell Pass, which takes off on the south side of the Finlay above Long Canyon. This valley runs almost in a straight line, northwestward, cutting through the mountains—the chord of an arc described by the Finlay. A man going towards the Fishing

Lakes by way of this pass ascends a stream to its source in a two-mile-long lake, passes over a low divide to another small lake, and returns to the Finlay down a shorter stream that falls into the river almost opposite Point du Mouton. The whole length of this bypass is about fifteen miles.

McConnell and his men reached the Fishing Lakes on August 28, 1893. Having observed and recorded the geological formations on the way up, McConnell put in two or three days at the lakes, climbing the surrounding mountains in order to fill in the gaps and solve some of his outstanding problems. Then he made his way back to his canoes. Travelling at his accustomed speed, he reached Quesnel on October 1, thus terminating a season of almost four months on the headwaters of the Peace.

The Old Slave, with the two Sikanni women and the children, took this McConnell Pass trail while Black and the crew worked their way out of Long Canyon and through Cascade Canyon. To lighten the canoe the two Sikanni women were burdened with very heavy loads. Every so often this would throw them into an unbearable rage, whereat they would fling down their burdens and yell and curse at the top of their voices—but there was no help for it: in the end they always had to pick up their loads and go on. Perhaps this heartfelt indulgence in what was probably very bad language did some good. At least it must have relieved their feelings. La Prise's wife also took this shortcut trail up Cutoff Creek. She carried her own bundle, but she seems to have kept herself to herself, not wishing, perhaps, to associate with the Sikanni ladies.

Early on June 4 the expedition emerged from Long Canyon into a broad valley. The passage of the canyon had been tough on the men. La Guarde was still unwell. La Prise had done his best but had less reserve strength than the rest: the effort was telling on him. The cold weather and the upstream work, forever in and out of water that came straight from the snow, were having a cumulative wearying effect on them all. And the river was still rising.

The canoe also had suffered: "To day and yesterday they have driven several Holes in the Canoe and cracked one of the Gun Walls but without any material injury." One of the difficulties in rough going, such as the canyons of the Finlay, is the loading and unloading of the canoe where there are heavy swells beating against the rocks—the beginning or end of a portage, perhaps, or at some enforced night camp like the one on the mountain slope. Men have to stand in the water and hold the canoe from being dashed on the rocks by the waves; and it's far from easy to lift it, when empty, out of turbulent water—or to launch it again—without inflicting some damage.

The broad valley was soon passed, and ahead of them they could see the entrance to Cascade Canyon, almost six miles long and in one place seven hundred feet in depth. They pushed on into the canyon and evening caught them at a portage over a point of rocks: "having broke and shattered a little our Canoe and the Men fatigued etc., we shall pitch camp for the night." Black and La Guarde climbed up the mountain behind camp after supper and dropped over into the McConnell Pass trail, and soon they heard the sound of voices. That was the Sikanni ladies, very dirty about the face and struggling along with their loads. The Old Slave was not with them (which was just as well for him), having gone off on the trail of some fresh caribou tracks. He had killed nothing and taken no fish, "the Sikannis not being Nimrodians or mighty hunters," and by now the women were hungry. That accounted for the frightful mess they were in: they were reduced to grubbing and munching bear's root by way of sustenance. This is the licorice root, at its best at this season and much beloved of bears. The women were digging the bear's root as they went along and they were, literally, mud up to the eyes, "for they never wash these roots before use; a rub or two on the leather doublet being sufficient preparation." Black sent the women over the hill to the main camp, where they could get a proper meal. He and La Guarde pushed on to the end of the McConnell Pass cut-off, where, on reaching the Finlay again, they found to their relief the river about as bad as usual but no worse. Somehow, they decided, they could deal with it. La Guarde was worrying about some point or cliff that the Iroquois hunters had described to him—the Iroquois Cap, a place where the Finlay was absolutely impassable. Black, too, had that on his mind; but the greater worry for him was their stock of provisions. "Our Indian Companions providing nothing for themselves," he writes, "we are obliged to share with them our staff of life, Pemican." And again, later: "They however made away with all our dried Deers Meat and cast a wistful eye on the Pemican, and requires some resolution to resist so many pleased faces."

Cascade Canyon proved to be the worst water they had so far hit and it took them two days to get through. They thought they must have passed the Iroquois Cap there—a cascade, "the Waters tumbling over a broken shelf as white as snow, here no means of making a Portage appearing ... La Guarde thinks this the Iroquois Cap from discription and that never man passed in such a place." Nevertheless, Black and the Old Slave found a narrow ledge, which they widened by means of felled trees—and somehow it went. They had quite a time getting the canoe out of the water, and then in again, without holing it—and they got away from that place on a double line, playing it as safe as they could. By this time the Old Slave had formed a high opinion of "the Whites Canoemanship" and was coming to think nothing was impossible to them.

Towards the head of the canyon they holed their canoe twice, patched it, went ahead on a double line—then scrambled ahead and passed the line. The rapids were wild. "La Guarde says his Head is dizzy looking at them, made WNW 1/3 [mile] one of the worst places we have yet met with, the River raging with great fury amongst large Masses of Rock."

In the end, thank God, they passed through a narrow gap and emerged suddenly into a fine valley that seemed to them like heaven after the bellowing hell of tumbling waters they had left behind. They made a good camp on the point where the Obo River enters the Finlay, and they named that place Point du Mouton from the Stone sheep that the Old Slave shot and brought in that evening. It was not a very big sheep but it was the first big game animal of the trip. Up to now, to eke out their provisions they had killed "very little, sometimes a Goose or a Duck and only Nine Beaver since the Commencement of the Voyage." The Old Slave's name for his sheep was *sason*.

On the opposite shore from that camp the upper end of the McConnell Pass trail drops down to the Finlay, and there, as evening drew on, the Sikanni ladies appeared with their loads, shouting and beckoning furiously. They were in a horrid temper, having eaten nothing since leaving the main camp in Cascade Canyon—not even the muddy licorice roots, for over the latter part of the trail the bears had been beforehand with them and had cleaned up the complete spring crop. The women and the two suffering children were ferried over and fed.

Prowling around in the dusk from the Point du Mouton camp, Black came on two winter campsites of the Sikannis, and also on an old pound or trap into which caribou had been driven. By this time he had come to the conclusion that the Old Slave knew a lot more about the country than he had been willing to admit, so he sought him out and questioned him directly.

Yes, the Old Slave said, some of the Sikannis did often winter here— a band which had for leader an old chief, by name Methodiates.[17] He thought that these Sikannis might even now be at or near the Fishing Lakes. Black told him to take a light outfit and one of the fishnets and go ahead on foot in the morning to find them. He was to warn them of the White men's coming and say that what they needed was information about the country and any help they could get in the way of provisions—meaning game. Black had not yet realized that these Indians lived almost permanently on the bare edge of subsistence. The Old Slave agreed to make the contact, warning Black that between Point du Mouton and the Fishing Lakes there was one stretch of river that was very dangerous—so much so that the Iroquois had never attempted it, and bad even to make a portage. He was speaking of the stretch of rapids and cascades that Swannell would name Reef Canyon.

That evening they set the fishnets in the eddy below the inflow of Obo River. There was no skilled fisherman in the party—Ossin, whose business that was, having deserted with Bouché on May 28. So La Guarde and La Prise took the work in hand and set all the nets: two of 4½-inch mesh and two of a smaller size, together with some night lines baited with pork. The Sikannis also set two of their nets, "made out of the filaments of the Willow Bark twisted into Thread." One would like to have seen them: they would be museum pieces now.

The Indian nets were brittle when dry, but when wet they were strong enough to catch and hold the medium-sized fish of those mountain streams. The thing that struck Black was that they were always more successful than the nets of European manufacture—and, sure enough, on the following morning they ran true to form: in the

White-man nets there was not a single fish while those of the Indians held five. Disgustedly the men took in the nets and set about drying them. That was not too easy on that cold June day, and it was late in the afternoon when they got away from Point du Mouton. They made between three and four miles—their course being west-northwest now, for they had passed the most northerly point of the big bend. "Camped late very cold, the Ice forming on the Poles." Yet that same frosty evening the men were cheered by a flight of songbirds on their way north, blackbirds and robins, birds of passage. The people were pleased when they saw them still around camp in the morning. And then, suddenly, the birds were gone, "just as if Nature had been jealous of the happy Scene of the morning ... In all our Travells amongst the Rocky Mountains, we never before or after last night and this morning heard the voice of a Singing Bird."

A savage-looking range now came in sight, snow-covered and with snow still deep low down and in the shady hollows. Black called the range the Peak Mountains, and by that name they are shown on the map today. The men went on, and before long they came to the foot of a cascade and to L'Anse du Sable, the Sandy Bay. Southwest from here, as far as they could see, the river ran between cliffs, a turmoil of foaming water shining white against the sun. Here La Guarde's resolution deserted him and he broke down and wept. He would not venture into this new and most frightful canyon, he said, until he could see the end of it and so make a complete plan of action. Black humoured him and calmed him down. "I know La Guarde to be a good Man and willing to do his best and an excellent foreman, but withall of a Mulish cast perhaps, therefore gave him his own way to go and visit the River and make his Report."

La Guarde had somehow got it into his head that the portage trail—or road, as they called it then—would be on the east side of the river, above the cliffs. So they made camp on that side opposite the Sandy Bay, and La Guarde departed in a hurry, to be seen no more till breakfast time, when he reappeared, despondent and hungry, having slept without food or blanket. Black, meanwhile, had gone part of the way himself and found it "bad enough but we have passed worse." Two frantic days of searching followed. La Guarde vanished once more—

this time with his camp on his back and with instructions to go right ahead to the Fishing Lakes and get in touch with the Sikannis there. Perreault took to the mountains on that same east side: he was to search for any travelled Sikanni trail and to shoot and bring in any game he might see. Black crossed over to the west shore, established the main camp at Sandy Bay and then pushed on upriver himself, above the cliffs, accompanied by La Prise and his wife. Manson remained in charge of the camp at Sandy Bay.

The Fishing Lakes lie in a wide valley, flanked by the Peak Mountains on the west and by gentler, more rounded mountains on the east. Here the tumult of fast water ceases and the Finlay becomes a lake, six or seven miles long and with an average width of two hundred yards. The current is slack. On either side (but mostly on the west) are minor lakes: tarns would be a better name for them—willow-ringed pools, the largest a bit over a mile long, some of them connected by winding channels with the river.

The whole wide valley with its muskeggy, balsam-studded flats must, in some earlier time, have been one large lake, held in by the rocks that now outcrop in Reef Canyon. Gradually the Finlay has cut these rocks down, and now the waters escape from the old lake basin by "a horrid Chasm, the River confined into a narrow stream as white as snow, rising its Watery vapours in the air."

In the fall of the year the wild animals frequent this valley or use it as a crossing place. Swannell writes: "The banks are tracked like a farm-yard." Harper Reed[18] told me that he had seen the silty shores "churned up like a muddy corral at weaning time." Swannell was speaking of late September, Harper Reed of October. It was in August that I walked down from the Stikine Trail crossing to the head of the Fishing Lakes; and there, after shoving through willows and tall, rank grass, I came on a place that had been a shallow pool through most of the summer—now just half-dry silt, barren as the surface of the moon. And not one inch of that oval lake bed was free of tracks. The pattern was so confused and overlaid that it was hard to pick out those of individual animals. There were the great, splay-footed hoof marks of moose—and two bears had walked across: that much was plain. The rest was chaos; and all I knew was that, in the surrounding mountains, there were three more large animals: caribou, sheep and goat. You could take your pick. Did these beasts, I wondered, come here to roll and shake and clean themselves? A Bushman, or a Navajo, or a black Australian tracker might have made some sense out of this jumble. I just marvelled at it.

A dead silence lay on the valley on that August day. Far above, some air must have been moving. A line of cloud lay along the black Peak Mountains; and from it, now and then, a vaporous fragment would detach itself, trailing a drifting streak of snow. But sunshine held sway over the valley and the wandering cloud would shred out to nothing against the deep blue of the summer sky. Only the silence would remain, all-pervading, almost a tangible thing. Even the echoes were withdrawn and remote. If you smote hard with the back of an axe against a lightning-blasted fir and then listened, there still would be no sound ... until, whole seconds later, from far away the answering echo came: *knock*!

On that June day of 1824, and at the other end of the Fishing Lakes, the evening echoes suddenly came alive and the silence fled before the roar of guns. Had not the Old Slave been sent ahead as ambassador, bearing messages of goodwill and offers of trade, then the quietly fishing Sikannis would most certainly have fled, too, from their pools and eddies. As it was, they just raised their heads and listened. Perreault also, away up on his mountain slope, must have heard the shots and wondered.

It was Black firing off his gun, trying to make contact with the Sikannis. La Guarde, too, was firing from somewhere on the far side of the Finlay. After a day of climbing cliffs and blazing trails through the bush, Black had figured out a route through Reef Canyon for the canoe; it would involve some "tight work" with the line, some dangerous crossings and four portages—but still it was a way and, as mountaineers say, it would go. Then, leaving "La Prise and Rib" to make camp (he had played them both out), Black had pushed on through the willows that lined the quiet river, firing signal shots—and at last getting answering shouts from two young Sikannis who were fishing.

Without La Prise to act as interpreter, Black's contact could be little more than a greeting. However, he mobilized his few words of the

Beaver language and, with them and by means of signs, he gathered that the Old Slave had arrived and was camped not very far away, fishing. He also was able to set his mind at rest about the course of the river: it held straight on to the south and did not turn, as he had feared it might, into the Peak Mountains. Easy on that point, he returned to where he had left La Prise, to supper and to bed.

The following day saw a reunion at the Fishing Lakes. Black came up again with La Prise and Rib; the Old Slave arrived by canoe from across the small lake where the two young men were still fishing; La Guarde came across the calm Finlay on a raft, having found no practicable way for the canoe up his side of the river and no possible portage trail. The Old Slave said messages had been sent to the chief, Methodiates, who was camped some distance away at a lake called Thucatadé.[19] He brought Black a dozen fish and said that if the Whiteman nets had been any good he would have had more. He would stay where he was and fish for Black, and he was also building a light canoe. Black noted again that the Indian nets were the best: the two Sikanni fishermen had taken fifteen fish in the night in willow-twine nets that were short but deep and about 2- to 2½-inch mesh. In their language the Fishing Lakes went by the name of Tototadé.

La Guarde was cheered to find that Black had found carrying places and a course for the canoe—and the party then returned to Sandy Bay, where they arrived about sunset. On the way they cut and blazed much of the portage trails. A little later Perreault appeared on the further shore and was ferried across. He came empty-handed. All he had seen was one caribou and he had been unable to get a shot at it.

They tackled Reef Canyon the following morning. Heartened by their rest, the men went at it with a will. Their strength was up by two manpower, Black having hired a couple of Sikannis at the Fishing Lakes; and the crew, as is natural with any team of men, were all out to show these strangers what they could do. Black had plotted a course that involved four portages—of 70, 60 and 1,450 paces, and one more that, in the enthusiasm of that morning, La Guarde scorned to make. It would have been the third portage, coming after the one of 60 paces. They took a look at it, but it was "a horrid place amongst Rocks and large Stones. Here the Gentlemen shot across, catching the Eddy on the otherside and got up with the line, this however is rather a dangerous Manoeuver in case of falling short or passing the Eddy, these fellows are geting courageous upon it. Recrossed the River, a bad Rapid bearing strongly on a Rocky Precipice, slipt up on the otherside wading in the Water amongst big stones." They were all pleased with themselves and Black with them: they "passed this place and some other tight places with labour and dexterity for they are good Bouts[20] when once into it." In the end La Guarde brought them safely, on the line, up the last rapid and to the foot of the Cascade of the Long Portage. Night found them with half the load across this carrying place.

About noon the next day they entered the calm water. Here was the first place since leaving Rocky Mountain Portage where the current was not fighting them, and this "so animated the men ... that the Canoe seemed to fly on the aqueous mirror of the Lake." This was the place where the two young Sikannis had been fishing, and the Sikanni camp was on a low, wooded ridge between the lake and the long quiet stretch of the Finlay. Here Black made his camp and here he remained for four days, talking, questioning, trading.

The Old Slave brought in a meal of fish for the outfit, complaining, as he did so, of the poverty of the fishing. A Sikanni by the name of Menayé brought a present of mountain-goat meat and told Black that the old chief was on his way. Cournoyer was sent back on foot with one of the young Sikannis to Point du Mouton to find and bring up some shot that had been left behind there. It had been covered over with branches and forgotten, an easy thing to do—just like Haworth's sack of dried meat ... And, later in the day, Methodiates arrived from Thucatadé River with the rest of his little band, some fifteen men.

Black and the chief embarked on a time-consuming series of speeches, discussions and questionings. They talked of the country, of its game and its fur, and of the surrounding tribes—the Thloadennis, the Trading Nahannis, the Carriers and the Beavers. Gradually it became clear to Black that this country of the Finlay–Stikine divide to which the Company had sent him was no fur-trade Eldorado, no "fur-hunter's dream." These denizens of the bleak uplands where the big rivers take their rise were an unwarlike, downtrodden people who had had bad luck. Together with their neighbours, the Thloadennis, they were shut off from the salmon rivers by the Trading Nahannis and the Carriers. And they were herded away from the grazing lands and the buffalo countries by the Beavers and the fierce Indians of the Liard. They were a poor people, grubbers of roots, snarers of marmots, cursed with fisheries that barely deserved the name, forever on the verge of starvation. If they wanted ammunition, guns, knives or metal cooking pots, these things were traded to them, a little at a time and at a vast price in furs, by the Trading Nahannis who themselves had traded them from the Thlingit, the Coast Indians—who, in turn, had obtained them from the Russians at Sitka. Beaver were scarce on the Sikanni lands and there was no dependable supply of fish or game by which a trading post could be maintained. And even if there had been, the country was hard to reach. Black estimated that, even knowing the

Black finally met Sikanni chief Methodiates at the farthest lake in the distance in this photo of the Fishing Lakes taken from the Bower Creek mountains. Black soon realized that Methodiates' followers were "a poor people ... forever on the verge of starvation."

rapids and with the portage trails cut out, it would take a skilled crew at least twenty-six hard days, starting as early in the year as possible, to arrive at the Fishing Lakes with a canoe-load of goods from Rocky Mountain Portage. And, if they were delayed till full high water caught them, the passage of the canyons might be impossible for a month or more. Furthermore, most of the fur that these Indians caught would find its way to Bear's Lake or Rocky Mountain Portage anyhow—so why, Black reasoned, go to all the trouble and expense of establishing a post in this faraway country?

Meanwhile here he was with a hardened crew, a load of trade goods and provisions, and instructions to proceed "to the Source of Finlay's Branch and North West Ward." And that was precisely what he intended to do, come hell or high water: get the canoe up to Thutadé Lake, cache the outfit there, and then take off into the unknown northwest. Who could tell? There might be better country there. And he began on the subject of carriers and guides with old Methodiates. The speeches the two of them made are interesting. They point the differences between the two races: the White man direct, demanding, knowing exactly what he wanted—and the Indian, evasive, shifting his ground, wondering in his heart what lay behind all this. After a later meeting on the same subject Black was to write: "Gave out some hints of our requiring some of them to go along with us to Guide us in the best passes and roads amongst the mountains and to hunt for us, to this they kept silent, but appeared uneasy ... nor did I press the thing, leaving them to chew the cud on it."

And there, for the time being, the matter rested, Black and the old chief having arranged to meet again on the headwaters of Thucatadé River.

The weather was becoming more like summer but, even so, on the morning of June 16 ice rimmed the lake shore. That day presented Black with a problem or two. La Prise, having twisted an ankle on the Long Portage, selected that morning to be awkward: he wished to be allowed to stay and hunt around the Fishing Lakes while the rest went on, joining with them again on their return journey. Quite obviously he was sorry he had ever left Chipewyan—and for two pins he would desert, build himself a canoe and get back there. Black talked him into a better frame of mind, "working a little on his Pride for this is the only Virtue he has to have kept him from returning to Fort Chipewean long ago."

Then there were signs of uneasiness, "at least a Vain of bad humour," among the crew, who had all been listening to Methodiates' accounts of the difficulties and dangers of the country to the northwestward. Black took a stroll by himself to think things over. His decision was soon made. He had finished his business with the Sikannis for the time being: he would break camp on the morrow and get going again; that would give the crew something else to do besides just magnifying the difficulties of the trail ahead and going sour on the job. "Returned to the Camp resolved on seeing the Source of Finlay's Branch and the Thloadenni."

That same day Cournoyer and the Sikanni returned with the shot.

21

Thutadé

It took them exactly six days to reach Thutadé Lake. It was at noon on June 23 that they poled up the last stretch of river and felt the current slacken; in a paean of victory Black joyously records the fact in his *Journal*: "Here we bade adieu to all the Currents Rapids shallows shelves Cascades and Falls in Finlay's Branch upwards of 200 Miles with little intermission, and by the Widening of the river Lake Thutadé opens in View with some round black Rocky Islands rising in it."

There had been nothing on the way from the Fishing Lakes to equal the drama of the canyons of the bend; nevertheless this last leg of the voyage had not been without its moments … First of all, the start had been delayed by old Methodiates returning for one last conference—ready, now, after all the turns and shifts of the last few days, to do exactly what Black had asked him to do in the first place: guide the fur traders to the northwestward as far as he knew the country and put them in touch with the Thloadennis. But let them first, the chief said, make their way to Thutadé Lake. There, with two of his men as guides, they could get their living by fishing and hunting about as well as anywhere in the country. He himself would be waiting for them at Thucatadé Lake after twenty days had passed—and by then the snow would have melted on the mountain passes, enough so that they could travel. At present there was too much snow.

So that was decided upon, and at noon on June 17, Black's party hit the river. They made more than ten easy miles that day and camped a couple of miles beyond the mouth of Thucatadé River. From there they had almost forty miles, following the windings of the river, to go to the lake, and they still had well over four hundred feet to climb. Next day the current quickened, and after a few miles of stiff poling they got into one of the worst places of the whole trip. This was a low canyon with a long, low island in the middle—always the worst kind of obstacle because, in such a place, the island splits the current, driving it against the banks or walls and undercutting them. There is no poling bottom or tracking beach on either side, and in this case they couldn't line from above.

La Guarde stopped and stared at the rapid, screwing up his eyes against the morning sun. This, for some reason, irritated Black: "The lofty brakers dancing majestically in the Sun beams before us have begun to dance in La Guarde's brain." So he called a halt for breakfast and then scrambled ahead with La Prise. Ahead, the river looked good. On one side of the island the channel was just a wild chute where the canoe would be "sweept off like a feather" and smashed against the rocks. On the other side, the west, the channel was deep, strong and narrow, driving beneath the undercut cliff. And at the head of the island there was a big driftpile. A wonderful prospect, whichever way one looked at it. It would, I suppose, have been possible to make a longish portage—but that uninspired way of tackling it seems never to have entered anybody's head. Black sent La Prise back with word that they would get on to the lower end of the island, line up it—and then somehow get off the point of it (which was the driftpile—frothing, foaming, a place that normally one would keep well clear of), paddling as if the devil were after them and catching, Black hoped, the tail of a favouring eddy. Then, having given his orders, he set to work to cut the trees on the cliff edge so that they could line around the first point of rock.

They made it. "Got the Canoe up to this Island ... and by taking out part of the cargo got the Canoe round to the extremity of the point and into the Thread of division of the two streams in which we all got famous duckings sliping off the ends of the trees under water, here placing the Poles and Paddles against the Projecting stumps, making a strong Effort. We got with much ado into still water, had we missed our aim and gone down its most probable we would have gone no farther." In other words, it would have been the end of them. My heart went with them when I first read, fourteen years ago, Black's wildly punctuated account of that morning's work. Travelling alone, on a bigger river and in far deeper canyons, I too have got off the points of islands, paddling like mad to catch the lower end of a beach or the tail of an eddy. The surface of the river seems to fly past beneath the canoe, the canyon wall comes nearer, the beach seems to be shooting hopelessly upstream. A prayer goes up with every stroke of the paddle—and through the back of your head you can hear, and almost feel, the curling break of the waves over the black reef below that will catch you, if you miss your aim ...

That afternoon they passed Delta Creek—on which we left Fleet Robertson[21] camped with his horses, looking for a way through the mountains. They made camp for the night on an island in the river and their keg of rum was opened almost as soon as it was brought ashore. Not only were they celebrating their safe passage through the canyon of the island, but they also had La Guarde to thank for the addition of a beaver to the larder and his pelt to the expedition's fur. La Guarde had shot the beaver in a small lake near the river and, since there was no other way of getting it, he had swum in after it and "brought it ashore in his Teeth a la Nage, for which feat he got a good dram, and we all joined in the beverage." Very neatly put—that is, assuming the pun was intentional.

Two Sikannis from Methodiates' band, together with their families, were with the party now, nominally as guides and hunters; however, little was produced by them for the pot on the trail to Thutadé: one porcupine, one beaver, and one very good trout taken in the basin at the foot of the Falls. Further inroads were being made into the pemmican. As for the river, Fleet Robertson's description of 1908[22] hits it off exactly: "below the Falls the river is very dangerous, being for miles streaked with rapids and strewn with boulders." There were several cascades. One of these gave them a portage of 164 paces; the rest they were able to pass with the line. On June 21 they breakfasted at the Firesteel River— a translation by La Prise of the Sikanni name. They were then about eight miles below the lake and four below the Falls. Regarding those miles, Black's *Journal* agrees wholeheartedly with Fleet Robertson's *Report*: "between the Fire Steel Fork and the Fall its one continued roar and rough murmur through the Gloomy Valley."

On the morning of the twenty-second they got the canoe into the basin below the Falls. The atmosphere was tense: a portage would have to be made, and to say that Black and La Guarde did not see eye to eye about this would be a gross understatement. The evening before, Black had left the crew coping with the continuous rapid that the infant Finlay had become and had walked ahead to the Falls.[23] From the basin he had climbed up a steep coulee and had marked out a portage trail of "about 950 Paces very steep hills at each end." The only thing wrong with it was that it ended in very swift water: they would have to reload the canoe there, and then cross the river immediately to catch an eddy on the far side. If they missed it they would be swept backwards down the rocky gulch and over the Falls, and Governor Simpson would be left wondering what had become of his expedition.

Meanwhile La Guarde, nerve-racked and harassed by the continual danger and the responsibility, had suddenly stopped the canoe in the rapids and, without so much as a word to Manson, had walked off to see if portaging could possibly be any worse than everlastingly lining and frogging the canoe uphill through a continuous boulder rapid. Black had seen him standing and gazing down on the Falls—and then he had somewhere passed Black in the woods without seeing him, or perhaps intentionally failing to see him. He arrived back at the canoe before Black did, still without a word to anybody, and gave the signal to move on. Soon afterwards they holed the canoe on a rock and camped for the night—La Guarde talking of a three-mile portage that he had mapped out on his jaunt through the bush.

Black let things simmer down till the cool of the morning. Then he took La Guarde in hand: too much of his own way altogether, Black said: a gross breach of Company discipline in leaving his post without a word to Manson: unwillingness in taking the canoe up to the Falls basin that very morning—and, as for a three-mile portage with half the timber in the country to cut out of the way, he could forget about that. The portage they were going to make was the one of 950 paces and now was the time to get busy and cut the trail out.

I imagine all this was said by this very large man without heat, with dignity and restraint, and in his usual deep voice. La Guarde listened. Then he asked for a new trackline, which Black issued to him. With that in his hand he went off to his work, muttering audibly that he was afraid of nothing living or of anyone, "which if designed for me," Black wrote, "I was pleased to take no notice of." And so the smoke blew gently away and tempers cooled, and the work of cutting and carrying went on ...

That was the last barrier. The four-mile canyon that followed Black's Portage was soon passed and the sound of the last rapid died away. Ahead lay only the sun-flecked waters of Thutadé, serene and unruffled.

This lake is the ultimate source of the great Mackenzie River. A drop of rain falling in the basin of Thutadé must travel 2,362 miles before it meets salt water in the Beaufort Sea. On the map the height of the lake is given as 3,625 feet above the level of that sea—a long descent for our venturesome raindrop, a rough passage and by no means an even slope. To reach the lake from Rocky Mountain Portage, Black and his men had lifted their heavily laden canoe 2,058 feet, with the strong currents of the Peace and the Finlay disputing every foot of the climb. The lake of Thutadé is twenty-seven miles long and shaped like a boomerang, with a shorter northern arm running due north and south, and with a main arm, sixteen miles in length, running northeast and southwest. The average width throughout is one mile. There is a narrows five miles from the outlet into the Finlay, and a second narrows where the boomerang makes its curve into the southwest. Black made his first camp at the first narrows which, according to the Sikanni guides, was a good fishing place. "Sent one of the Indians a hunting and the other put his Lines in the Water. La Guarde and La Prise got our Nets in the Water and also some lines baited with Pork which we suppose will be an extraordinary treat to the Thutadé Trout."

The Sikanni hunter was back that same evening with a caribou tongue, and in the morning Perreault and Tarrangeau were sent out to bring the meat in—a hundred and twenty pounds it proved to be. La Guarde and Cournoyer inspected the nets and lines and brought in seven good trout, the largest being fourteen pounds, and ten carp. The fish "will not look the way of our Pork and have preferred a Gulls head, the upper bill bent in such a manner that it succeeds as both Hook and bait, this is an Indian Contrivance." The Indians also had hooks completely of wood hardened in the fire; other hooks partly of wood but with a barb of bone spliced on to them; and lastly—and these were the best—hooks made entirely of bone. Fresh carp was their best bait: "They flay the Fish leaving part of the Flesh on the skin and cuting it in pieces sew them slightly on the Hooks in the form of a small Fish never minding covering the point of the hook." Their lines were thongs of caribou hide cut fine; some of their nets were also made of fine caribou thongs, and others of twisted sinew—but always the most successful were those of the willow fibre, "but this is a tedious process twisting the filament on their Thighs, nor will they sell them for love or money, besides they are not very strong, a large Trout brakes them in pieces."

They stayed on the lake a couple of weeks, spending five nights in that camp. But the fishery steadily deteriorated and the caribou moved away. La Guarde shot a couple of siffleurs—marmots or whistlers—lean, miserable things at that season. A Sikanni child (not one of those who had made the long march from Pete Toy's Bar[24]) died of croup. "It was a stout fat infant and must have been the application of Wet Moss to the surface of its Body which I had observed several times coming along the River." The poor mother made the dawn hideous with "a kind of convulsive laugh and repeated yells with agony of mind." The father took it more philosophically "and requests to make a coffin for it and bury the child in the same manner the Whites do which shall be complied with." For some time now "the Musquattoes" had been on the war path, and in this camp they were very troublesome. In fact everybody had had enough of the place, and they moved to the second narrows on June 28.

Two days saw the fishing there begin to go down and Black, seeing no profit in having the whole crew watching nets and lines, set out to circumnavigate the southwest arm, leaving Manson and La Prise behind to care for the gear and to fish. Reaching the head of the lake where Thutadé Creek comes winding across the flats from the small glaciers of the Tatlatui Range, the men took the canoe up one of the channels until they were stopped by a beaver dam. Questing around for a possible way to pass this, they saw "a large Buck Rein deer his head barricaded with a noble pair of branching antlers of one yard in length." La Guarde and Perreault made their stalk: La Guarde missed and Perreault got the caribou with a neck shot. The meat was excellent.

One wretched trout of a blackish hue was the sole product of the nets and night lines at that head-of-the-lake camp, and they kept on travelling. The next excitement was half a dozen goats on the mountain slope. Again La Guarde and Perreault took off, this time without success. The sound of their shots re-echoed amongst the cliffs while the goats—just as they did with Haworth—climbed, unhurriedly and with dignity unimpaired, out of range. Meanwhile Black, who had landed and gone along the foot of the mountain on the chance of heading the goats, had been brought up short by a loud, clear whistle, the usual signal of hunters when some animal is not to be disturbed. Hastily he concealed himself—but the minutes passed and nothing happened, no shot came. So he went on, imagining he had heard the cry of a lake gull. Suddenly another whistle sounded, clear and piercing, and Black obediently dived for cover. However, just as he did so, he spotted "a little Grey Animal, nearly about the size and colour of a Raccoon, resting or rather standing on its hind legs on a large stone … in the act of rising its throat and shrill whistle as a Signal to its companions of my intrusion into their solitary retreat."

Black's interest was immediately aroused and he carefully examined the burrows and the little beaten trails. It seemed, he wrote, that these new acquaintances of his were living in a hamlet of only a few families. Had he been there in the fall he would also have seen, neatly arranged outside the burrows, semicircular rows of alpine flowers and grasses, stems towards the holes, all curing in the sun but ready to be pulled in under cover if thunder and rain should threaten. No one could be more fussy over his haying operations than the marmot, the whistler of the stony heights. And while he is putting up his hay for the winter he doesn't fail to take good care of himself as well: nibbling away at the best and the rarest of this sweet-scented alpine herbage, he becomes full and fat—a delicious meal for the traveller, or for the grizzly bear, who will spend hours digging and upheaving rocks in order to get at him.

From the marmot colony Black angled down and across the mountain slope to catch up with the canoe, which had gone slowly on for two or three miles. The going was terrible; mere words, Black wrote, were inadequate to express the vileness of that trail: deadfall with tough, stunted alpine fir growing up through it, every storm-battered tree with branches like steel springs; patches of melting snow; bogs overgrown with water herbs and flowers—and the low, crawling type of fir, knee-deep and treacherous, concealing every hole amongst the rocks in one smooth, green carpet, one of the most miserable obstacles of the timberline country, and the best-designed for the breaking of a leg in its tangled network of branches. "And such," Black wrote in his exasperation, "is a true discription of the Bonney Glens of the Rocky Mountains." Thankfully, at the last, he waded out into the shallow water and took his place in the canoe.

Creeping quietly along with the shore close on their left hand, they put another couple of miles behind them. Then they quickly, but still quietly, sought the shelter of a small bay. A commotion in the lake in the far distance had been puzzling them. Distorted by the mirage, it might have been caused by a flight of gulls—but, as the canoe drew nearer, it had resolved itself into a band of caribou, "frisking in the Lake near the shore." There, in plain view, was meat just where it was most convenient; and the men quickly made their plan. The most skilled hunters would land and go quietly ahead through the trees till they were level with the caribou. The canoe would follow, a short distance behind the hunters and close in to shore. If all went well the caribou would be cut off from the land and would fall an easy prey to gun or axe.

La Guarde and Perreault stepped ashore and vanished into the bush. The men in the canoe waited for a little while to give the others a start; then they dipped their paddles and the canoe slid gently out of the sheltering bay. Sitting absolutely rigid and in dead silence, they urged the canoe towards the caribou, hugging the shore, plying the paddles with wrist and forearm only, never lifting them from the water ... Then something must have given the alarm: either it was the moving canoe that looked queer to the animals or else it was some suspicious movement among the trees. Suddenly alert, the caribou made for the shore beyond the hunters; two guns roared from out of the bush; paddles flashed in the sun and drove deep and strong into the water—and the canoe leapt forward. Wild shouts burst from the voyageurs and somebody broke into song ... That is the picture that I have formed of the scene from the reading of Black's *Journal*.

Things went without a hitch and they got the lot—five head of young caribou. "With Fire Arms and hatchets they were soon all dispatched tho' not before a Couple of them got nearly across the Lake, so fast do they Swim."

And that is all. That is the maddening part about Black: sometimes he will devote a complete page to geology or natural history and then dismiss an incident like this in a few words. One would have liked to know more: who shot what and how—was it in deep water or in the shallows? Did Black shoot from the canoe? And the two they pursued and killed—did they skin them on the far side of the lake and bring the hides and meat back to where La Guarde and Perreault were working? Or did they fetch the dead animals across, and skin and cut up all together? Probably that was the way they handled it—all together on the northwest shore. In any case they had a bunch of experts on the job and it cannot have taken long. "Embarked our Deer Meat and skins," Black writes, leaving the rest to our imagination—and four more miles saw them back to the main camp on the far side of the lake at the bend of the boomerang. There they found Manson and La Prise in good shape: "They made a good Fishery this morning, took 14 Trout and 6 Carp."

The next day the good weather went to pieces: cloud drove in from the southeast and a cold rain poured down. The wind blew keen and hard and the snow crept further down the mountain slopes. As best they could, the men got on with splitting and drying the caribou meat—on racks over fires, sheltered from the rain by coverings of hides. Black went off shooting and got "some Partridges and Ptarmigans, now brown with white tiped Wings and other white Feathers. I saw a pair of the Grouse kind also ... they had a covey of young Pouts, the Hen defended with so much spirit and fury and came so near me I could easily have killed it with a stick or Stone if so inclined."

He had made up his mind by now as to the futility of trying to establish a trading post on Thutadé Lake. For every beaver in that upland country there were at least three on the lower part of Finlay's Branch; and as to feeding the personnel of a post, there did not seem to be enough dependable game in the country and the fisheries were not good enough:

"They seem to be good only for a few days at one place. Perhaps by changing about a few people could live for the Summer Months."

In camp through those four rainy days they fed their Sikanni hunters, as usual, on meat that they themselves had killed. The Sikanni women cut up two of the green caribou hides into thongs for snaring siffleur and two more into fishing lines—all for the use of the Whites. The Sikannis did not forget to demand payment for each individual service performed, and the only real hold that Black had on these Indians as guides and carriers was by keeping the men short of ammunition for their guns—that being the one thing they really wanted and were prepared to work for.

On July 5 they moved camp about five miles north up the east shore of Thutadé to the mouth of Attichika Creek. It was just about time to be getting on the trail in search of Methodiates—and here, at this little river, were "dry Sand Banks and a fit place to make caches to secure the Property and some provisions we are not able to carry with us on our projected Tour to the North West Ward through these blessed Mountains."

After some deliberation they decided to make two caches of completely different construction. One would be in the nature of a small, windowless cabin, built of heavy logs and with dovetail corners—heavily roofed and made waterproof with layers of freshly peeled bark. "This cache may be made double and enclosed with prickly Brush wood to circumscribe the approach of animals ... and a few Trees may be thrown down over it in different directions." This type of cache was evidently designed to defeat the wolverine and the grizzly bear by sheer weight and strength of construction.

The second cache would be excavated in the sandbank and lined with a shell of wood, the logs again being dovetailed. It would be roofed much like the first one and again waterproofed with bark. Finally, after the goods had been placed in it, the roof completed and the sand shovelled back over it, a fire would be burned on top "to elude the keen sentiment of wild Beasts of whom the Wolverine is most to be apprehended ... the Most destructive animal in the Country." Black put two men on each cache and the work took most of two days. Meanwhile, "La Prise and Lady erected a Scaffold to finish the drying of our Deers Meat," and Black and Manson sorted and apportioned the loads to be carried. These were heavy, ranging from 120 pounds, plus personal gear, to Black's own pack of 50 pounds—a featherweight in comparison, light so that he could go ahead of the party, pick the camping places, keep an eye open for game, climb any mountain that promised a viewpoint and make notes on the country they were passing through.

The outfit was placed in the caches on the morning of July 8; all was made secure, and a fire was lighted on the trampled sand. The party then embarked with their packs and crossed the lake to the mouth of a small stream where they laid up the canoe in a place of safety. There they breakfasted. Then, sitting down, they eased themselves into their heavy packs, turned over on to their hands and knees, and slowly and with difficulty rose to their feet. A shake and a grunt, and they were on their way—up a steep hillside, deep in moss and set with firs.

Early in the evening of the following day they came to the Firesteel River. It was rapid and full of boulders, impassable at that point for men on foot, so they followed the river upstream for a mile or so till they came on a place where it had forced its way, in a narrow canyon, through solid rock. Immediately on escaping from the rock walls it had expanded into a wide basin with a strong eddy on either side but with an equally strong current down the centre. The water in the basin was full of movement, as in the basin below Deserters Canyon, but the surface of the stream was unbroken. Once again it was a matter of catching the eddy, for the strong centre current swept on down into a boulder rapid that foamed among huge stones. Black frankly admits that "the business was tight to manage," but there didn't seem to be much prospect of anything better. So they set to work, in teams of two, to make their rafts.

La Guarde and Cournoyer got theirs finished first and made two trips across with the greater part of the gear. Manson and La Prise worked together and got over safely. Perreault and Tarrangeau, the inseparables, made a good, stout raft, so Black embarked with them "with a small Keg of Powder covered with Green hide and some Balls." The men got everything safely over in spite of the strong current in the centre which forced them downstream till they barely caught the tail of the eddy on the far side—and that only by jumping into the shallows with the line and snubbing the rafts as they started to drift away.

The Sikannis were by no means in such good case. They were accustomed to cross their lakes and rivers in small, temporary pine-bark canoes—and here, sad to relate, the country had been recently burnt over by a fire that had got away from one of Black's camps on the Finlay. So the trees were charred and blackened and the bark was hanging from the dead spikes in shreds and brittle fragments, useless for building canoes. The Sikannis, creatures of habit, were disinclined to make rafts. Canoes were what they used for crossing this river. Now let the White men (who had set this fire) do something about it. And they stared, disconcerted and depressed, at the desolation that had been, till these strangers came, their green forest and their source of canoe bark.

They came to life, however, when the rafts were completed. "One of the Indians and two of the Women threw themselves on the Mens Rafts, the other Indian with one of his Wives remained to trie their fortune by his own skill." These two got to work and built a raft—rather a light affair by Northwester standards. Well after sunset, and with the rest of the party watching from camp on the far side, they shoved out from shore and sailed up in the eddy. Then they hit the millrace in the centre—and that was another matter entirely. "The Indian was not able to manage his raft and was swept off down the Current like a Feather in the stream. The poor Sikanni seeing himself in jeopardy began to roar out as if he had been going down the Falls of Niagara, but fortunately (for a ducking at least) not being yet far advanced into the stream, with some exertion he Paddled back and got ashore some distance below his starting place." And there he remained for the night.

In the morning Black, musing on the awkwardness of these Indians when afloat, sent La Prise and one of the other men over with a raft to rescue the castaways. Then, about an hour and a half after sunrise, they moved on. They made, that day, about eight miles under a blazing sun—through swamps and over stony screes with the mountain torrents roaring, unseen and inaccessible, through the rock slides beneath their feet, a tantalizing sound to thirsty men. They got into green, unburnt country and they camped that night by a narrow lake, "tormented with musqueetoes."

The dawn broke cloudless and clear, and soon the day was hot. The camp was utterly silent—and still Black and Manson slept on, slowly waking to find themselves alone. La Prise and the Sikannis had gone off early on some fresh caribou tracks, and the crew had roused themselves at sunrise from sheer force of habit, shouldered their packs and silently departed into the dew and the coolness of the early morning. Hastily the two officers of the Company, the chief trader and the clerk, packed up their stuff and hit the trail—which had been clearly marked for them by blazed trees, broken branches and handfuls of turf or moss stuck up in the tops of small firs. This was the morning on which La Prise shot the bull caribou[25] that Black found, "unsuspecting of danger in his solitary Glen." That cheered the company mightily and gave a lift to the day—and they breakfasted by that two-hundred-pound caribou. "A reasonable quantity of its meat was devoured on the spot, for a Sikanni can eat as much as he likes and the Mountain air and travelling seems to have a wonderful effect on us all." Then they went on, camping early in the afternoon close to timberline on the approaches to a pass between the Firesteel and Thucatadé watersheds.

The scene of that camp was one of unusual beauty. The mountains on the east side of the valley were banded with vividly coloured strata, soft and friable and variously mineralized. Snowfields still lingered there—but they were not shining white and dazzling under the summer sun. The winter winds had been at work, eroding the gaily painted bands of the mountains and depositing the coloured dust on layer after layer of snow, mixing the tints and brushing them out in sweeping curves. As the snow melted, these dust layers had blended again as they settled and became one, the colours becoming always more intense. All this caught Black's eye and aroused his curiosity.

"These colored Earths having been driven by the Wind on the now melting snow, create the most beautiful Tinges imaginable, Purple and blues, Carnation and Red hues, and the Flows and Blossoms seem to partake of and emulate their Tints. Having stoped Early in the afternoon, I ascended the mountain ... following a Gullie full of snow."

Up Black went, stamping out steps in the painted snow. In some sunless cleft, on that ascent, he found, imbedded in the ice, "a Stone downed and feathered like a young swan." It was covered with delicate frost crystals "exactly resembling feathers, some of them several Inches long." Beneath him, as he climbed, a stream of water was booming down the couloir with a muffled roar, hidden under its snowy covering—a dangerous sort of a place unless the mountaineer keeps close to the rock walls. But Black came out safely from the head of the couloir and walked across the stony summit of his mountain. Suddenly he fetched up on the brink of a precipice and found himself looking down some 3,000 feet, almost sheer it seemed, into the deep green vale of the Thucatadé River. There, on the edge of the drop, he sat down and rested.

Beyond the deep valley of the river and its lake rose the tumbled mass of the Peak Mountains, which he had named. "Peaks, pinnacles, pillars," black, forbidding and splashed with snow, they seemed to lean forward and almost to overhang the sombre forests of Thucatadé—"an impregnable barrier to the approach of man." Chafing his hands in the sharp, cold wind that whispered in the crannies of the rocks, Black felt in his pocket for his notebook. "They look," he wrote, "like a Wreck of Worlds ... "

A hard day on which they made only five miles brought them to the Thucatadé River. They had broken trail through the snow on the pass, eased themselves and their heavy loads down a steep and narrow coulee, tramped along a deep valley awash with melting snow, sinking deep into the soft ground where spring water rose to the surface. They were strung out and spread all over the flats of the wet valley—and now those in front were up against the deep, slow-flowing river. They built a raft and crossed over, to find on the far side a well-beaten trail over which, judging by the trampled grass and faded flowers, a body of men had passed some eight days ago, heading west up the river. Black, Manson, La Prise and the two Sikannis—the first party to cross on the raft—interpreted the signs. It was old Methodiates and his band that had gone by. They had exhausted the fishing on Thucatadé Lake and had killed no big animals. Hunger had forced them to move and they had gone west towards the Thloadenni lands. But they would not have gone far —probably only to Metsantan Lake, which was just over the Stikine divide, no more than two days' travel. The only thing to do now was to follow them ...

Two days later, assisted with their burdens by Sikanni women who have been sent to meet them, they reach the head of the Thucatadé River. They keep on westward, following the well-marked trail over an imperceptible divide, picking their way on the swampy ground, a wild-looking procession that puts Black in mind of the wandering gypsies of his native land ... A lake shows close ahead and the smoke of many campfires rises from its shores. They hold on towards it, straight into the evening sun, black plodding shadows against the blaze of light ... But we may follow them no longer, for they have gone beyond the furthest sources of Finlay's River and into the country of the Stikine. A long trail lies ahead of them[26] and we shall not see them again until the autumn comes—not till they return to Thutadé Lake and their canoe.

They are men to remember and to honour in the roll call of the river—they and their leader, that strange man: hard, yet at the same time a romantic; capable of sudden anger, yet kind and compassionate; a ruffian and an outlaw to his enemies in the war between the Companies, but to Father Morice, the historian of northern British Columbia, "a good-natured man who saw life through rose-coloured glasses and had not a little sense of the ludicrous"; one who troubled himself little with the generality of men, but who was deeply attached to his great friends, Ogden and John Stuart, each one a fellow Northwester. Governor Simpson wrote him down in his secret *Character Book* as "the strangest Man I ever knew."

To this day Black still remains the only man who has led an expedition by canoe from the mouth of the Finlay to its ultimate source in Thutadé Creek—right to the beaver dam where Perreault shot the caribou with the nobly branching horns—and then down again in one hard and dangerous summer.

22

Bower Creek

A sudden shaft of sunlight came streaming into Ludwig's cabin, found my humped-up eiderdown and concentrated on it. I crawled out, cursing myself for having overslept, lit a fire in the stove and cut some bacon. Then I brought in the trout, which had spent the night hanging by a wire from the gable of the cache. Breakfast was fit for a king.

The morning was busy. I baked a couple of bannocks, sliced bacon and sorted out grub for about a week—say eight days for good measure—and made up my pack, which seemed to me to weigh about fifty-five pounds. I sharpened my little 1½-pound Hudson's Bay axe till it was like a razor and cleaned my rifle. Then I slid the canoe up into the shade of the trees and tied it there, and packed everything else, bit by bit, up the ladder and into the cache. This caching business was a frightful nuisance but it was on Ludwig's advice. Some of the Finlay River Indians were no longer the unspoiled children of the woods that they had been in Butler's day, when a cache was a sacred thing. This cache, fortunately, didn't need to be sacred: it had a padlock on it that would have puzzled a crowbar; and anyway, locks were still respected. "Put your stuff in there and lock it up," Ludwig had said. "Then give the Indians the key when you've done with the place."[27] So I did as he said and left the cabin swept clean as a whistle but well stocked with wood and kindling. Then, on in the afternoon, I hit the trail up Bower Creek. I went about seven or eight miles and camped by the good pool at the foot of the cliff that Alan and I had seen. This time I had plenty of line with me and, after discovering that it's pretty well hopeless trying to manipulate a spinner in almost-still water from a height of ten or eleven feet when one is wedged in between the Jack pines, I took to a fly and again got two nice trout.

Almost immediately next morning the creek and the trail forked, the main stream of Bower Creek coming in here from the south. I followed the trail that headed west, up the smaller fork—sloshing through wet places, jumping from tussock to tussock among springs, crossing the creek to the south side on a logjam, and then climbing steeply, as up the side of a house. I passed by what Ludwig had told me was his third cabin—and then the trail, after so much climbing, levelled off to such an extent that I was convinced I was over the summit and heading downhill towards the upper Finlay. I swung contentedly along, heading west, with the creek some distance off on my right flowing silently through small meadows gay with long-stemmed asters. I kept on till I came to an ideal place for a camp: on dry ground between two pines that were just the right distance apart for my lean-to shelter; and there I dumped pack, axe and rifle— thankfully.

The first thing on the list, even before setting up camp, was tea—lots of it and soon. To my utter amazement, when I got to the creek with the tea pail I found the water was still flowing east to Bower

Patterson consults a map as he relaxes in camp.

Creek. I stared around at the valley and the mountains, wondering if I was going mad. I could have *sworn* that water was flowing uphill, so sure had I been that I had crossed the hump and was dropping down again to the river. I have seen one or two other places in the mountains like that—it's something to do with the lay of the country and the dip of the strata and they fool a stranger every time.

Thunderheads had been banking up in the west all that afternoon. Now they were climbing high, great masses of cumulus, anvil-headed, blotting out the sun. Not a breath of air was moving, though here, at 4,000 feet above sea level, it was cool and no mosquito hummed. I made a good job of that camp: I stretched the lean-to between two pines and pegged it down solid; I unrolled my bed beneath it and laid in a good supply of dry wood and a pile of resinous pine branches that would flare up and give a good light. And after supper I refilled my mug and tea pail from the creek and set things handy for the breakfast porridge ... and that was that. With a sigh of contentment I took my mountain boots off and put on an old and beloved pair of moccasins, old favourites made for me long ago at old Fort Nelson on the Fort Nelson River. They had been several times refooted and the colours of the porcupine quill work on the insteps had faded a little, but for me those moccasins had become a sign that camp was made and the day was ended. Twiddling my toes in the soft moosehide, I lay on my bed by the fire, staring at the dancing flames, watching the fading light in the western sky, going over the day's trail again. I made a few notes on that in my diary, enough so that I would always remember it. Then I threw a handful of pine branches on to the embers and pulled out Norman Douglas' *Together*. Feeding the small blaze with twig after twig, I lay there and read that delightful book by the firelight while the sky grew blacker and heavy with the threat of storm ...

Sometime in the night the earth shook to the crash of thunder and rain roared down on the lean-to. I opened one eye—just in time to be almost blinded by a blazing flash that lit the mountains and the trees. Hastily I shut that eye again and pulled my blanket over my head: the canvas, I thought, was good; the leather thongs were sound—now let it roar and rain and see just how much it could do. And I slept on—and the grey light of dawn showed only the grey curtain of the rain still falling, though the thunder had ceased. So I went back to sleep again, hoping for better things. What else was there to do?

It poured. With some difficulty and a fair amount of smoke under the lean-to I cooked a good breakfast. Then I sat there for a couple of hours, occasionally raking the embers together and putting on another log, reading that happiest of Douglas' books while the rain hammered on the canvas above my head. Time passed unheeded, for I was far away, lost to the world in that lovely Austrian valley which, twelve years later, I went to see simply because I had read *Together*... Dimly, sometime in mid-morning, I became aware of a change: the rain was easing off. This brought me back with a thud from the Walserthal to Finlay's River and the Caribou Hide trail. A patch of blue sky sailed over; the heavy clouds were rent and broken. I made more tea and downed some bannock, raisins and cheese. Then I set forth again into the dripping willows, the sodden grass and the sunshine, which picked out each water-laden tree in a sparkle of diamonds.

A recently blazed tree caught my eye and I went up to it. Here was another of those comments on life and things in general that the Sikannis were always leaving. "April 25. 1949," it ran. "Snow too deep for dog hard trail from Ft Ware BC oh I sure have hard time now I go home." The poor guy—he must have had his dog with him, carrying a pack the same as he was doing, and it was probably warm and they were breaking through the crust and sinking deep into the spring snow. I surely sympathized with him.

A strongly flowing stream, running in a deep watercourse, next barred the way. I crossed it by a log bridge—if you could call the arrangement by that name. Somebody, long ago, had dropped two trees across this creek. Now one was rotten and almost ready to go and the other was slippery from the rain—just the sort of place to slip or overbalance and fall with pack and rifle down into the creek bed, breaking some bone in the process. I hurled the axe over, landing it in the yielding willows so that the blade wouldn't slice through the leather cover. Then, holding the Mannlicher in both hands in front of me and trusting to my nailed boots, I did a balancing act and got across on the sound log—though not quite perfectly, for almost at the far end I lost my balance and fell, with all the routine imprecations, into the big willow where the axe was. Thank God, the willow received me gently with its green, bendy branches, and the axe kept well out of my way.

The trail began to run downhill in the valley of a small stream. It was dry and gravelly, and it went winding through the Jack pine, becoming ever steeper in its descent. But it seemed pointless to carry all this stuff right down this very steep hill to the Finlay. I had no time to cross over and go on towards Metsantan Lake and Caribou Hide: what I wanted to do was to see the Fishing Lakes. There must, now I come to think about it, be some magic in that name for I was not the first to be drawn by it—nor the last, for several have questioned me about that place. Samuel Black and La Guarde had got the name from the Iroquois hunters, and it acted as a magnet to them—just as it did to Jim Alexander ninety years later. Those men were *determined* to get to the Fishing Lakes. So was I. But I would do it the easy way: I would make camp at the first good place and then go to the lakes on the morrow. I could make it there and back in a day, travelling light.

So I set up a good storm-proof camp on a level point between two streams. Then I wasted what remained of the day climbing the slopes to the south of camp, trying to get a view of the Finlay valley and the Peak Mountains. Nothing went right: the slope was too gentle, there were too many trees—it almost seemed that the further I went the less I could see. Finally I gave it up and slid down the hillside through the timber, returning to camp frustrated, tired and hating trees ...

The dew still lay heavy on the rank growth of grass and flowers when I got down to the Finlay. A cabin stood by the crossing— somebody later told me it was known as the Stolberg cabin—but nobody had been there since the spring, and the grass was untrodden save by the odd moose or bear. The river was quiet. It flowed through spruce flats, unbroken and without a sound, rippling on the near side of the trail crossing over a bar of fine gravel. Over against the further shore it was deep. Upstream, above the tall spruce that lined the east bank, a high mountain could be seen, its rocky summit streaked with snow. That mountain was probably just below the mouth of Delta Creek, and it must have been somewhere near this trail crossing in the quiet water that Black camped on June 17, the day he left the Fishing Lakes for Thutadé.

The growth here was tremendous: grass that was breast-high, fireweed that was even taller, each plant still holding in its channelled leaves a generous shower bath. There were asters and goldenrod—and redcurrants, on which I browsed as I walked around; one had to be careful in all this rank stuff: the ground was completely hidden and one had to feel and make sure of every step.

Full of red currants, I pushed on down the frightful river trail towards the Fishing Lakes. A couple of miles downstream the Thucatadé River entered the Finlay from the west, brawling over the stones in two main channels with a wooded island in between. Driftwood littered its delta, just as it had done in Black's day. Here I scared a cow moose and calf into the Finlay. They swam it and came out into a dry channel of the Thucatadé, vanishing into the trees with their awkward-looking, deceptive stride … I came in the end to the head of the Fishing Lakes— and it was there that I found the dry lake bed covered with animal tracks that I have already described.[28] That was as far as I went—about forty-five miles, or a bit over, by trail from the mouth of Bower Creek. To go on would have been useless, for it was impossible really to see the lakes from the dead level of those flats. The best thing to do would be to go back up to the Bower Creek divide, camp there and see them from the mountain heights on the east side of this upper Finlay valley. So, with that decided upon, I turned for home—which, just then, was my camp on the little flat between the two streams. At least, in the tradition of La Guarde and Alexander, I had reached the Fishing Lakes.

I camped for three nights near the head of the west fork of Bower Creek, putting in two whole days above timberline on the ridges that look down on the Fishing Lakes. The first of these days was the best— the one I spent walking over the southerly spurs of this range.

Four miles from camp and about 3,000 feet of a climb put me on top. The going was not too bad: the lower slopes were just at the right angle so that one could pick one's way, avoiding particularly those stretches of mountainside that were overgrown with tangled mats of creeping fir. All went as planned—and then came the moment when the first black fang of the Peak Mountains heaved up in the west above the stony skyline of the Bower Creek upland. The slope eased off and I hurried on, picking my way through old drifts of last winter's snow, anxious, as always, to see. I crept cautiously over the summit, keeping hidden among some big rocks and using the glass, hoping to get a sight of sheep or caribou. But there was not an animal anywhere near, so I planted myself snugly between two huge blocks of stone just below a big snowdrift, and proceeded to enjoy the tremendous view. The day was cloudy and cool and no mosquitoes were bothering.

Right opposite me across the deep valley of the Fishing Lakes, a good five miles away but looking only half that distance, rose the Bronlund Peak, holding high in its cirques its small residual glaciers. That peak was named by Swannell in 1931 on his last expedition to the Finlay, when he surveyed the river downstream from Thutadé Lake, tying on to his furthest point upstream of 1914. The man for whom he named the mountain was Emil Bronlund, a Norwegian who prospected and hunted here in the depression years of the early thirties, now a well-known mining engineer. To right and left of the 8,500-foot Bronlund Peak ran the black, jagged Peak Mountains, ending in the south at the Thucatadé River and in the north at the big valley of Thudaka Creek, close to Black's Sandy Bay. Of the wild waters of Reef Canyon nothing could be seen: beyond the foot of the Fishing Lakes the Finlay vanished from sight, hidden by the green forest and the canyon walls.

Turning now towards the southwest, one could follow the course of the Finlay for many miles, pretty well to the mouth of the Firesteel River. From there the eye was led on through an opening in the hills towards Tatlatui Lake, but the basin of Thutadé lay concealed by a group of high mountains. About twenty-five miles away in that direction a line of red cliffs was caught in a stray splash of sunlight; those must have been the rocks that Black saw the evening before the expedition reached the Firesteel fork: "The declining sun ... shining on the red-colored Rock, creating vivid red mixed with purple hues more bright and glorious than the rainbow."

Small snow flurries were circling around Bronlund Peak. Occasionally one would be wafted out over the valley and a few stray flakes would come drifting down on the rocks where I was sitting. This moisture seemed to rouse to strenuous life a fine hatch of small mosquitoes, right out of the snowdrifts. I turned my collar up and flicked away at the pests with a spray of heather, holding the glass in my other hand. The country was not completely devoid of life: a couple of moose were grazing on meadows by the Fishing Lakes, and half a dozen goats were pursuing their leisurely way in single file along a thread of a trail under the rimrock in the Peak Mountains. Below them a vast scree swept down towards the timber; and the plodding pinpoints of ivory, distinguishable at this distance only by their movement, seemed to maintain, I noticed, about a three-goat interval—an object lesson in caution to the frenzied motorist.

And on my side of the river a bear suddenly appeared, deep down in a creek valley, going as if the devil was close on his trail. Now what, I wondered, could have got him moving like that? A hornets' nest? And how many animals were there, all around and in plain view, that I had failed to see? Partly obscured by trees, perhaps; camouflaged by their backgrounds; lost in deep cloud shadow—but none the less visible if only one could recognize them for what they were.

I moved on southwards along the rounded summits of the hills, tramping over patches of white heather, finding a blue creeping gentian, seeing once more the green cushions of the moss campion, *Silene acaulis*, covered with its deep-pink flowers. They grew, I thought, much better in the southern Rockies: you must look for them in July on the North Kananaskis Pass if you want to see moss campions at their best ... I went on from that place by the snowdrift until I had passed the end of the Peak Mountains and could see far up the Thucatadé River—as far, I now think, after looking with a magnifying glass at my photographs, as the mountains where Black found the rainbow-coloured snow. Then I turned eastward and headed across the summit towards the west fork of Bower Creek and camp. The mountain dipped steeply in a convex slope so that it was impossible to see far ahead: one just had to trust to luck for a good descent.

And the luck was out: I ran into a patch of creeping fir. It was sparse at first so I kept on, hoping it would peter out. But it didn't; the curve of the mountain became a steady slope so that at last I could see downhill—and acres and acres of the stuff lay ahead, springy, absolutely unbreakable and dangerous, covering with one innocent-looking green carpet a slope that was strewn with big rocks and honeycombed with deep cracks and potholes. It was impossible to tell whether one was going to put a foot hesitantly down on the greenery and find a firm rock two inches beneath the surface, or whether a six-foot, crevasse-type crack was lurking there below the prostrate branches—waiting for a man to go crashing into it. A good half mile of this stuff lay ahead and it stretched to right and left as far as I could see. To go back at this late hour of the day and try elsewhere would be a most wearisome job. One might as well go straight on down.

I had no staff with me. I had to use the long-suffering, rubber-shod Mannlicher as a staff and probe around with it at every step. A finer set-up for the breaking of a leg I never saw—and I couldn't risk a fall, for I was alone and completely dependent on myself. So I prodded away and stepped cautiously—but it was a damnable descent, slow and wearing; and evening was coming on and I wanted my supper and several mugs of tea. Somehow I got down through most of a mile of the bending yet unyielding growth: an invention, surely, of the devil, for while every tree at timberline, tortured and twisted into stubborn perversity by the winter storms, seems to have branches like springs of steel, this malignant scrub makes the rest of them appear, in comparison, fragile as any spider's web—and lies flat on its back into the bargain, a tangled net, a snare and a booby trap for the tired mountaineer.

At last I got out of the rocks and the juniper and onto blessed, barren gravel—and then into the welcoming trees and the small meadows by the stream. Somewhere on the way down I passed through a clearing where tall asters grew, waist-high and swaying a little as the west wind stirred them. Nothing else grew there: no grass, no other flowers, only the asters in their thousands—an eddying pool of gleaming purple in the evening light. Everything in that meadow must have been to their liking—a rich soil, shelter from the storms, and rain in its proper season—for never elsewhere in the mountains have I seen asters of that size.

Camp was as I had left it, unmolested by bear or wolverine. I celebrated the homecoming by having a good wash in the creek—by which I mean that I washed my face, or the greater part of it, for the first time since leaving the canoe. The mornings had been sharp and sometimes frosty, and up to now I had been content with a hand rinse in the cold water and a quick dab in each eye to wash the sleep out of it.

I had with me no soap, no towel, no shaving things—nothing in that line but a toothbrush and a small comb. I must have looked like a wild man; but, after all, this was my trip and nobody else's: there was no one around who had to look at me. And—weight mattered. Washing was a luxury that could wait till I got back to Ludwig's cache.

After supper I stretched out at ease on my bed, laid a pine branch on the fire and reached for *Together*. Automatically, as the flames leapt up, I looked around camp to make sure that all was in order ... And all was not. There, about sixty yards away, beyond a little knoll by the stream and seeming to shuffle forward with the halting gait of the very old, was the Thing—just where it had been the night before. In the flickering light of the fire you could plainly see it moving in its crablike apology for a walk. I had meant to destroy it—but I had come in late and hungry and it had gone clean out of my head. Now dusk was thickening, the waning moon had not yet risen and only a faint afterglow lingered in the west. The old hag had been out of sight and forgotten till the crackling glare of the pine branches had fetched her hobbling out of the shadows—a beastly shape, the sort of thing that the initiated might hope to see at a witches' coven.

The offending object was a dead timberline fir—a dwarf fir, very old and only about seven feet high. The extreme tip had been broken off, perhaps by a moose horning away at it; and the bare, silvery-grey branches, dry and hard as iron, flared out in a truncated cone beneath which the moving light from the fire created the semblance of a face— a hideous face, that of a malignant crone of some Coast Indian tribe— a face lined and distorted by an incredible weight of wickedness and years. The whole thing had put me in mind of a picture I had seen somewhere of a Coast Indian medicine man, horribly masked and decked out in conical hat of woven spruce roots and ceremonial robe of cedar bark, or some such material. Only this was a woman. Somehow I *knew* that the Thing was a woman—and up to no good, one could also be certain of that. I had noticed her the night before while reading late by the fire; and for the first and only time in a thousand solitary camps I had been bothered by a silly idea, an impossible juju of the shifting shadows. It was horribly lifelike and somehow it had been difficult to refrain from looking up at it ...

Anything that gets in between me and a good book is my enemy, and that old fir was not going to bother me again. I threw some more branches on the fire and picked up the axe. I knew the thick trunk of that ancient tree would be like iron, but down it was coming even if I chipped a dime out of the axe blade. And I walked towards it; and when I got there I gave it a shove, just to see—and without a sound it keeled over and fell: it had been standing there, dead, for many years; its roots had rotted away until it was balanced only on its great squat trunk and the grey skirts of its pendulous lower branches, waiting for some whirlwind to lay it low. I was pleased to have the damn thing out of the way, there was something uncanny about that old tree. Now it would help to feed the fire while I read in peace; though I would not cook with it, for the amount of oily soot those timberline firs can spread on tea pail or frying pan is frightful and wonderful to behold— a menace to everything in a clean, well-ordered pack.

In the morning I went north from camp, getting above timberline by the easiest route and building a little cairn on top in case I came back that way—for I was absolutely determined that there should be no more in my life of that infernal prostrate fir. From the cairn I skirted around the head of a big coulee that fell away to the Fishing Lakes, and then I scrambled on northward along the ridges, keeping an eye open for game. This was not primarily a hunting trip, but I did want, at that time, a good Stone sheep trophy—a first-rate head, and nothing else would do. These hills were, or had been, a Stone sheep range, and this northern interior of British Columbia had produced some notable recorded heads. Black's people shot several sheep on their march into the northwest, and Black saw one ram with splendid horns on him, "as big as a mans Thigh above the knee and would have made a famous Bugle horn." He went on to speculate whether it was mountain sheep horns the ancient Jews used to blow down the walls of Jericho. It may well have been, for the wild sheep of the world ranged all the way from Corsica through Asia and North America to end in Mexico. But what one would dearly like to have seen is the impact that was made by that lively and discursive *Journal* on the Governor and Committee of the Hudson's Bay Company in London. A report of an exploration, when written by an unseeing, unimaginative man, can be as dull as ditchwater.

But this one has everything—from the sidelong, come-hither glances of the Thloadenni maidens as they danced, to the precise whistling notes of the siffleur and the dimensions of mountain-sheep horns, together with a few excursions into Jericho, geology, classical mythology and kindred subjects. A valuable record and human document now—but what did they think of it in 1825?

The going got tougher—a narrower crest and more scrambling amongst the rocks than on the day before. And while I could see a number of animals down by the lakes and across the Finlay, not a sheep or a caribou, not even a bear, showed up on these empty hills. There *ought* to have been game here, even making allowances for hard hunting by the Fort Ware Indians. And then there were all those tracks that I had seen in the dry lake bed by the Fishing Lakes—they had to be accounted for somehow. However, the only thing that I saw worthy of note was a golden eagle hurtling down out of the cloudy sky like a falling stone. He disappeared for an instant into a hollow in the rocks—and when he rose again a small marmot was in his claws. The marmot was alive, I could see him moving. That was the last trip for that luckless whistler, and he was travelling further and faster than ever before in all the days of his life—to who knows what inaccessible ledge in the Peak Mountains?

By early afternoon I was almost opposite the lake where Black met Methodiates when the West was young. Below me and stretching away towards Reef Canyon were the hills where Perreault hunted: he stalked a caribou there, but was unable to get within range. He must have heard, from these very heights, Black and La Guarde firing their signal shots in warning to the Sikannis of their approach.

I wish I had known about Black and his voyage when I made that walk. There is always so much that is worth seeing in the wilderness; but if that wilderness has witnessed the passage of men of one's own race—raiders, traders or explorers—then something is added to the scene and it comes alive through a human association, a past that we can share and understand. It is no longer just a beautiful piece of wild country with the vacant stare of a picture of mountains on a Christmas calendar, and with nothing behind it except, perhaps, the long-forgotten wanderings of strange migrating tribes.

Further north, and in years gone by, I have walked into a country where all then was blank on the map except for the alluring words: "Mountainous country, unmapped." I have picked my way through a range of nameless mountains there, wondering, with something of a thrill, who, if anybody, had gone before me through that pass between the granite outcrops and the small punchbowl of a lake that so nearly barred the way ... And I have walked, not so long ago, up the old road, the Ruta de Francia, now gone to grass and sheep pasture, on the Somosierra Pass in Spain. That was not a particularly inspiring pass—just the rock outcrops, the stony slopes with the first green of spring coming on them, and the little stream tumbling down northwards, keeping company with the road to France. Nothing remarkable—just an old track over the sierra north of Madrid, abandoned now for the modern highway on the far side of the narrow gorge.

But up that green road on a November day of 1808 went the Polish Light Horse of Napoleon's Guard, charging the Spanish guns—one of the famous charges of history. If you knew something of that affair you could see the manifest impossibility of it, marvel at the spirit of those horsemen from the great plain of eastern Europe who carried it through to success, hear the drumming of the horses' hooves, the wild shouts, the thrash and flap of saddle leather and the roaring of the guns ... These things can be felt, they have entered into the rocks and the stony soil, and it is impossible to come to such a place without a quickening of the heart.

That is why, as long as great deeds are remembered, such places as the winding defile of Somosierra must mean more to civilized man than the grandest pass in some trackless wilderness where nothing has ever happened, and where, most likely, nothing ever will. And that is why I wish it had been possible for me to read Black's *Journal* and to meet Swannell and Emil Bronlund before I went along those ridges above the Fishing Lakes. Then there would have been life and the memory of human endeavour in those mountains—impressive piles of rock and beautiful in their own wild way, but lacking the ultimate adornment of legend or history.

On my way back to camp in the late afternoon I kept more to the eastern slope of the range. On my left as I came south were deep coulees containing the heads of streams that flowed away into the northeast, draining down into McConnell Pass where Black and La Guarde found the Sikanni ladies, mud from ear to ear and competing with the bears for licorice root. These streams all united to form Cutoff Creek—and it was about these headwater coulees that Bronlund told me a tale … I have already said that he prospected and hunted here in the early thirties. In those years he and his partner decided that it would be handy to have a cabin between Cutoff Creek and the west fork of Bower Creek. A trough through the hills makes a natural passageway for a trail between the two streams, and it was almost on the divide, at an altitude of about 4,000 feet that the two men began to build. They had been to some trouble in selecting the site, and eventually had found exactly what they wanted: a place in the green timber that was handy to flowing water and well hidden even from the surrounding hills. They never cut any trail to that cabin and no trodden path led to it, for every time they came there they approached it by a different route. They were particularly careful to leave no signs of cutting or human habitation in any place that was visible from their trail between McConnell Pass and Bower Creek. And their precautions were effective: no Indian, no White man ever got to know of the cabin. Nothing was ever interfered with there.

The years went by and the two partners moved away from the Finlay. Then came 1952, and Bronlund, working for a mining company now, came riding with his packer and their pack train down Ruby Creek. They came to the Finlay, crossed it by fording and swimming the horses, climbed the hills and dropped down (as Black and La Guarde had done) into McConnell Pass. From there Bronlund turned south up his old trail through the hills towards Bower Creek. And nothing had changed: the trail was little used and the bush was untouched by fire or axe cut.

They reached the divide and Bronlund turned his horse off the trail and into the trees, wondering what had become of his cabin after all these years. "And, by God, it looked just the same as we had left it: windows boarded up, roof good and door shut. And not a track around; nobody had ever found the place and no bear or wolverine had got in. So I went in; and it was a queer feeling, after twenty years. We hadn't *known* we were not coming back and we'd left everything fixed up right. Kindling handy, plates and mugs on the table, all ready for a meal—even the candles ready to light. It was like looking back on your own youth again."

"But Emil," I said, "packrats, mice, weasels, squirrels and all that gang—hadn't *anything* got in? And what about rain and damp? What sort of a roof did you have?"

"We took trouble over that cabin. Everything fitted snug and we always kept the surroundings clean. No junk or bits of grub were ever thrown out, and I guess there just never were mice or packrats around. And the site was good and dry. As for the roof—there was first a layer of split poles laid from the ridgepole to the walls, flat face to flat face and staggered—you know how. Then there was a layer of pine bark, like you'd put on a cache. Then sod and earth. Then a layer of moss. And then more sod. There was never a drop of rain came into that cabin … "

Not with a roof like that on, there wouldn't be! And the place was certainly well hidden from anybody on the hills. I looked carefully over all that country with the glass and not a sign of any cabin did I see. Not, of course, that I was looking for one … Bronlund went on to tell me of a trip he and his partner made over this same trail in the days before they built the cabin. They made camp where the trail hit the west fork of Bower Creek, and as they ate supper they noticed a couple of scarred spruces across the creek. Bronlund's partner maintained that the "scars" were old blazes, and being of a curious turn of mind he went across later on to investigate.

Sure enough, they were blazes; and one of them seemed to have something written on it. He cut that blaze out and brought it back to camp where he sat for ages by the fire, working carefully away at it with axe blade and knife. Layer after layer of gum had to be removed until, at long last, the writing became clear. It was simply the initials of three men and the date, 1887. Now that was indeed early for this wild country. It was ten years before the very first of the Klondikers passed through; it was six years before McConnell came, three before Fort Grahame was founded. There was nothing on the river then. And all that remains of that trip is three sets of initials and a date in some notebook of Emil Bronlund's. What happened to those fellows? Which way did they go from there?

It was late when I got back to camp. I must have walked about twenty miles that day and it was good to get home and find everything in order—the green tarpaulin stretched between two trees and the stuff stacked away beneath it, sheltered from rain or sun. Since the expression "lean-to" must convey little to those who have never made this type of camp, I may as well explain here exactly what I carried with me on this and similar trips. The "tarp" (which I still have and use) is 8 feet 8 inches long by 6 feet 8 inches wide and is of green, proofed "Willesden" canvas—an English product. On each of the two long sides of this tarp are set three brass eyelet rings, one in each corner and one in the centre. In the rings on the side which is to be on the ground are braided three large leather loops, using a foot or over of latigo lace for each loop. In the rings on the other long side are fastened three of the longest latigo laces obtainable—and the ones in this tarp at the moment average about 7 feet 6 inches. That is all, and the whole thing, which is completely waterproof, weighs about 4½ pounds. To this outfit I always add three more long latigo laces which I carry with me in my hip pocket. They are useful in a dozen different ways: for tying things together for a portage, for bringing in a trophy or for making camp.

The latigo laces are long, finely cut leather thongs, taken from a big hide: any good saddlery outfit will cut them for you. The Spanish word *látigo*, like a lot of other words associated with the western saddle and rider, is an importation from Mexico that has drifted into Canada via the western States: it means "whip." These thongs are best kept well oiled with neat's-foot oil. This keeps them flexible; rain and sun have no effect on them, they are amazingly strong and are lighter and more compact than their equivalent in cord.

To set up one's tarpaulin as a lean-to shelter the ideal spot is on level, dry ground between two trees. The trees can be anything from nine to over thirty feet apart, since the ties on the tarp can always be extended by adding to them the spare latigos. One simply takes a turn around each tree with the oiled leather at a height of 4 feet 8 inches from the ground—which I measure by levelling with the breast pockets on my bush shirt. Then draw the tarp absolutely tight and loop the latigos so that they can be undone with a single pull. To tie is unnecessary: you are not using cord and the oiled thongs never slip.

The ideal spot for a lean-to camp is between two trees, but with enough extra thongs it can be put up anywhere, as can be seen in this photo of Patterson's camp on the old riverbed of the Omineca, just below the Black Canyon.

Then cut and point three tent pegs—of hard, dry wood if that can be found. Twist them into the big leather loops at the base of the tarp and drive them into the ground as far back as you can—and there you are, snug. The remaining long latigo in the centre of the upper side can be tied to an overhanging branch, if there is one, as an extra precaution against wind. Or it can be lengthened with one of the spares and passed forward over the campfire to hitch on to some tree beyond— thus making a good line on which to dry socks or moccasins and an even better guard against wind. Be it understood, of course, if you do this, that your fire is not a dude or trail-ride bonfire, best suited for setting the country ablaze, but the small fire of a man accustomed to the bush, just big enough for cooking, warmth and light. This shelter can be put up in next to no time. With enough extra thongs it can even be set up where there are no trees at all, as is shown in my photograph of camp taken at the Black Canyon of the Omineca. The lean-to can be faced in any direction, having regard to the wind and the rain, the need for sunshine or shade, the advisability of keeping one's canoe in sight or keeping an eye on some game trail, and sometimes just the beauty of the view.

That is, basically, the lean-to camp. Under certain conditions it can produce a few tricks from its sleeve, and these can easily be anticipated and frustrated by means of a forked stick here or a brace there, and an extra pull on the thongs. The only good course in that sort of thing is the one I graduated from—experience. I can thoroughly recommend it.

Underneath the lean-to the mat of spruce or fir branches is laid, withdrawn a little from the fire. On that mat the bed is unrolled and some sort of a pillow contrived by humping up the greenery at one end. My bed on this Bower Creek trip was not the heavy Woods eiderdown that I had been using on the Finlay: that lay securely in Ludwig's cache. I had with me a contraption that I had found in, of all places, a famous store in Piccadilly in London. Having acquired the Christmas present which was the object of my visit to Fortnum's, I gravitated from the frills and fripperies department by a process of natural absorption into their out-of-doors section, just to see what they had. And there I found this beautiful sleeping bag—at a most reasonable price. It had been specially ordered by an Australian: it consisted of three pieces of the finest Jaeger blanket, each about 3 feet by 6 feet 8 inches, sewn together in a sort of triple envelope so that a man could sleep in it with two layers under him and one over him, or vice versa, according to the weather. It was an excellent rig for packing, light and warm—and the Australian had never come back to pick it up. I took it and had one change made in it: I had one side cut down about two feet from the head end so that I would not be completely encased in the thing like a chrysalis in a cocoon. I had it fixed so that I could partly close this opening by means of large and splendid buttons, which, I found in practice, I hardly ever used. It was a wonderful bed and I carried it around over hundreds of mountainous miles. It was on this bed that I lay that last evening on the west fork of Bower Creek, lazy and content and wearing the old porcupine-quill moccasins. In a bit I would wake up the fire and read another chapter of *Together*. But not yet. It was so comfortable just lying there, occasionally prodding the glowing embers, watching the stars come out one by one in the evening sky.

My next camp was away down Bower Creek below the junction of the west fork and the main stream. No Indians had come this way since

I came up, but my own tracks were overlaid by those of moose and one small bear. The night was starry and still and turning to frost, and around ten-thirty, as I was reading by the firelight, there came a crash from the bush, no more than twenty yards away: some large animal, suddenly aware of strange things in his domain, had changed course and was getting out in a hurry. The sounds died away in the distance, leaving once more only the quiet murmur of Bower Creek.

It was down the main fork that Fleet Robertson and his party came in 1908 from Delta Creek. We left him there, ages ago it seems, camped seven miles up from the mouth of that stream and with unknown country ahead of him.[29] That was on August 2. Next morning one of the men, L. M. Bower, prospector and trapper, was sent out with the Indian packer to look for a pass that would lead to some stream falling into the Finlay below the bend. On that first day nothing was found except a lot of rugged country and valleys that led nowhere; and on the fourth of August, Bower set out again, this time alone. The rest of them watched him disappear into the mist and the rain. Then they set to work digging and panning gravel. Camp was beside an old beaver meadow on which the horses were grazing, and at some earlier date the ground had been tested for gold. Pits and trenches had been dug down to the shallow bedrock by "prospectors unknown"—perhaps by the three men whose initials Bronlund's partner found on the blaze—and no record of this old activity had ever reached the outside world. Robertson carefully retested but found "no serious amount of gold," and the little that was obtained was very fine. Yet a story persisted that a large amount of gold was once panned out on Delta Creek and cached near the mouth, the owner then meeting with disaster and never returning. A Scotsman travelling with Bronlund had this yarn firmly fixed in his head, and when, on some occasion or other, they camped where Delta Creek enters the Finlay, he proceeded to do some excavating in likely places, seeking for the buried gold. A shout of triumph went up when he struck something that seemed to be a metal container. And container, indeed, it proved to be but, sad to relate, only of gravel and sand: it had been thrown away by somebody and then buried by flood or landslide. But the Scots are a strong, persistent people and this one was no exception to the rule: he kept on digging ...

Towards dark on that miserable fourth of August, Bower returned to Fleet Robertson's camp, having put in the whole day in the mountains in storms of rain and hail. He had found a way over a divide to the headwaters of a stream which, he felt sure, was the one near the mouth of which he had built a cache a year or two back. And that was when Bower Creek got its name: Fleet Robertson, delighted at finding a way through the mountains of the bend, named the stream after the discoverer of the pass.

The next day the whole outfit moved another seven miles up Delta Creek to the head of the north fork, where they made Camp 36 of the trip on a long flat summit, the divide to Bower Creek, at an altitude of about 5,000 feet. The grazing on this summit was excellent: good meadows of hard upland grass, the best thing the horses had seen for weeks. By this time two of the horses were completely played out by the long hard trail from Hazelton and the poor feed. The packer, Jack Graham, decided to leave those two here on the meadows to fill up and recuperate. He would salt them here, and cache at this camp all he could of the provisions that he and the Indian would need to see them back to Fort Babine. Then with the rest of the string he would take Robertson and the outfit down Bower Creek to the Finlay, leave them there and pick up the two abandoned horses on his return with the pack train.

So on August 6 they started down Bower Creek, and the tuckered-out pair on the pass watched them go without making the half-expected effort to follow. They were all right where they were: they had salt, water, companionship and all the feed in the world. They would remain and be content.

The rest were soon into trouble. The first two or three miles down Bower Creek are quite all right for a man on foot but impassable for a horse, the valley floor being composed of great sheets of volcanic rock that drop off in sheer steps about six or eight feet high. So the pack train swung out onto a shoulder of one of the mountains, which here rise about 3,000 feet above the pass. The people soon found themselves a good thousand feet above the valley of the giant steps, and the creek all the time falling away from them as hard as it could go. They had a hell of a job getting down: there are places in the mountains where it's a whole lot easier for a horse to go up than it is for him to get down—and on some of these dangerous slopes they would have to give the horses a boost from behind and send them sliding down half squatting and with forelegs braced. The fellows just hoped no horse would break a leg; and in the end they got them all down safely. It was dark when they made camp beside a small slough with only a very little coarse grass around its edges for the horses—but nobody was worrying that any of them would stray back along the homeward trail in search of better feed; not that night, anyway. In a long, hard day they had come only four miles in a direct line from the meadows on the pass.

It must have been of that day's travel that the story got around that they had lowered the horses over steps in the rock. Bronlund told me about it, but I can find no mention of it in Robertson's *Report*; nor is it at all probable, since the pack train had to go back up the way it came down.

The next three days were spent looking for a possible way, cutting trail and moving by very short stages. Progress in miles was slow, and not until the morning of August 11 did they reach the mouth of Bower Creek and make Camp 41 on the point between the creek and the Finlay. No time was wasted in sitting around and congratulating themselves: as soon as the horses were unloaded Jack Graham and the Indian hit the trail with the pack train, with instructions to be at Fort Babine to meet Robertson and the party on September 11. Meanwhile Bower and Irish had already set to work to build a raft.

A. M. Irish had a cabin about two miles above the mouth of Bower Creek and on the far side of the Finlay. He had left a big canoe there, and he and Bower crossed over on the raft and walked up through the woods to get it and bring it down. The canoe was big enough to take the party of four and all their stuff to Fort McLeod, and from there they could get Indian horses and packers to Fort St. James—and so, travelling by the lakes, they would be at Fort Babine to meet Graham and the pack train in exactly one month's time. All nicely laid on—and by God, when they got to Irish's cabin the canoe was gone! Stolen by the Indians, they decided promptly, and, as things turned out, correctly.

They would probably have been reduced to rafting it down to Fort Grahame had not Irish happened to have at his cabin some long boards that he had whipsawed out for making sluice boxes. Having adequately cursed the Indians by bell, book and candle, they called these boards into service, and in two days they had an eighteen-foot, flat-bottomed, straight-sided boat, pitched with resin from the trees, and five paddles made. The boat was capable of carrying four men and the eight hundred pounds of baggage, and it was absolutely watertight. All was once more reasonably well.

On August 14 they hit the river with their box-like boat. Two days' travel saw them some seventy miles downstream, making camp for the night at Barge Camp alongside the old scow that had been, ten years earlier, the Klondikers' ferry. And five more miles in the early morning brought them to the head of the portage at Deserters Canyon. Here they made their boat fast and then walked ahead to look the situation over. The river was at the normal late-summer stage and the canyon was not too bad. The trouble was, as usual, the first chute at the entrance to the canyon. Here the current drives on a submerged reef and a nasty, curling wave is thrown up, not squarely across the river but at an angle of about 45 degrees, sloping away to the right and downstream. Hit that with any kind of a craft that is too awkward or too small and you are liable to be turned over to the right and upset as you run up the wave. If you do get over, you may well find yourself broadside on to the next wave—which is smaller than the first but quite large enough. And it's impossible to hit that standing wave square. A big canoe or boat can run right through, but many men with only small craft must have looked longingly and vainly at that first chute, trying to figure out a way to tackle it—and in the end probably decided to play it safe, as Robertson's party did.

They portaged the complete outfit and then lined their empty boat down that chute—no easy job of lining. Then they paddled down through the canyon to the beach by the big pool where the outfit was stacked and where they reloaded. They camped there that night and arrived at Fort Grahame in the afternoon of the following day, to be welcomed by Fox, who was in charge.

Irish didn't have to take back anything he'd said about the Indians, for there, drawn up on the beach, was his canoe, battered a bit but still sound. The Indians who had made free with it had very considerately left it at Grahame, since they were returning upstream and, not being any more skilled with the canoe than they were in Black's time, preferred to make that journey on foot by way of the river trail.

The men spent August 18 gumming the canoe—going all over the seams with heated spruce gum mixed with animal fat and a little powdered charcoal. Then they said goodbye to Fox and Fort Grahame, and in two days' time were through with the Finlay and at their Camp 47, a couple of miles up the Parsnip ... It is worth recording that, after all their delays and after losing still more days owing to gales and a rough sea on Babine Lake, to say nothing of the "borrowing" of yet another canoe by Indians, they arrived at Fort Babine on September 12, only one day late, to find waiting for them Jack Graham, who had got there with the horses one day early, on September 10—a long-range, wilderness tryst that was well kept.[30]

23

The Surveyor

For the evening of the day I got back to Ludwig's cabin I see a note in my diary: "Bathed, baked bannock, good supper, bed—thank God!" That pretty well takes care of the evening—and in the morning I went on to do a large-scale Chinese laundry and then took a look in my shaving mirror. I was shaken by what I saw. A nasty-looking tough glared back at me: bright blue eyes stared unwinking out of a copper-coloured face and eight-day beard—and nobody knew better than I did that the copper was about thirty per cent woodsmoke. So I shaved this fearsome apparition, removing thereby a certain amount of the carbon deposit. That left things a bit uneven, so to make up for the week's neglect I laundered face and head in the gold pan, doing a very thorough job and getting about the normal amount of soap in my eyes in the process. Then, feeling literally a new man, I sat down in the sun and cleaned my rifle with boot dubbin (being, for the moment, unable to find the gun grease), wondering whether to go on upriver after lunch, or whether to stay here, get a fool hen or two for a mulligan and pull out in the morning. Wondering also why no Indians had come up from Ware to take over the cabin: I had half expected to find some of them here on my return. Still undecided, I went over to the trees where the canoe was lying in the shade and carried it down to the beach, just in time to be confronted with a raft-load of Indians in midstream, poling, sweeping, lurching towards the beach by the canoe.

This was the entire Massito (or was it Massiter?) family—two brothers, the wife of one of them, and various children. They had nothing with them, of course, the normal Indian greeting on the Finlay at that time being, "Good morning. I'm starving"—the cue for you to produce something from the inexhaustible stock of provisions you were naturally carrying in your pack or in your canoe. The two men were going up Bower Mountain after sheep while the woman and children camped here. In the cabin, I thought, would be the best place for them: they seemed to have no tent. And there was not going to be any peace around here, anyway: I would sling my camp into the canoe and leave for upriver.

While I cleared my stuff out of the cabin I made tea with lots of sugar in it for the incoming tenants, carrying on a running conversation at the same time. One of the men, who had been gazing around, suddenly said, apropos of nothing in particular, "I don't think gold in Long Canyon." I was puzzled for a moment—then I saw the gold pan sitting on a stump outside, dry now and burnt out, and I understood. So I was a prospector. Well, if that was what they thought, why argue about it? It would be no use telling them the truth—that I just wanted to see a little more before turning to run down the Finlay to meet Marigold at the Forks. So it was as a prospector that I waved goodbye and poled away up the river. The trackline, which had been doing duty as a washing line, was back in its place, tied to the ring in the nose of the canoe and to the rear seat, the balance of it neatly coiled and lying on the tarp ready to grab and pay out in a second. Most of the stuff was still in Ludwig's cache and what I had with me was loaded a bit carelessly—but it would do well enough for a fine day and a few miles. The gold pan and the cooking pots were flung in all anyhow, and over the thwarts and the front seat and any old place was draped the laundry, drying in the sun. The canoe was riding light and slipping easily over the water but, from the point of view of the purist, it must have been quite a sight and it would have given my old friend and teacher, Albert Faille, the horrors. However, that is the way a prospector travels on the Finlay. Having been one, I *know*.

The day was perfect and I tracked happily up the river, stopping now and then to fish and getting a couple of nice Arctic grayling. All I wanted to do was to go up as far as I could without portaging and find some nice camp by a good fishing pool where I could take a "Sunday"—that is, a day when one didn't move camp, a day of rest and small chores. Then I would turn and run down to Ware, to Deserters Canyon and to the Omineca.

At the red cliffs, Long Canyon closed in on the river and soon the dancing water of a long riffle came in sight. That must have been the place that Haworth, on his raft trip, called "a long chute down which the river plunged at tremendous speed." Black noted it as "a strong rapid." I did some rather tricky lining and got the canoe up the northeast shore almost to the head of the riffle. The smooth, unbroken water was very close and only one obstacle stood between me and it—a huge boulder close in to shore. The water banked up behind this rock and poured round it in a green, curving chute. I couldn't frog the canoe past the boulder, it was too deep there and I would have been swept off my feet. I couldn't line the canoe past it because that called for two men: for one man alone it was impossible. It was pole or portage—and portaging was barred. So I pulled the canoe in to shore, coiled the trackline and picked up the pole. Poling in short thrusts I passed the big boulder and began to turn in towards shore again—just a little too soon, for the current caught me and seemed about to send me piling, broadside on, against the upper side of the boulder with the whole force of the Finlay boiling into the canoe. With a thrust at an angle I turned the nose of the canoe out again—rather too much, and in a fraction of a second I was away down the riffle, broadside on to the river. I had a most exciting passage down that small hill of water, balancing and gradually turning the canoe, just getting it straightened out in time for the big waves at the foot of the slope. I tried twice more—on the third attempt almost losing my balance as the lightly loaded, lurching canoe sheered out above the boulder and I sat down to change from pole to paddle.

Three times ... Well, obviously it was useless going on trying. I should have liked to get as far as the place where Haworth built the raft, which cannot have been more than half a mile ahead. But for that little distance it was not worth taking the time to portage—so this was *Ultima Thule*. And now for some more fishing and a nice quiet camp and a Sunday.

I floated around for some time in an eddy which, my memory tells me, was the one at the foot of the long riffle. I got one nice fish and I was intent on getting a second, which I could plainly see down through the very clear water. I had a paddle in my left hand with which I was keeping the canoe quietly moving in the eddy—and I half noticed, out of the corner of my eye, a black thing that had got into the eddy with me. That dimly registered, and I found myself automatically thinking: charred log—forest fire away upriver? Or somebody extinguishing his campfire and rolling a burning log into the water? I had done that, myself, many a time. Then some odd movement from the black thing made me look—and it was a bear and it seemed quite anxious to come aboard.

The fish was forgotten: the rod hit the tarp alongside the pole and the paddle swung over my head and into the water at my right hand. I drove it into the water in reverse, at the same time throwing my weight back. The canoe slid backwards and spun on her tail, the nose sweeping through the air in a half-circle and coming down on the water with a smack, facing downstream, as I once again leaned forward. Then I got out of that eddy, racing downstream faster than any bear could swim. As I wrote elsewhere of that meeting, "a grayling couldn't have moved quicker."[31]

After a short run I stopped and looked back: the bear was on dry land and climbing the steep rock slide as if his life depended on his speed. What gets into their heads I can't imagine, but they seem to lose all judgment when it's a case of human beings on the water in a boat or canoe. If they plan to swim a river, then they swim it and be damned to their two-legged enemies. And this one, I suppose, had been crossing the Finlay from the far side, making for the eddy, and then had got a whiff of the two grayling and the trout on the floor of the canoe. It was an experience that was well worth having, if only because my mention of it, years later in a camp in the Northwest Territories, brought to the mind of an old-timer a bear story that was rich and strange and beyond the price of rubies.[32]

There was no camping place in this lower end of Long Canyon: the rock slides ran straight down into deep water. I dropped downriver, passing on the left what may have been Irish's cabin and making camp some distance above Bower Creek. There was a good sandy beach there between two rock points, and a fine fishing pool at the foot of a strong riffle. And there I spent my Sunday—reading, fishing, hunting fool hens and making one sound pair of khaki drill trousers out of two ruins: that walk to the Fishing Lakes had pretty nearly wrecked one aged pair. Now I had one stoutly patched pair of hard-duty pants on my legs, and one good one in the strategic reserve—something decent to end the trip in ... That evening one of the Sikannis appeared, Frank Abu. He had a small boy and a girl with him and he came from a camp about a mile below to set a night line in this eddy.

I got out of that camp early in the morning. This bit of country was getting overcrowded and I was all for fresh fields and pastures new. Frank Abu, I noticed, had a dead trout on his night line and I left a can of bacon fat by his willow rod for him to cook it with, covering it from the sun with spruce branches. There was no sign of life at his camp as I slipped by and not a soul was moving at Bower Creek. I cleared the cache and was packing the stuff down to the river when an Indian girl appeared, a newcomer: one, at least, who had not come over in the *Mayflower*—not in that first raft-load. "Good morning," she said. "I'm starving." So I gave her a can of Australian bully beef, thinking that I could replace it at the Hudson's Bay post at Ware. Then I took some colour pictures of the place and shoved off down the Finlay. The day was perfect: summer dropping into autumn, preceded by the first gorgeous heralds of decay: the shining gold of a birch lighting some green hillside—the little poplars flaring yellow on the bars.

That afternoon I fished in the Seven Mile Pool, the big eddies where Alan caught his trout and grayling the day the mail plane came. There again, deep down, were the fish, and I couldn't get them interested in anything—fly, spinner, baited spinner, bait. After wasting a lot of time I tried trolling a black gnat with some split shot on a very long lead, and that fetched them. Pretty soon I had eight Arctic grayling on the floor, every one of them a good fish. That was enough, and I ran on down the gently rippling river to make a flop camp opposite to, and a bit above, Prairie Mountain. A "flop" in the parlance of Gordon Matthews and myself on the South Nahanni was a camp made right beside the canoe on some shingle beach or sandbar. No shelter is put up, no sheltering trees are near, nothing is carried further than five yards from the canoe and only the most knobbly rocks are picked out of the way of your bed. It's quick, easy and lazy and saves a lot of time. One essential for a flop is a perfect night, and that was what I had at that camp by Prairie Mountain.

It was towards dusk when I cleaned the eight fish, working on them and rinsing them in the shallows. As I did so there was a splash and a surge and a big Dolly Varden came rushing in amongst the stones and took the fish guts almost out of my hand. This went on while all eight grayling were cleaned; there were three or four Dollies on the job and not one scrap of anything was left. Four of the grayling went straight into the pan together with some wild onions, and that, with some bannock and a pail of tea, was supper. As I sat on my eiderdown in the twilight, eating, a voice came to me from the river: "Hullo!" it said, softly and huskily. I looked up to see one of the Massito brothers sliding by, paddling a small raft on which a dead animal was loaded.

"Hullo," I replied. "So you got something?"

"One sheep," came the answer. "Bower Mountain."

So now, I thought, there'll be meat in the cabin at Bower Creek and babies eating marrow out of broken bones—but still the greeting will be unchanged.

The dawn broke cloudless, clear and still. Breakfast was the usual porridge with raisins in it and brown sugar—but only two of the grayling. Four had been something of a tight fit—and in saying this I am not referring to the frying pan. Afterwards I sat for a while on my rolled-up eiderdown, examining Prairie Mountain with the glass. I could see where Alan and I had gone up and I thought I could see where Haworth might have run into his steep cliffs. Swannell also went up Prairie Mountain and his only comment was: "Steep, smooth grass slopes and bluffs, flattish top." From this shingle bar in the middle of the valley I could also see the long eastern spur of Bower Mountain about ten miles away up the Finlay. Swannell and Copley climbed it, too, on August 29, 1914. The mountain rises to about 7,000 feet and they found it very cold and windy on top. Even when its legs were firmly planted and steadied with rocks, the transit was shaken by the gale and it was impossible to read angles except in the intervals of lull.

Black never climbed Prairie Mountain. His mountain climbing was all done on his march northwestward from Thutadé Lake, and for very practical purposes: to see all he could of the country and to plan the next day's trail. These two men, the explorer and the surveyor, were up against quite different problems. Black went up in June with the ever-increasing flood of the river against him, and often with next to no tracking beach. On the other hand, he had a comparatively light birchbark canoe that could be lifted and carried through the woods, away from the river, and he had enough people with him to help in the search for portages, cut trail, hunt and carry the loads. His crew was the more volatile in temperament, sometimes riding the crest of the wave, sometimes downcast and in the very depths. But, counting Manson and himself, he had seven men who, from years of constant use, were all familiar with the handling of a canoe. And two, at least, of those seven, La Guarde and Perreault, were highly skilled men. In Swannell's party only Jim Alexander could have held his own with them.

Swannell started into Long Canyon on September 2. By that time the river had dropped, and while the lower water had fetched the reefs closer to the surface, he had at least plenty of tracking beaches. His main trouble was a large and heavy cottonwood dugout which four men were unable to lift or carry. Their only way of moving this awkward craft on land was by means of laying skids and shoving and pulling to the limit of their strength. All four were united in their determination to get to the Fishing Lakes and as far beyond as possible, and they were not subject to the same temperamental ups and downs as were Black's French Canadians and half-breeds. Nor were they worried about going into unknown country. In fact, in that respect, Swannell had rather the better of it: he was at least able to read, before setting out, the *Reports* of McConnell and Fleet Robertson and to pick up on the way any information he could get from trappers and prospectors, whereas Black had only the information given him by the Iroquois hunters.

But the chief difference between the two expeditions was the matter of the survey. The explorer, having taken and recorded his compass bearings and having set down his estimate of distances, was then free to write up his copious and exuberant *Journal*—free to describe all that he saw, from the dress and habits of the Indians to the fears and petty jealousies of his crew. He must have written in camp in the evenings, on the summits of mountains, and at the halts on the river for the *pipe* of the voyageur. Nothing was left out from that record, not even the queer shapes of the mountain peaks and their fancied resemblances—to a human head, to an animal, to a temple of old Greece or Rome ...

On the surveyor, however, figures bore heavily, leaving him no time for poetic fancy. There were the daily temperatures to record and the barometric readings—but there was also the map. The *Diary* is terse, a concise record of events; and one can well understand that, for progress up the river was marked by a series of angles and bearings—forward bearings and back bearings, an endless chain of angles linked by distances and expanded by bearings to mountain peaks. Detailed, meticulous and time-consuming work. These had to be converted, every so often, from a closely written mass of figures in a field notebook into something that even a layman would recognize as the beginnings of a map—and so it is that one reads in the *Diary* entries such as:

Sunday, Sept. 13. Day 136. Camp 75

In camp, plotting up map.

No move was made that day, and yet the work was going forward and the day-by-day traverse of the Finlay was becoming, on paper, a pair of sinuous lines, spreading apart or approaching more closely as the river widened or narrowed, accompanied on either side by things that looked like fingerprints but that were really mountains indicated by embryonic contour lines. Lines like wavering antennae would be springing from the main river: these were the tributary streams, Ruby Creek or Porcupine Creek, to give them their original names—creeks that had been traversed for six or eight miles up from the Finlay. Beyond the survey the creeks would be continued, but only as dotted lines representing, perhaps, a view from the summit of a mountain and fading away into the emptiness that concealed a sea of unknown peaks and no man knew what besides ... In this way was a map born in that last golden age of the explorer-surveyors, in the days before the airborne camera laid bare the hidden places of the North.

Whole days passed in that sort of work; days, too, on mountaintops trying to read angles in a gale. All these things add heavily to time spent on the road, as the following record shows:

Black reached the Fishing Lakes in twelve days from his camp below the Kwadacha.

Swannell reached the Fishing Lakes in one month and a day from his camp below Fox River.

Swannell put in five days at Bower's cache, one mile below the mouth of Long Canyon. A Sunday was taken; Copley and Alexander hunted; Bower Mountain was climbed and the creek was traversed up to the forks. The survey was completed up to Long Canyon, and Swannell arranged with Nep Yuen what supplies to take on and what to cache. And at that camp Jim Alexander, after one or two weeks of careful consideration, arrived at a decision. That five-dollar pair of pants that had been bought at Fort Grahame[33] —he found himself unable to wear the things. The pants had cuffs on them, turn-ups, something he had never seen before. Forty-six summers had passed over his head and he was too old now to bother about keeping abreast of the fashion. Furthermore, he drew the line at what he called "sissified stuff"—and so he sold the pants to Copley for a dollar.

So, in one way and another, they made ready to tackle the most difficult part of the river. I don't propose to record in detail Swannell's upstream passage of the bend: a photograph or two, an incident here and there, and, having already been once over the trail with Black, one can easily form a picture of the voyage of the dugout canoe.

They left Bower's cache on the second of September, as I have already said. They passed by the Old Man, "a bad drop and broken water surging against the rock." If Jim Alexander had not been under the weather that day they would have reached the head of the canyon. As things went, night caught them, just as it had caught Black when La Guarde was ill, on an inhospitable scree—no landing worthy of the name, no level place on which to cook or sleep. And no Sikanni ladies to bring down moss from up above. They spent a godforsaken night there, each man sleeping curled around a tree to prevent himself from rolling down into the deep water.

In drizzling rain they pushed on: Alexander may have been unwell, but there was nothing else they could do. The rain continued and fresh snow fell on the mountains. They passed by the mouth of Cutoff Creek, recognizing it for the road taken by McConnell in 1893. Sunday, the sixth day of September, found them in Cascade Canyon, and on that day they made no move. All morning it rained and all day Swannell worked on the map. Copley and Alexander went hunting when the rain stopped, but the luck was out and no game was seen. At this camp they were above the main cascade, which is shown in the photograph where they are manhandling the canoe over the skids and up the fall. Swannell is on the left, in the lead and leaning forward to pull; Alexander, in the light-coloured shirt, has just reached back to grab hold of another thwart; Nep Yuen is in the water with his shoulder under the tail of the canoe. No picture, and certainly no words, can convey any better idea of the wildness of that river.

On the ninth, Swannell gave the men a holiday while he figured out the traverse. They broke a beaver dam and added one beaver to the menu. Then uproar supervened and the voice of dog Dick was heard from the bush. Quite obviously he was after something. The men grabbed their rifles and waited. A moose shot out of the bush and into the river—just what they needed most; only the dog dashed in after him and "we are afraid to shoot for fear of killing Dick."

By September 12 they were camped opposite the mouth of Porcupine Creek—now, on the map, Obo River. This was on the other side of the Finlay from Black's Point du Mouton and they spent three nights in that camp. On the last day there Swannell and Copley crossed over the river in the canoe and cruised for some miles up Porcupine Creek. They had dog Dick with them, and it was on their return to the Finlay, when they were clambering over the deadfall of an old fire, that he started another moose. The hound gave tongue and the moose took off down Porcupine Creek through the down timber and the young growth, making for the river. The din alerted Alexander, and by the time the moose came out on to the beach he was waiting on the far side of the Finlay with his rifle at the ready. He shot—but only wounded the moose, which then took to the river and began to swim across, being carried downstream by the current. Alexander, wild at the thought of losing and wasting so much good meat, dropped his rifle and plunged in, closely followed by dog Caesar. He reached the wounded animal, climbed aboard and bestrode it, cutting its throat with a hunting knife. That left him riding down the swift river on his unusual and unhandy craft at some considerable speed, and with dog Caesar swimming alongside, frantic with excitement and nipping at the dead beast's flank. The whole peculiar outfit went downstream a quarter of a mile before Alexander was able to pole and guide his moose on to a shingle bar by means of a driftwood stick he had snatched up as he rushed into the water. All hands then converged on the kill and the meat was back in camp by 7:30 P.M.

This is not a tale from a boy's book of the turn of the century. It is simply the bare bones of the story as it is tersely recorded in a surveyor's sober diary, along with the Fahrenheit temperatures for 5 A.M., noon and 5 P.M., plus the aneroid readings for the day and similar prosaic details. An episode in the day's work ... They cut up that meat and then smoked it as opportunity offered—and four more days of rapids that were "like going upstairs" found them at the foot of Reef Canyon.

That was Camp 78 and they arrived there about noon. Swannell and Copley spent the rest of that day scrambling on through the bush, sizing up the river. They went up the right bank,[34] which was the east bank, the one La Guarde took, keeping above the cliffs. And what they saw was far from encouraging. Swannell's photograph of the upper part of Reef Canyon shows, better than any description could do, what they were up against: a confused turmoil of whitewater; reefs running transversely to the river, thus making a series of steps; rock outcrops, scattered boulders and at least two cascades. They almost abandoned any idea of pressing forward by river. However, they knew that, since he was a boy, Alexander had listened to tales of the remote Fishing Lakes with their banks tracked like a drovers' road by hundreds of game animals. They knew that he had set his heart on getting there, and they decided to work on that. They thought they could talk him into tackling the canyon ... They needn't have worried: they had no difficulty at all. It was going to take more than Reef Canyon to stop Jim Alexander.

Late that night it began to snow. The snow continued through the morning, turning later to a cold, miserable rain. The day happened to be a Saturday. That was near enough for these wild regions, and it was unanimously voted to be Sunday. They stayed in camp all day and kept warm.

On Sunday, September 20, they hit the canyon. They didn't get far that day and they met with a disaster. They arrived at a very bad piece of water, which they later came to call Kodak Cascade. They portaged,

Swannell's photograph of the upper part of Reef Canyon shows what he and his companions were up against: a confused turmoil of whitewater; reefs running transversely to the river, thus making a series of steps; rock outcrops, scattered boulders and at least two cascades. (Photo courtesy of F. C. Swannell.)

or so they thought, the whole outfit, but the rocks of the shoreline were at too steep an angle for them to slide the empty canoe up on skids past the cascade. So they had to line it up a narrow chute between two rocks—and, as they did so, the bow dipped into the curving, downhill rush of water and the canoe half filled. To their horror they saw the chronometer box floating about in the wash—but, since Swannell was there and I was not, let him tell the story: "We had forgotten to empty the wee forecastle built in the bow to house chronometer, aneroids and camera. The chronometer box floats out and we save it, undamaged—but the camera is water-soaked and the shutter ruined. This is a major disaster, as henceforth I can only take pictures by lifting on and off a wooden cap whittled to cover the lens."

The next day they worked their way, in mist and rain, through a lot of very bad water almost to the head of Reef Canyon, keeping mostly to the right bank. Their greatest difficulty was lining past the jutting points of the cliffs, but they dealt with that by passing the line. Alexander added a caribou to their store of meat that afternoon—which was all to the good, since they were working hard and eating like horses and some of their supplies were running a bit low. And on the following day they came to the Fishing Lakes.

Whether the lakes came up to Alexander's expectations or not, I never heard. The riverbanks certainly did their stuff: they were trodden like the stockyards at a shipping point—and the fellows saw some caribou, so that part of the tale came true. But I still think the best picture of the Fishing Lakes must be the one to be had from above—from the hills whence not only the long, slack-water stretch of river can be seen, but also the small lakes on either side and the whole green floor of the valley with its meadows and its browsing moose.

On September 26 Swannell made his furthest camp—Camp 85, about a mile above Delta Creek. A short distance above that again he brought the river traverse to a close, marking the exact spot by means of a squared spruce stump with the number of the station on it. For safety's sake he also brushed and marked a "bearing tree" a little way off, a six-inch spruce having on its blaze the true compass bearing and the exact measured distance to the centre of the squared stump. That should hold it, he and Copley thought, at least until some more permanent monuments could be placed along the route ... Seventeen years were to go by before Swannell would come again to that squared stump and the bearing tree—this time from above, from Thutadé, thereby completing his survey of his river.

That day they ate the last of the oatmeal.

A crisp, sunlit morning followed and, after breakfasting on caribou, Alexander and Copley each selected and cut down a tree. Cutting the required lengths out of the trunks, they set to work to hew, "à la Robinson Crusoe," two long ten-inch boards—scoring and chipping out and smoothing again and again—and then fining down and smoothing once more with the axe, till the hewer could squint along his board and pronounce it perfect—well, as near perfect as made no matter, anyway. These boards they nailed along the gunwales of the dugout canoe, giving them an outward flare. Besides providing more freeboard, these flaring extensions of the gunwales would tend to fling the broken water in the canyons outwards and away from the canoe. That was a thing of Alexander's devising, and it undoubtedly saved them from swamping and drowning in the wild water that they had to run.

Meanwhile, Nep Yuen cooked and fished and Swannell cruised, track-traversed and sketched for six miles upstream along the river trail. He turned for home where a sixty-foot torrent entered the Finlay through a swamp in which there were several beaver houses. On the way back he stopped to look again at the grave of a Stikine Indian that was close by the trail. A flagpole had been raised over it. From its peak a windtorn wisp of some material still dangled limply in the sunshine, motionless on this quiet autumn day, and to the base of the pole was secured the dead man's rifle. Swannell would be a man of over fifty when he saw that grave again, no longer young but still with the vigour of youth, and with exciting years behind him.

On that day the sugar came to an end.

From that camp they ran down in rain and snow to the lower end of the Fishing Lakes, to the end of the slack water. They landed cold and miserable from sitting in the canoe. They carried their camp on shore, made their fire and ate a hot meal. Then they gave their undivided attention to Reef Canyon.

Copley writes: "We ran this canyon at the peril of our lives—we were very short of grub and didn't want to take the time to portage, which would have delayed us two days. We looked the water over very carefully, then walked back to the upper end and went into conference—and finally decided to take a chance. If we had upset we would all have been drowned as no one could possibly have lived in that turbulent water."

What happened after the conference was that Jim Alexander took each one of them aside and asked him separately if he would take a chance with him. He got hold of Copley first—and he agreed. Then he asked Swannell, and he said yes. Nep Yuen also agreed and he gave his reasons, which ran more or less like this: "Better I go with you. No good watch you fellows drown and then starve and freeze to death in the bush. Better I drown, too. So I go." This frank statement cheered everybody up and was known from then on as "the logical remark."

The next day, September 29, was fine, and after a good breakfast they got at it. The worst place was Kodak Cascade, and they ran ashore just above the chute to size up the situation from close quarters. The bad feature of that place was in the turmoil below the drop where an intermittent wave rose and subsided, a six-footer. They watched this wave carefully for a while, timing the intervals between its appearances and trying to figure out just when to hit the cascade so as to get through when the wave was down. And when they thought they had it taped beyond any possible shadow of doubt they walked back to the canoe and took their places.

Shakespeare has put the matter in a nutshell:
There is a tide in the affairs of men,
Which, taken at the flood, leads on to fortune ...
And we must take the current when it serves,
Or lose our ventures.

They watched the wave and counted the seconds ... Now then! And they shoved out into water no man was ever meant to travel. The big canoe came quivering over the drop and the way lay clear ahead. But, alas, they had mistimed it: they had underestimated the speed at which they now rushed downward on that foaming chute. Suddenly the frothing water heaved and the wave—which, according to the book, should by then have risen and once again subsided—rose dead in front of them. The canoe tried to rise to it but failed, and they shot straight through that curling wall of water. As Swannell writes: "The wave arose—I, in the bow, had it break over my head ... The smother went clean over the canoe. We shipped six inches of water ... "

Fortunately they were able to drive ashore in the eddy below a big rock on the right bank and bail out. They were all wet, of course, but no one was wetter than Nep Yuen. This cascade, he must have thought, was the end—and Copley writes: "When we swept down, Jim Nep lay down in the bottom of the canoe and got properly wet. I was in front of Jim Alexander and split the wave at this point." Nep Yuen had been asked by Alexander to walk down from the head of the cascade to the foot of the canyon, to be picked up there—but he flatly refused. Having voiced his agreement and stated his reasons, he was now going to stick by the ship, sink or swim, and run the rapids in his own queer fashion—in this case flat on the bottom of the canoe, sloshing about in six inches of water and with his eyes tight shut.

They careered on down the centre of the river, running over submerged reefs that were just like the riffles in a sluice box: this time it was like coming *downstairs*. Below a huge flat boulder that lay in midstream the two currents around it converged, making a ridge of whitewater like the tossing mane of a bucking horse. They got on to the crest of this race and rode it down, making for a flattish, exposed piece of reef, grinding up on this and coming to a standstill with the river roaring all around them. It was impossible to run the channels on either side, so they dragged the canoe in the lapping water across this shelf of rock, launched it again with great difficulty below the reef and went on.

About a mile further down, and still in Reef Canyon, they came to a place where the whole force of the Finlay piled head-on into a cliff face, the river here making a right-angle turn. As before, Swannell was in the bow, making ready to avert the coming smash, dropping his paddle and reaching for his pole. "Jim Alexander didn't think he could make it and shouted to me to stop the canoe with the pole—that is, by tilting like a Knight with a lance at the cliff. The impact threw me overboard, pole and all, but George grabbed me and hauled me back into the canoe."

It was risky work and full of incident, but six hectic hours of wild canoeing saw them through Reef Canyon and camped a mile below Thudaka Creek. In those six hours they undid the work of three and a half toiling days of upstream travel.

I asked Bronlund if he had ever gone by boat or canoe right round the big bend; and he said, "No. Thudaka Creek—that was as far as I ever went by river. Frank Swannell and his bunch are the only men that ever ran that canyon. And they ran it because they had to: there was no other way for them with their heavy canoe. Otherwise a man would be insane to try it."

Black came down Reef Canyon by making two out of his three earlier portages. He was travelling much lighter than when he went up and his men were moving like horses that are headed for home: they must have almost run with their loads over the portage trails. In one long September day they completed the long portage (they had started on it the night before), made one other carry, ran the rest of the canyon and camped late down at Point du Mouton. "We move pretty fast," Black noted rather complacently in his *Journal*.

The next bit of serious trouble was Cascade Canyon. Black and Swannell dealt with the main cascade in slightly different ways. In each case there was what Swannell calls "rather a ticklish crossing" to be made just above the actual fall—and here Black had a narrow escape. Running down the rapid above the fall, the canoe, in spite of the efforts of the men, "was swept about broadside driving down the strong stream bearing on the Cascade." Then, as they lurched sideways over the waves, all hands were momentarily overcome by the paralysis of panic—and for a second or two they sat there inert and helpless, mesmerized by the roaring cascade that was rapidly approaching. Had not Black roused them from their trance with a stentorian bellow, they would have been swept over the fall and drowned. He saw that there was a chance of getting to shore "before too far into the suction of the fall or too late to right the Canoe to cut across to the opposite side." He ordered the men "to pull strongly ashore, and all hands obeying, we again got to Terra firma, and righting and taking the proper course, shot across the Rapid and won down the Waters edge with the Line to the Portage. Made this Portage and Breakfasted on the Beaver we shot yesterday which proves fat and Fur good."

So much for Cascade Canyon. Long Canyon gave La Guarde little trouble except that the canoe shipped water once or twice—and they camped that night, with the big bend behind them, on an island near the mouth of Fox River. All over that island ran well-beaten beaver trails and the place was a tangle of felled trees. On landing, Black "took a turn around this Island and only found one Beaver House with 4 Inhabitants, its amazing the quantities of wood these little animals cut down."

Swannell got moving early from his camp below Thudaka Creek; it didn't take him long to run down through the islands, and then he hit Cascade Canyon. Where Black ran the rapid to the head of the cascade, Swannell came down more cautiously on the line. Then he made, with his heavier craft, the same dangerous crossing, and lined down to the head of the portage, almost swamping on the way. In the rapids below the cascade the dugout struck rocks twice, and towards evening "George is dragged into the river while ashore lining, but Jimmy[35] drags him out, reeling him in like a fish." A note added to the *Diary* here by Copley, thirty years afterwards, says, "Yes—and George's clothes froze solid by the time we made camp." This was a clear case of history repeating itself, since it was about here that Cournoyer slid into the river while lining from a point of rock—he, too, being hauled in clinging to the line.

The next day was October 1, and the dawn broke on a valley white with frost. Without further incident they ran through what remained of Long Canyon and passed through the red gates into the plain swift water of more open country. The first thing that caught their eyes was a long pole leaning out from the bank over the deep water. To the end of the pole a canvas-wrapped bundle was tied, and from the very tip a red flag fluttered, a bit of old red shirt. The whole rig had obviously been put there by some trapper who knew they were upriver, above the canyons. Perhaps it was a message to be taken out—and they headed for it.

They undid the canvas wrapping and an old, rolled-up newspaper of early August came to light. They unfolded it—and then they stared at it in a stunned silence. Then they turned it this way and that, almost tearing it, and stared again. "War!" they said. "War, by God—and with Germany!" And as they went on down the Finlay they could think and speak of no other thing. They camped that night at the mouth of the

Kwadacha, and both there and at Fox River they met trappers coming in for the winter, full of stories about the war. But if it hadn't been for that newspaper, Swannell tells me, they would have been certain the whole thing was an elaborate hoax got up to make fools of them. They wouldn't have believed a word the trappers said.

Towards noon on the third they came to Deserters Canyon. The river was a bit high for October and the awkward waves at the head of the canyon were little less awkward than they had been in July: it was therefore decided to portage most of the stuff and run the canoe through light, Copley and Nep Yuen walking. Nep Yuen took this hard. Having survived Reef Canyon, he now considered himself an amateur of rapids and wanted the fun of running Deserters Canyon. He became very angry with Swannell—but that got him nowhere, and it was with furious resentment that he walked over the portage trail, a riverman out of his element and on dry land ... And so, in the afternoon of the following day, a Sunday, they came to Fort Grahame.

They put in four days there, surveying for the Hudson's Bay Company, and then they went on downriver. On October 10 they came to the settlement at the meeting of the rivers—and it was on that afternoon that they decided to run the Finlay Rapids, simply in order to get some good photographs. However, "Copley, stationed on a boulder as photographer, is so entranced at our speed that he forgets to trip the shutter—so we line back up and repeat the performance."

Sunday was spent at the settlement and Jim Alexander parted from them there to make his way up the Parsnip and home to Fort St. James. The other three went down the Peace, headed for Peace River Crossing in Alberta, four hundred miles away. They passed through the Rockies, leaving behind them the wide valley of the Trench and the reefs and the wild cascades of Finlay's River. And there we should say goodbye to them as they slip silently through the high mountains—were it not for one thing ...

After three days' travel they came to Cust House at the head of the Rocky Mountain Portage. And there to greet them, drawn up above high-water mark, lay the cottonwood dugout with the good lines that they had made at Fort Grahame in the autumn of 1913, the canoe that should have been waiting for them at Fort McLeod in May. They hailed it as an old friend and they arranged to have it hauled by wagon across the portage to Hudson's Hope. At least they would make the last three hundred miles or so in their own canoe. As for the old warrior, the battered and lopsided dugout that had carried them so far in such dangerous waters—no one else should use that, nor would they sell it. They put rocks aboard as ballast, and then they turned the old canoe loose and watched it as it started down the Peace alone, headed for the narrow portal of the Rocky Mountain Canyon through which no boat had ever been ...

On Sunday, October 18, the outfit and canoe having been safely hauled over the portage, Swannell and Copley walked up the river from Hudson's Hope to the foot of the canyon. They scanned every eddy along that shore, and at last, somewhere above the "flower-pot" islands,[36] they found what they were seeking: a fragment of the gunwale with a bit of hand-hewed, flared-out board still spiked on to it. Along with the beaver cuttings and all the debris of the far-off forests of the Trench, it was circling quietly in the dark water.

Part Four

Downriver

24

Deserters Portage

From my flop camp above Prairie Mountain I ran lazily down to Ware, tied up by Pattie's boat and went up to the Bay house. I wanted to thank Pattie and Mrs. Pattie for their kindness and also to say goodbye. That developed into quite a visit and it was midday before I got going again on the river. I was still minus bully beef. Art van Somer would be bringing up the fall outfit for the Hudson's Bay post, but that wouldn't be till on in September, and meanwhile the shelves were getting a bit bare—canned meat being represented by various nondescript compounds of God-knows-what, paraded under snappy, monosyllabic names, and most of them scarcely fit to feed to a dog. It was going to be trout and bacon for me till I hit Finlay Forks, I could see that. But I got some cheese from the Bay—and, while I was in the store, in came an Indian with a desperate cold in the head. "Where did he pick up that beauty?" I asked Pattie after the Indian had sneezed his way out again. "Oh, it's been going around," he replied. "Somebody must have had one on that plane that brought the nurse in, and every Indian in the place has been sniffling. There's never any cold or flu here that doesn't come in on the plane."

I lunched late, somewhere downriver, off the last two Prairie Mountain grayling, and then ran on through a gorgeous afternoon and evening, making a good camp in a fine stand of spruce a little above Del Creek, the place where Ludwig had put in his night's torment in the superheated cabin.

My next camp was at Pesika Creek, about four miles above Deserters Canyon. That was another perfect day in a long spell of good weather—thunderheads showing to east and west, climbing over the walls of the Trench, but never a cloud over the river. I fished at the mouths of small streams and caught lunch, supper, and the morning's breakfast. And I hunted around, near a cabin that Ludwig had pointed out to me, for a trail that took off from there for the Pelly Lakes. I had thought of caching the outfit there and walking in to the lakes, but in the rank summer growth not a sign of that trail could I find. That settled it: I would spend the days that I had in hand up the Omineca at the Black Canyon, dropping down to Finlay Forks on September 10, the day the mail plane was due into the country with Marigold on it. So I went on to Pesika Creek, and from there, in the morning, I ran down the few miles of fast water and beached the canoe at the head of a vast shingle bar on the left bank, just above Deserters Canyon.

The river had dropped a good six feet in the three weeks since Art and I had relayed that load through the canyon, and I was not sure just where I could best land the canoe on the further shore for the portage. If one missed the landing place one would be swept on down into the canyon, and it was very doubtful whether the little seventeen-footer could run it or not. All I really knew was that Haworth and Joe Lavoie never even considered running it: they portaged both outfit and canoe. So I walked down the big bar a good half mile till I was opposite what I thought must be the landing place. I stood and looked across at it for some time. The water was broken there and very fast. The landing was between two big rocks, and even the beach there was nothing more than a steep slope of shattered rock. And if you missed it, that was that: you could just kneel low on the floor, straighten the canoe and prepare to take the big waves of the first riffle ... I got the landmarks well fixed in my head, and then I walked back towards the canoe, a tiny grey speck on the sunlit desert of rounded stones.

The Finlay makes a long left-hand bend around that bar. I came down that bend at a rare speed, close to the right bank and keeping my eyes skinned for the two big rocks and the opening between. There they were, racing up to meet me—and I swung the paddle over to my left side and put the canoe's nose slightly in towards the shore. At the last moment I drove the paddle in hard and set the canoe straight at the beach. She rushed in between the rocks, I threw my weight right back—and then forward again, and she landed with a crash, plumb centre and halfway up on the broken rocks. Hoping that I hadn't bust any thing, I stepped ashore and regarded my handiwork. If ever a man landed a canoe dead on target, I thought, I had done it this time and made a real job of it.

The first thing to do was to find out if it was possible to run the canyon with a reasonable chance of success. I walked down a little way and scrambled out onto a point of rocks from which I could get a close view of the first riffle. And there it was with its big, curling waves slanting across the river at a horrid angle. I looked at it just as Fleet Robertson[37] had looked at it—and many another before and after him. It didn't look at all good.

I poked on down the canyon, keeping along the cliff edge, climbing out onto the points. And after that first riffle there was nothing else that I couldn't run. That was the maddening thing—and perhaps when I went back, I thought, I might be able to figure out a way over or around those great waves—great, anyway, for a small canoe. And I went on down, all the way to the big pool at the foot of the portage. A trapper's cabin stood at the top of the slope that ran down to the beach. The cabin was on a neck of land that connected the portage trail with the high promontory, the Gibraltar Rock, at the foot of the canyon. That trapper must have been a man of sensibility, for he had chosen his site with care, just as a great landowner of the eighteenth century would have done. The ground fell away from the cabin on either side, and the builder had taken advantage of this to cut a lane through the trees in each direction, so that he had a clear view, from one window, upstream far into the canyon, and, from the other, downstream across the big pool, between the twin capes of rock and down the Finlay. A wonderful site—even if he did have to pack his water up the hill from the pool, maintaining a waterhole there through the winter ice—and even though the north wind must have blown keen as a sword blade across that exposed ridge on days of storm, piling the snow into great drifts down among the trees ... Meanwhile this was late August and the wild raspberries by the cabin were ripe and almost ready to fall. I spent some time among them.

A second look convinced me that I had better forget about running the head of the canyon. Lunch was eaten by the canoe, and as I ate I considered how best to manage the portage. The immediate problem was how to get the canoe up on to the portage trail. I think I must have run further downstream than the usual portage landing, since the only path off this beach was a very steep zigzag climb. I couldn't carry the canoe up that path, I would be certain to overbalance and come crashing down with it on to the rocks. Nor could I drag the canoe up without damaging it. And everywhere else the bank was a twenty-foot cliff.

Above the cliff a stout little birch was leaning out at about the right angle. Now, I thought, if I just had the trackline running over that tree, as though on a pulley, I could probably talk to the canoe on even terms ... Down went the last of the cheese, bannock and tea, and I scrambled up the stony path carrying the trackline. The birch proved to be solidly rooted into the rock, and the line was long enough, so I doubled it and left it dangling over the white trunk of the little tree. Then I slid down to the beach, unloaded the canoe and carried it up to the foot of the cliff. I ran the doubled trackline round the small forward thwart and tied it there. And then I began to pull on the free end of the double line. It slipped easily over the smooth birchbark and the nose of the canoe began to rise. I lifted the tail close in and pulled again and the canoe rose to the vertical. Then, lifting and pulling, I next had it dangling from the birch tree a couple of feet off the ground. It was a horrible-looking sight, my only means of transportation dangling in mid-air, above sharp rocks, from a double line of waterworn sash cord. I gave the canoe a gentle tug, just to see. The cord still held.

I rammed that canoe up with my right hand and pulled down on the line with my left until the nose was a bit above the level of the cliff top. Then I tied the free end of the line to a heavy drift log and tore up the zigzag trail, wondering what I was going to do next—for the trackline, which had helped me up to now, would soon be hindering. I also prayed the line would hold, for if anything went wrong now the canoe would drop on the rocks and smash.

Arrived on top, I grabbed the nose of the canoe and hauled it in, and on to the moss of the forest floor. After heaving upwards I got the tail end to rise—but I couldn't get the canoe over the point of balance because the trackline was now holding against me. Hanging on like grim death, I thought that one out—and then I remembered the two nine-foot leather thongs in my hip pocket. With one hand I got them out, and with that hand and my teeth I tied them as one to the ring in the nose of the canoe. I somehow twisted them into a spiral for mutual support—and then came the ticklish bit: gently I let go of the canoe and took the whole weight on the thongs. And the thongs held. Thank God, they did, for a hundred pounds of dead weight falling would have snapped that double line and the canoe would have crashed. Moving slowly back and keeping the twisted thongs absolutely taut, I made them fast to a young spruce.

Once more I slid down the stony trail, this time to unloose the trackline from the drift log. I did that, and I looked up at the canoe, two-thirds of it in mid-air and held from destruction only by two slim latigo laces. I was not happy till I could get my hands on it again and, with one frightful heave, drag it over the point of balance and lay it level on the moss beside the trail. Then I went and got the paddles and a jacket and a sweater from the pile on the beach. I lashed the paddles crossways to the thwarts, padded them with the jacket and sweater, upended the canoe and walked away with it—to lay it down, after much grunting and groaning, on the shore by the big pool. Not too bad, I thought as I did so, for an old fellow of over fifty years. But there is something humiliating in all that fuss when one reads now of Black's downstream passage of that place on September 13: "Arrived at deserters' Portage about 2½ hours before sun set, run down this Rapid easily."

I next carried a load of hardware over the portage, stuff the animals wouldn't bother, and then I returned, via the raspberries, to make a flop camp on the beach by the outfit. All the energy seemed to have faded out and I slept there that night, at the head of the portage, with the clamorous uproar of the river close beside me.

In the morning I felt disinclined for any activity—and I called to mind that sneezing Indian at Fort Ware and laid a few left-handed blessings on his head. Flu picked up last year at Telegraph Creek, and this year a cold in the head at Ware: truly the North was not what it used to be, with germs being freighted all over the place in riverboats and planes. However, I took my time over breakfast and then made a trip or two and got the rest of the outfit carried over to the beach by the canoe. Then I made a comfortable lean-to camp on the sand, close to a little cottonwood, intending to spend the rest of that day, and the following morning if need be, getting a good series of pictures of the canyon in colour and in black-and-white, and in doing a bit of fishing.

But it didn't work out that way exactly: I found, after lunch, that I didn't care if I never took any photographs of the place, and I spent most of the afternoon sitting on the sun-warmed rocks near the entrance to the canyon, reading. The book was *Triple Fugue* by Osbert Sitwell and, much as I admire and enjoy most of his work, I got little pleasure from that one. All I can now remember of it is a rather sordid tale of murder in which the murderer is ultimately given away by an eyewitness, the victim's parrot—and I may have got even that wrong. No book, anyway, to read alone in the bush with a feverish cold in the head, even in bright sunshine. Gloom of spirit deepened, and finally I consigned all literature to the devil and went fishing from the canoe, circling around in the eddies. It was the wrong time of day and for a while I caught nothing. Then I hooked and netted a whale of a Dolly Varden, far more fish than I could eat for supper and breakfast, so that finished fishing. I ate a section of that fish for supper, admired the writhing pattern of the eddies under the light of the young moon and went to bed early.

But not to sleep. I was just dropping off when I was roused by a frightful scuttering noise from the lean-to—a pattering sort of row like heavy rain. It subsided—and then it came again. Dimly I considered this. Then, with slowly returning wits, I realized that it was field mice charging up the lean-to roof and down again on to the gravel. God knows what they were doing it for: fun, I suppose, because there was nothing else to be gained by it. I did some more deep thinking and a little figuring. It was a hundred and twenty-five years since Samuel Black had come to this place in May of 1824. In that time hundreds, possibly thousands, of men had landed here and made the upstream portage. And on every occasion some box or bale or sack had leaked a little, scattering a few grains of rice, some sugar or rolled oats, a few raisins. One sack that Art and I had handled had left a trail of sugar behind it. Gradually the portage bay had become a mouse's Eldorado.

A roar of pattering feet—and up to the roof peak and down again went a couple of squadrons of mouse cavalry. This sort of thing couldn't be allowed to go on all night or there'd be no sleep here. And I sat up in bed and waited for the next charge.

It came—and just as the mice were nearing the peak I caught the inside of the canvas a resounding smack with the back of my hand. Most of the cavalry immediately became airborne. With faint cheeping squeaks of protest they flew through the moonlight to crash on the stones some ten or twelve feet back. It must have been a rough landing. So rough that after one or two more involuntary flights they gave it up as a bad job and peace reigned. And in the morning there were no signs of mice.

To complete the mouse saga: the following evening I, somewhat recovered, settled myself by the fire to grapple once more with *Triple Fugue*. Before tarping things up for the night I had routed out the two mouse traps that always formed part of the outfit and set them, baited with cheese, one by the cottonwood and one behind the lean-to. Barely had I started reading when two loud smacks and a convulsive rattle indicated that two mice had paid the last forfeit. I got up, took the traps down to the water's edge, hurled the dead mice out into the pool, returned and reset the traps. Two or three minutes later the whole sequence was repeated. The moon was at its first quarter, and the canyon gateway and the whole of the portage bay were bathed in its clear light. I threw the dead mice into about the same place as the first pair—and almost immediately there was a boil in the water, and then a second surge, and the surface of the water was broken ... and the mice had vanished. That went on and on till I had thrown almost thirty mice into the water, leading a school of huge Dollies that were like sharks closer and closer to shore. I know they were Dollies because nothing else would act like that and because my party caught a couple, two years later in the Northwest Territories—one with seven mice in him, and the other containing six mice, one lizard and one small fish.

I broke camp and got going on the river late the following afternoon. Loafing about in the sun for a couple of days at the foot of the portage had more or less shifted the Fort Ware cold, flu, whatever it was. Clambering over the canyon rocks in slow motion, I had got a good set of pictures. And it was time to be going, anyway. The idea of fishing for Dollies that were busy digesting a load of trap-flattened mice had no appeal. I would drop down to Hamburger Joe's cabin, make camp somewhere near there and have a go at Deserters Peak in the morning. So I ran down the two sunlit miles to Joe Berghammer's, helped myself to a few sticks of rhubarb from his garden, and then drifted down a short distance to the mouth of a little creek, where I made camp and promptly caught a good grayling for supper. A trail of sorts ran up this creek from near the cabin and I hoped it might lead to Deserters Peak. The mountain rose 5,500 feet above the river and from its slopes, I thought, there should be a wonderful view of the Trench.

Breakfast next morning was eaten by the light of the fire. A stiff neck, a dry throat and something of a headache all more or less vanished under the onslaught of porridge and tea. And with the first light I walked up to the cabin, found the trail and followed it up the creek valley. It was not much of a trail—just a pathway made by the game and improved here and there by the slash of an axe. The sky was cloud-covered with scattered patches of blue; then, as the sun climbed higher, the clouds began to roll away and a deep blue sky spread over all of the great valley. I shoved ahead through the dew-laden trees, climbing all the time by the little stream.

When I had gone nearly a couple of miles the stream forked and I took the left-hand or larger fork. Another mile went by and the trail forked, the smaller, less-used trail going straight on alongside the stream while the larger, plainer fork turned half left and began to climb. I could see nothing on account of the trees, and the map was of little help, but I thought that surely I had reached the base of the mountain and I took the uphill trail. And I climbed steeply upwards, my nailed boots scraping on the rocks, rasping in the loose gravel. I had the aneroid in my pocket and at 2,000 feet above the river I still could see nothing, the little trees were all around me. The trail was a game trail now, there were no more axe cuts—only the work of an army of energetic bears: every anthill had been clawed apart, every rotten log bashed to pieces, almost every rock overturned. It's amazing how one can travel so far through the bush, which is obviously inhabited, and yet see so few of its people.

Up I went, with feet that were getting to be like twin lumps of lead and a throat that was like a lime kiln. At 3,000 feet by the aneroid the trail came out of the trees. It ran northwards along a semi-open western slope, still climbing—and then it came into an area of lightning-blasted, fire-killed trees, grey and old. The winds had uprooted the dead trees and laid them low, and in their shade and shelter the sweetest of raspberries had grown. Never have raspberries tasted so good—I think they saved my life that day, for there was no water along this foothill ridge and I had none with me. From there the trail climbed again, heading for a lonely, wind-twisted, contorted pine. And when I reached that tree I found that I was on the rocky, knife-edge crest of the ridge and I saw what I had done. Blinded by the trees I had climbed, not Deserters Peak, but a great, guardian foothill lying immediately to the west of it.

The old pine had its huge, crawling roots set firmly into the rocks, which it had split apart as it grew. I laid my pack and rifle down and settled myself comfortably in the shade, in between the roots, almost as if in an armchair. The place was perfect and so was the day. I alone was feeling out of touch—a bit weird and almost light-headed. Probably lunch would put that right; and I opened the useless tea pail and soon was munching away at a bacon-and-bannock sandwich, eased down with cheese and raisins.

From the river the green, unbroken forest swept up in a long curve almost to the rock ridge where I was sitting. But if I turned round and looked behind the pine, then the ridge dropped away sheer, almost a thousand feet, into the valley of a little stream. And beyond, quite close as a bird would fly but hopelessly out of reach for me, feeling as I did this day, rose Deserters Peak. I was about 3,500 feet above the river and the peak topped me by about 2,000 feet—but it might as well have been the moon for all I could do about it. I turned away and gave myself up to the marvellous view: the western mountains, the dense forest of the Trench, the Finlay winding its way through this green carpet like a silver snake, whirlwinds dancing on the bars beyond Fort Grahame, sending the sand aloft in yellow spirals that rose and fanned out to nothing against the blue of the sky. I swept the glass this way and that over the valley—from the winding river to the emerald lakes west of Deserters Canyon ... The sunlight was surely strong up here, I thought. It splintered on the shining needles of the old pine into a thousand dazzling pinpoints of silver—and if one just closed one's eyes for a moment ...

God knows how long I slept between the comfortable knees of the pine. A cold wind roused me and I blinked sleepily, with screwed up eyes, at a strange world, wondering for a moment where on earth I was. Gone was the blue sky, gone the blazing sun. From rim to rim the Trench lay under masses of heavy cloud that moved slowly out of the west. Twin thunderstorms had formed in the western mountains and were trailing dark curtains of rain across the valley. One, in the northwest, had blotted out the faint, far shape of Prairie Mountain. The other was crossing the Finlay somewhere near Collins' Flat. Lightning flashed from it, and its dark shadow crept on towards the Rockies. In between the storms a strange yellow radiance that was not the direct light of the sun penetrated the cloud canopy. It stalked across the valley in vague, unshaped columns, making darker the darkness of the storms. The effect was weird, and the whole fantastic scene would have made a famous backdrop for the last act of some sinister play.

I roused myself with a shiver and took a photograph of the cloud-shadowed Trench. Then I slung my little pack and got going. I stopped to eat a few handfuls of raspberries—but who or what took me on and into camp from that berry patch I have never known. Two nailed mountain boots, with feet in them, slid and crashed down the stony trail, but they seemed far away and somebody else was directing them. Even the sound of their going was distant—but they took me in to camp, God bless them, and rarely has camp seemed sweeter. Straight from my pocket came a curl of birchbark, and in seconds the fire was flaring and the tea pail swinging on its willow. While the water boiled I polished off what remained of Hamburger Joe's stewed rhubarb, and the sugared sweetness of its juice was like nectar. Down went the tea, heavy with sugar; and then I threw myself into my eiderdown and slept—and slept. Somewhere in my sleep there was a rumble of thunder and a heavy drop or two of rain fell on the lean-to. But nothing more, and I slept on.

That sleep must have lasted for nearly four hours—and the queer thing is that I woke clear-headed and hungry and without a trace of fever. Even my feet, as I laced the moccasins onto them, seemed once more to belong to me. That was well, for it meant that the Fort Ware Indian's curse was lifted. The sky, too, had improved: not a cloud was to be seen. In the west was the last faint afterglow of the sunset. In the east the young moon was almost over the wall of the Rockies. And, in my camp by the Finlay, very soon there was feasting: hot cakes, bacon and maple syrup—and coffee for a treat. All was well; and a new day, with all its wonders, lay ahead.

Fast water and a perfect morning brought me to the mouth of the Ingenika. I made the noonday fire there, caught a couple of nice fish and went on. From the Ingenika to Fort Grahame the Finlay is a maze of islands, bars and driftpiles. In places it is up to two miles wide from outside channel to outside channel. Through this patchwork of islands the canoe traveller threads his way, trying to pick the main channel, trying also to figure out what really lies ahead when the mirage is making small, white-crested ripples look like tremendous waves, and when a light-coloured, waterworn log of drift can appear, from a distance, as a twenty-foot sandbank shimmering in the shifting light. The only thing to do is to stand up in the canoe and thereby change the angle of vision. Slipping silently down the river, standing upright and steering with the tip of the paddle, one listens intently to the sound of the approaching riffles as they divide on the point of an island. Then, suddenly, the pattern becomes clear. All doubts are resolved and one can sit down and swing the canoe into the right channel. Down the noisy riffle at the head of the island, and then a sweep past a curving, cutbank shore, dangerous with a tangle of sweepers and beaver cuttings, shaded from the winking sun by giant cottonwoods which next year's flood will uproot and take away—the pattern is repeated time and again but it never loses its charm. Later on that afternoon the west wind got up and it was hard to make headway into it on westward-flowing reaches of the river. I landed and put a rock or two into the nose of the canoe, thereby making it quite clear to that wayward craft which of the two of us was running things.

Towards evening the wind dropped and the lonely, tenantless buildings of Fort Grahame came into view. I was slipping along, close under the right bank of the Finlay, when I saw a man walk down to the landing at Grahame. He was carrying something on his shoulder that he laid in a black-painted, open riverboat that was tied up there and that I hadn't noticed. Then he disappeared again into the old house, to emerge from it with another load. I had just spotted a good camping place on my side of the river, close to the foot of the trail that ran up the mountain to the old mica mine project: I might have camped there and taken a stroll up the trail in the morning, but now I rather wondered. I was pretty sure the man was Shorty Weber, whom Alan and I had met at the Warrens' house on the Parsnip. I didn't think he had seen me yet—but if he hadn't, he soon would; and he most certainly would when my fire smoke drifted out on to the river. It would then look a bit odd, my camping here: probably I had better go on and hail him. And, fortunately, that was what I did.

It proved to be Shorty, and I got a most friendly welcome and an invitation to stay the night with him. Just one more load, he said, and then we would get going for his cabin, which was a little way downstream and on the west bank at the foot of a big snye. He would give me a tow—and with that he disappeared over the bank again, while I threw the rocks out of the canoe and made sure the trackline was running free. Shorty came back, this time with a load of heavy linoleum, and soon we were speeding down the river, the trackline tied to the nose of Shorty's boat, and myself in the canoe, holding the two rivercraft apart. A neat cabin, built of brightly shining, peeled logs with dovetailed corners, hove in sight. Balustraded steps led up to it through the grass, and the pathway from the landing, running over soft, yielding silt and sand, was thickly strewn with willow branches, laid crossways and giving a firm footing. To the right of the cabin, as one walked up from the river, was an oblong levelled area carpeted with spruce boughs and rimmed round with heavy spruce logs. Shorty had had his tent set up there while he was fixing up the cabin, and now, while he was getting supper going, I carried up my eiderdown and laid it out on the level spruce mat. Then we set up Shorty's big mosquito tent around it, a palatial affair, a bug tent on a glorious scale. In the slack water of this snye, he said, and with its silty beaches, there might still be the odd mosquito. And, when all was done and the canoe tarped up, I went up into the cabin, which was as neat inside as it was outside and spotlessly clean.

Frank Weber (I wonder if his given name was Franz?) was born in Germany in 1887. He came to Canada in 1911, and to the Finlay in 1913. He worked for Swannell on the Hudson's Bay Company's survey at Fort Grahame in October, 1914. Swannell has a photograph of that survey party, and from it a young Shorty Weber looks straight into the camera with an arrogant stare. On his head is a battered homburg hat, set at a jaunty angle, and Shorty's face is decorated with a full-length, old-time moustache. He was clean-shaven when I met him thirty-five years later, one of the oldest of the old-timers on the Finlay.

As with many people who live much alone, Shorty's character developed a few kinks as the years went by. Quite recently Swannell told me a tale that illustrates the truth of this. Shorty, in 1931, had a cabin that was about six miles from Deserters Canyon, and to this cabin Swannell came in the summer of that year. He wished to enter for some reason—for shelter, to cook a meal, or whatever it may have been—and he took a look at the door. There was no handle or lever on the outside, just a pivoting screen of wood covering a round hole beyond which, inside the cabin, the latch string was dangling. Swannell swung that aside and was going to put his hand through to pull the string

Swannell's survey party relaxes at Fort Grahame in October 1914. Left to right: I. Robinson, D. Forbes, F. C. Swannell (with hands in pockets), Steve Redey, Jim Alexander, Nep Yuen, Shorty Weber, G. V. Copley (with dog). (Photo courtesy of F. C. Swannell.)

when something inside his head said, "Don't!" So he shoved a stick or an axe handle through and felt with it for the string. He got it and pulled down—and there was a loud, metallic clang from inside and something heavy landed on the axe handle. I don't know what the exact arrangement was, but Shorty had it fixed so that, while he could get in, a stranger pulling on that latch string would liberate a heavy crosscut, arranged to pivot on a five-inch spike driven through one of the handle holes, and to descend like the blade of a guillotine, with all its weight and its jagged teeth, on the wrist that had unwarily reached through the hole. A murderous contraption. Swannell and his assistant got in—and Swannell was looking around the cabin when he realized that his man, also a German, was busily collecting bark and kindling and laying them in a pile on the floor. "What's all that for?" Swannell asked. "I'm going to burn the goddam shack down," replied the assistant, "and maybe that'll teach the little bastard a thing or two." Swannell pointed out that, while the idea was a laudable one, it would do more harm to the forests than to Shorty Weber—and there the matter rested.

The stories about Shorty were—and still are—legion. He was an energetic little pack rat of a man, a gatherer of anything that was lying around loose without a string on it. Hence these acquisitions from Fort Grahame. The various fittings and furniture might conceivably have been destined for Ware but Shorty was taking no chances. "They'll leave it there till it's too late," he said, "and then, if there's another flood like last year, all of Grahame'll go down the river." He needn't have bothered to justify himself to me: it was none of my business. But his depredations worried him towards the end. He confessed as much to Marge McDougall when he was being taken outside in his last illness. He was wondering if St. Peter would hold these things against him.

Supper was excellent, and we sat afterwards by the window in the cabin, talking and watching the Rockies glow in the sunset light and slowly fade. I know it was well after eleven when I went out into the moonlight and to bed in Shorty's splendid tent ... I mentioned to him the habit the Fort Ware Sikannis had of writing messages or comments on blazed trees, and that set him off on an old Indian of Fort Grahame, old Toma. It was Toma who once shot a cow moose, a forbidden thing. Rashly he recorded the event; he blazed a tree and wrote on the blaze:

"Here I killing cow moose"—and signed and dated the statement. The next time he went that way he was attached to the game warden's party during a tour of inspection. The game warden regarded Toma's old blaze for some time in silence. Then he turned to the old Indian: "You wrote that, Toma?"

"Yes."

"Then here I fining you—" and he named the penalty. I suppose that, being a game warden, he had to do something about it, but my sympathies have always been with Toma. There was plenty of meat on the hoof in North America before the White man came, and one cannot blame the Indian for any scarcity of it today.

Shorty told me that his trapline was up the Ingenika at Wrede Creek. He could get that far with his boat and it was a good country, easy to get around in and no devil's club with its festering spines. From Wrede Creek we got on to Pelly Creek, another Ingenika tributary, and the Pelly Lakes—and that brought Shorty back to old Toma.

"He's up there now, hunting," he said.

"Hunting what?"

"Sheep. They're in the mountains on both sides of Pelly Creek—the grey sheep. When the Bay was closing Grahame this summer, Toma was there. The district manager had come in to oversee the job, and Toma hit him up for a couple of boxes of shells over and above his other debt. The post manager might have fixed him up if the big chief from the outside hadn't been around—but Toma's credit was used up and he got refused. 'Well,' Toma said, 'I am an old man now but I can still get sheep with the bow and arrow.' And that's where he is now: up Pelly Creek with his family, living on sheep."

From sheep we got on to moose; and Shorty, who had been long enough on the Finlay to form an opinion worth listening to, held that the moose population varied from scarcity to plenty in a definite cycle that had little to do with wolves. I don't have all his dates, but he was definite that in 1911 there had been no moose and that in 1949 we had reached that point again—meaning by "no moose" that only the odd one was seen or killed. But three times between those dates the moose had increased to a peak of plenty, the last time being in 1944. If he was right, the complete cycle from peak to peak would be ten or eleven years.

Shorty Weber stands in front of his cabin, which was built of brightly shining, peeled logs with dovetailed corners. Stories about Shorty were legion.

By bedtime we had worked over just about everything on the Finlay including the Indians: it was a great evening and, to crown it all, when I went down to my small eiderdown in Shorty's vast bug tent, a splendid aurora was streaming across the sky, a river of green fire from some hidden source beyond the Rockies.

We had breakfast at six, watching a cloudless sunrise climb over the Rockies and spill its reflection into the calm water of the snye. Then we went out, and I was shown the new store where Shorty would be trading that coming winter with the Indians—and Shorty inspected my outfit and especially my old rifle, a .375 Mannlicher carbine. He admired its lightness and was astonished at the size of the bullet. "But," he said, "a large-calibre rifle is too big for one man who is on the move in the bush. He can't eat all the meat it can kill, nor can he carry enough of the shells. Give me fishing tackle, a good .22 with plenty of shells and a good dog that can carry a pack, and I'll walk from here to the Yukon." And there's sound sense in that. But the trouble is, the perfect gun for every job doesn't exist and never can.

Around half-past eight we said goodbye and I ran on. All through that sunlit September day I travelled, fishing only in one place, a creek mouth where I lunched—and then, in the afternoon, picking my way through a network of islands. I passed through the Picket Fence and one sunken, anchored sweeper rose beneath my canoe like a great grey shark, but I touched nothing. Then the islands came to an end, the river bunched together and the current slackened, and I knew that I had got, without realizing it, into the Deadwater, the twelve-mile stretch of slack current. The jungle came down to the water's edge and stayed there, and there was no place to land. The sun sank into the west and still I slugged madly on down this ditch of a river. At last, towards eight, a small gravel bar showed under the right bank. There was wood there, and somebody, long ago, had cut a sleeping place out of the alders beneath a huge old twisted birch. Thankfully I drew the canoe up on shore and called it a day.

It was not till I moved on from that camp and paddled on down interminable, calm, wooded reaches, with never a landing place of any kind, that I realized I had made the only possible camp between the head of the slack water and the mouth of the Ospika River. A couple of young men, Sikannis, were camped there by the Ospika with a bunch of horses. The sound of the horse bells came to me across the Finlay as I passed by, and the men waved to me. I brandished the paddle in salute; there was nothing else I could do, for thunderstorms, black as ink, were blowing up out of the Rockies and a squally wind was twisting the canoe this way and that. A few heavy drops of rain fell. And then the sky cleared again and I turned into the mouth of the Omineca. Fast water welcomed me, racing between the bars. Knowing that, somewhere, not far upstream, I should find a good camping place, I waded ashore with the coiled trackline paying out from my right hand.

25

The Black Canyon

The morning of September 4 was perfect, and I loaded up, flicked the canoe out into the current on the end of the trackline and started to walk up the bars. And it wasn't long before I began to fall foul of the driftpiles. McConnell makes a few comments on the huge driftpiles of the Omineca. The Finlay, I had thought, had gone the limit in piling up these obstacles to navigation, but I soon found that the Omineca, in proportion to its size, was far worse. Often one couldn't line round them because the line tended to snag on some projecting spar—and, anyhow, it's hard to climb quickly across them and control a canoe that's away out in the river. And more often than not one can't pole around a driftpile because the riverbed tends to scour out underneath, and then you've got no poling bottom. But somehow I got up. In one maddening place a great long sweeper lay from a shingle bar far out into the stream. I could almost paddle round the end of it but not quite: each time I tried I was swept back. I couldn't pole round it: I couldn't touch bottom there, it was so deep. And I couldn't get up on the far side of the river because of driftpiles. So I unloaded the heavy stuff and then lifted the canoe with all the small things in it, and laid it on top of the big sweeper. Then I climbed over myself and slid the canoe into the water again on the upstream side, loaded up once more and went on. I was permanently wet up to the waist on that trip, but it was such a lovely day that it couldn't have mattered less.

Then there was a place where huge driftpiles lined each shore. It was impossible to paddle up and, as usual, there was no poling bottom. And the driftpiles stretched away back over the shingle, right into the bush: to portage would have been horrible. But there is usually some way—and here a long, narrow strip of shingle bar ran right down the centre of the Omineca between the driftpiles. I could drive the canoe on to the tail end of it with the paddle. Now, if only I could get off the top end and make land just above the driftpile canyon, all would be well. So I landed on the long thin island and walked up to the head to see: and it looked as if one might just make it without being sucked under a driftpile—but only just.

In the middle of my slip of an island there was a shocking great pile of dead and shattered trees: it looked as though a mad, gigantic beaver had built his house up there. I lined the canoe up to it—but to line the loaded canoe round it was so nearly impossible that I couldn't afford to try. Two men could have managed, but not one. So I spent most of an hour there carrying the heavy stuff over that damnable ram-down of trees and on to firm beach beyond. Then, balancing like a tightrope walker on slender, swaying spars, I lined the canoe past that barrier. Nothing went wrong, and, with much delicate jiggling and careful placing of the feet, I made it. But there is only a hair's breadth in a place like that between victory or defeat. One slip and you may be in the river, driven by the fierce current into the tangled abatis of dead, peeled snags. One untimely gust of wind and the canoe, lightly loaded, may be out of control or snagged and out of reach. *Everything* must go right.

There remained the head of the island—and there, by wading upstream on the submerged bar till the canoe was almost level with my shoulders, and then jumping in off the bottom of the river with a gallon or two of water in my clothes, I just made the open shore about three feet above the head of the driftpile. It was what one might call a crash landing: I stood up in the canoe at the last moment, threw the paddle far onto shore, and jumped for the steep shingle bank with the trackline in my hand. As I hit the shingle the canoe hit the first log of the driftpile. Rolling over into a sitting position I regained control with the line—and then just sat there on the warm stones, looking at the little grey canoe which floated so gaily on the intense blue of that clear river. No profound thoughts afflicted me: only the conviction, firmly held, that it was a damn good job that canoe was close-ribbed.

The Black Canyon

Making his way up the Omineca requires Patterson to engage in some acrobatic moves in order to get past the obstructing driftpiles.

Acrobatics of that description, and portages and things, all take time, and the Black Canyon is some eight or nine miles up from the Finlay. Evening was coming on when at last I rounded a bend into a beautiful reach, free from driftpiles and with a good tracking beach. There seemed to be cliffs in the distance, golden yellow cliffs: they came closer, and then the current slacked off, and for the first time that day I was able to go upstream on the paddle, nosing up into the canyon.

For me this was a place of pilgrimage, and had been so for almost forty years. It was early in 1910 that I first read that book of Butler's and marvelled at its wild pictures. How do I know that it was in 1910? Because that was a hard winter in the north of England and the snow lay deep outside. Arched over the pale, cold sunset was the gleaming crescent of the Daylight Comet, and Halley's Comet also was due to pay the earth a visit. All these things marked the year that I found that book in my grandfather's library. He had a first edition of it, and

I read it there in the evenings by the wavering light of the fire, as was fitting with a book like that, myself being sprawled comfortably on the hearthrug and almost in the hearth ... Many a winter had gone by since that year of the two comets, and now here I was at last at the Black Canyon. I had been a long time on the way but I could see that I was not going to be disappointed.

I dropped back to the mouth of the canyon and made camp on the south bank in the silence of the quiet water, on the fine gravel of an old bed of the Omineca: it had changed its course a year or so before in a tremendous flood, bursting through a wall of tall old spruce that may have seen Butler go by, and leaving high and dry its old channel. The weather was perfect, so the lean-to was set dead facing the North Star to provide shade for the grub and outfit at noonday.

Here, but on the north bank of the river, Butler camped on May 11, 1873. The river then was high and swift with the spring runoff, and the canyon was roaring. "We looked," he says, "a moment at the grim gate which we had to storm on the morrow, and then put in to the north shore, where under broad and lofty pines, we made our beds for the night."

Any forebodings that they may have had were more than justified. The weather was hot and fine, and the heat was melting the mountain snows. The Omineca was rising fast and the difference, in a narrow gut like the Black Canyon, half a mile long and varying in width from a hundred to two hundred feet, between the calm tranquility of September and the foaming torrent of May and June, can easily be seen. At the head of the canyon I found indications of a thirty-foot rise from the September level.

Butler and his three companions set forth into the Black Canyon on the morning of May 12, and crawled up in the eddies close under the cliffs. "In the centre ran a rush of water that nothing could stem. Poling, paddling, clinging with hands and nails to the rock; often beaten back and always edging up again, we crept slowly along ... " They came, at the end of a morning's work, to the foot of a "wild cataract of foam," halfway through the canyon. Here there is a very steep portage trail up a coulee in the canyon wall, rising over a hundred and fifty feet, and up this trail in the sweltering heat they carried their camp and outfit to the head of the canyon, the canoe being too heavy to portage.

They came back for that, and, from the foot of the portage trail for a little way upstream, a certain amount of beach made tracking easier. Somehow they wallowed forward, half in the river, half on the rocks of the shore, lining, pulling and shoving the canoe. The beach on the north shore then came to an end and they were faced with a desperate crossing—a straight shoot across a wild rush of water in the centre of the canyon to try and catch a small eddy on the south shore. If they missed that small eddy they would be swept backwards against the cliffs and into the worst rapid in the canyon: it was the old game of "catching the eddy" and, as usual, the longer they looked at it the less they liked it. So they tried it: they drove in their paddles, there was a bewildering whirl of water and "a wild yell of Indian war-whoop from Kalder," and in a couple of seconds they were safely across. On they went, lining from rock to rock, till they reached the foot of the last fall—and the stiffest one: above this and on the far shore lay their camp and outfit.

Here disaster struck. Butler, with two men, floated a line back round a massive promontory to Kalder, who was holding the canoe in the eddy. This line Kalder made fast to the nose of the canoe—and a second line also, which he coiled loosely round his waist. Then he nosed the canoe out of the eddy into the current with a long pole. And then everything happened in a flash—the men up above hauled, the canoe sheered out into the flood, and the upper line broke. The full weight now came on Kalder, who extricated himself from the coils by a miracle, grabbed his line and hung on. His line snapped and away went the canoe, taking with it their meat and tent. "We crouched together on the high rock, which commanded a long view down the Black Canyon, and gazed wistfully after our vanishing boat." Night was coming on, they had no axe, no grub and no canoe, and camp was on the wrong side of the Omineca.

They walked back to the lower end of the canyon and, while Butler and two men set to work to construct a raft out of the logs of an old cache, Jacques, the miner, who had no faith in the raft idea, went on downstream to look for the canoe. The party of three somehow managed to get across, the raft going to pieces on an island, and made their way back to camp, to a well-earned supper and to bed.

This is the head of the Black Canyon, looking downstream towards the place where Butler lost his canoe, which contained the crew's food and tent.

Early next morning, May 13, they heard Jacques shouting from the far side. The canoe was on an island four miles below the canyon and not much the worse—a wonderful piece of luck. Down they went again to the canyon mouth, where they built a big, strong raft, picked up Jacques, and so reached the canoe. By evening it was landed once more behind the rock from which they had made their famous crossing of the previous day. The sun blazed down, the cottonwood leaves were coming green and, that morning, they had seen the first hummingbird in camp. And the Omineca was still rising.

On the 14th, after breakfast, they went back to the canoe, this time with a decided feeling of uneasiness. They shot out of the eddy to make the crossing, but now the increased weight of water was too much for them. "There was a moment's wild struggle, during which we worked with all the strength of despair. A second of suspense, and then we are borne backwards ... until with a rush as of wings, and amid a roar of maddened water, we go downwards towards the canyon's wall."

As Butler says, they might as well have tried to stop an express train: they smashed into the cliff and split the canoe to the centre, but it still somehow held together. "And now, ere there was time for thought, we were rushing, stern foremost, to the edge of the great rapid." And this must have been the moment immortalized for posterity by the Victorian artist in his splendid conception of the Black Canyon.[38]

But it was not the end. They went over the drop, the whitewater surged and hissed around them and the canyon walls whirled by—and in a few seconds they were safely down in the quiet eddies, soaked, half swamped and, for a while, speechless. They held a council of war. To try the canyon a third time, they decided, would be a folly after this escape: wearily they portaged their outfit back to the canoe and ran down once more to the canyon mouth, determined "to seek through the Parsnip River an outlet to the South."

However, the luck had turned. Just below the canyon mouth and on the right bank they caught sight of gaudily coloured blankets, and landed hastily to find a pile of gear—traps, beaver, flour—and a pair of miner's boots which Jacques, after careful examination, decided must belong to the Cornish miner, Pete Toy, who was evidently portaging his stuff from the upper to the lower end of the canyon. Pete soon appeared carrying a huge load, and when greetings and news had been exchanged he set to and cooked the sodden voyageurs a right royal feed. All was soon arranged: Pete's canoe was above the canyon and theirs was below. "Happy coincidence! We would exchange crafts: Pete would load his goods in our boat, and we would once again carry our goods to the upper end of the canyon, and there, taking his canoe, pursue our western way." So they set out, late in the evening, "to stagger for the last time to the west end of the portage," and next morning they were on their way towards the gold mining settlements of the upper Omineca. "Behind us lay the Black Canyon, conquered at last; and as its sullen roar died away in the distance ... I drew a deep breath of satisfaction— the revulsion of long anxious hours."

In that way Capt. W. F. Butler[39] (as he then was) dealt with the Black Canyon—an incident in his long and adventurous journey from Fort Garry to Quesnel and Victoria in 1872–73, all so vividly described in *The Wild North Land*.

And now it was 1949: sunset was deepening into twilight, and supper was still to get. Butler and Pete Toy and all those heroes of an earlier day were memories now, but the story of their deeds and their endeavour and their high courage was a tale that would stir the blood and quicken the heart for generations to come. Soon the fire smoke was drifting out on to the quiet river (it must have been on this very spot that Butler and his men enjoyed "the feast of Toy") and the scent of trout and bacon was rising from the pan. During supper a great round moon shouldered its way out of the Peace River Gap in the Rockies and climbed into the sky over Mount Selwyn; and when all was finished and put away I walked down to the water's edge and looked up into the Black Canyon—a study in black and silver, broken only by the pale moonlit gold of the little birch trees on the ledges. There was no movement save, here and there, widening rings in the black water—no sound save the gentle lap and fill of some deep eddy ...

Next morning, after breakfast, I paddled across to find the portage trail. Up a steep creek coulee it went, and a message cut on a tree showed that three men had dragged their boat over it in July of this same year; and a nice job that must have been, even with skids and rollers and block and tackle, for the trail rises some 160 feet before dropping again to river level in its half mile of length. The descent to the river at the upper end is gradual, ending over sloping rock—and there, above any normal high water, a canoe was cached, set around with a stout little corral of logs to keep it safe from falling trees, or from a playful slap from some passing bear. A dwarf Michaelmas daisy made this head of the portage into the gayest of rock gardens; to the west the Wolverine Mountains showed fresh and clear cut in the light of the rising sun, and on the portage trail every twig and every autumn leaf glistened under the heavy dew.

Across the river and a little way downstream was a deep bay between rocks, piled high with enormous banks of golden sand. There, next day, I found the ruins of a cache, sluice boxes and flume—and, upright, forlorn and immovable, a great slab of golden schist, the fireback of the fireplace of a vanished cabin, swept away, I was told later on, in the great high water of 1948, which had also, it seems, floated the canoe out of its log corral at the head of the portage and laid it high up in the bush.

I walked back to the canoe, paddled across to camp for fishing tackle and a tea pail, and headed up into the Black Canyon. Time lost its meaning in that place of quiet waters. The sun rose and set, and one golden day followed another, and still the canoe lingered in that enchanted spot, passing from the eddy to the stream and back again, even as the trout and Arctic grayling did down in the clear depths, playing along the shadow line. Sometimes there would come, stealing down the canyon, the very faintest whisper of a breeze, warm, scented with autumn and the clean smell of pines. Down would flutter a red leaf from a chokecherry or a golden leaf from one of the little birch trees that glowed on the ledges like so many Chinese lanterns: the red and the gold leaves would drift lazily on the green water, and the ripples, stirred by the breeze, would set their bars and patterns of light climbing the gleaming walls of micaschist in a maze of flashing colour. And then

Time lost its meaning as one golden day followed another at Black Canyon, the "place of quiet waters."

all would be still again except for the drip of water from the paddle or the drowsy chuckle of an eddy as it filled and overflowed.

I spent five nights and four cloudless, perfect days in that camp, and a full moon was with me to lend enchantment to the nights. No wind blew to strip the trees of their golden leaves and never a cloud came climbing into that summer sky. On the third evening the faint sound of a distant outboard came from downriver, borne on some moving breath of air. Then the engine stopped, and for a long time there was silence. And then it started up again, only to fade away into the distance till I could hear it no more. Some trapper bringing in his winter supplies, I thought—and I wondered why I hadn't noticed his cabin on my way up from the Finlay.

Meanwhile I explored the river upstream and downstream and on both banks—but it was never long before I came back to the Black Canyon to drift up and down there in the canoe and fish. The place fascinated me. I have had fishing where you simply hurled a line into a pool and the water would boil with sudden life—and you pulled out a fish, just as easy as that, and every time. But in this place the shadow of the cliffs plunged deep down into the clear water, and there, twenty feet or more below the canoe—which also threw a shadow—the rainbows and the Arctic grayling would be swimming quietly, passing from the sunlight into the shadow and back again into the sun. A black gnat was what fetched them—and when I had enough fish in the canoe I would put into a little bay of fine, untrodden sand, the only opening in the canyon walls. There was no driftwood there—but I had thought of that and there was always plenty in the nose of the canoe. Soon the smoke would be curling upward and the tea pail would be dangling over the fire on its green willow. Trout and bacon, tea and bannock—and the September sunshine setting the canyon walls on fire: crimson and gold, blueberry and wild rose, dwarf willow and small, twisted, flaming birch. Even the canoe with its nose slid up on the sand, half in the shadow of the cliff and half lying out on the sunlit water, seemed to be floating on an emerald pool of light. Four whole days, did I say? I wish it had been forty.

One evening, as I was baking bannock and making my way to the end of *Triple Fugue*, my gaze came to rest on the camp kettles. Those old cooking pots, a roughly nesting set that we had accumulated at odd times—they had followed our fortunes by pack horse and canoe for almost twenty years. And now, after a summer's use, they were blackened and horrible. The driftwood of the Finlay, the smoky alpine fir of Bower Creek, the cottonwood of Summit Lake and the Crooked River—everything had added to the coating of carbon on those pots. I was ashamed of them. Something would have to be done before Marigold set eyes on them. And in a wild fit of enthusiasm I stagged the ends off my campaigning trousers (which were disintegrating, anyway, in spite of expert patching) and took water and wood ashes and rubbed and polished till I had the solid old pots shining like silver. No man could do more than that and few would have done as much. When all was finished they looked a bit unnatural, standing in a row on the rocks by the fire just like a bunch of wedding presents. I hardly dared to cook my porridge in the porridge pot, it was so devastatingly beautiful.

On the last afternoon I took my rifle and went down the old, abandoned bed of the Omineca on which my camp stood. There were fresh tracks of moose and bear and I thought it would be nice to have some fresh meat to take down with me for the McDougalls. I had gone about a mile down the grey waste of stones when I heard the distant sound of an axe biting into dry wood. I went on—and I came to a cabin set into the trees on what had been, till June of '48, the bank of the Omineca. Below the cabin was a good boat landing where now no boat could come, and in the cabin, setting things in order, was Gunnar Loving. Roy McDougall had brought him up a couple of days ago and they had landed the winter's outfit where the abandoned riverbed swung around and met the new river. It was a long carry to bring all the stuff from there to the cabin and Loving was just leaving for another load. We talked for a few minutes and then went our separate ways, promising to meet again in the evening.

Loving appeared at my camp, carrying his rifle and with his dog following, just as I was starting to cook supper. He most kindly brought a present of six eggs (from a farm near Prince George) and three fresh peaches. He always brought in two or three cases of fruit, he said; he hated canned fruit and he was going to spend tomorrow bottling. And would I care for some fresh bread, just as a treat after bannock? He had already baked a batch, and if I would just walk back with him I could have a crisp new loaf, as good as any woman could bake.

All this, mind you, was from a man I had met for the first time that afternoon, for ten minutes—or it might have been for fifteen. He spoke in the precise English of the educated Scandinavian.

I asked him to supper but he had already eaten. All he would accept was a couple of the grayling. "They are welcome because, you see, I live on dry land now. That was a piece of bad luck for me, that flood of '48 and the changing of the river. And this old course on which you are camped—it will all go to bush soon. You have noticed the seedling trees?"

One couldn't help noticing them—millions of tiny trees poking up among the stones: willow, cottonwood and poplar. Slowly, and with their fallen leaves, they would build up the soil. Then, in the end, the pines or the spruce would take over, killing the older trees, and the cycle would be complete.

We talked for a long time. Loving agreed with Shorty Weber on his dates: there had been plenty of moose in '44; now there were almost none. Wolves, he thought it was—wolves killing moose calves all the time, and often the mature animals as well. Now the wolves were on the move: they had already reached and passed Prince George. He had seen and counted a pack of twenty and they took to following him as he worked over his trapping trail back towards the Wolverines—fearless at first, especially as he had been stuck with some dud ammunition. Using those shells, the rifle made a sort of a crack and the bullet somehow fought its way out of the barrel, only to trundle feebly through the air and flop into the snow about fifty yards away. Great stuff. And the wolves sat back there among the trees and just about laughed at him. It had him worried for a time—but then he got some good honest shells from Roy McDougall, and a dead wolf or two made the rest of them see things in a different light.

Caribou came into that talk by the evening fire—and the moose cycle, and Pete Toy and his buried gold, and the floods of the Omineca when the water would rise thirty feet in the Black Canyon, sending great uprooted trees twirling and thrashing down the river as though they were no more than little sticks—important things, all of them. But of the news of the outside world—who had become president of what; what particular mob of students had just finished smashing the embassy windows of whom; which political party had seized power in what recent upheaval—of these things not a word was said. And sitting here by the quiet river with the last rays of the sun climbing high on Mount Selwyn, one realized that the whole frantic Punch-and-Judy show didn't matter one solitary damn.

We sat drinking coffee till the moon rose above the Gap, and the last I saw of Loving he was walking away down the old bed of the Omineca, his rifle slung over one shoulder, two large fish on a willow twig in his hand, his dog at his heels. Two winters later he disappeared: went through the ice, perhaps, or met with some accident in the bush in the intense cold when a man is not allowed even one mistake—no one ever knew.

Meanwhile something had been happening to our weather. Faint mares' tails had appeared, as we talked, in the northeastern sky. Dusk had shown long black clouds racing along the Rockies—and in the night it poured. Breakfast was a wet, cold, smoky hell, and a freezing rain drove down straight out of the north—and what could a man do but curl up under the lean-to and mend his moccasins and read? But it eased up in the after noon and the sun peered forth again, though a wild battle of inky clouds was still raging around Mount Selwyn.

I loaded up and ran for it down the racing Omineca. The wind was rising again now and blowing sand off the bars, and twice a whirlwind caught me and spun the canoe end for end. And then the wind dropped again and the clouds vanished and I turned into a little snye and made a snug camp in thick old spruce about half a mile from the Finlay. The only open side of that camp faced west, and as I sat by the fire at suppertime I could look back towards the Wolverines, utterly clear and sharp against a frosty sky. Somewhere in that direction lay the shadowy, gleaming pleasance of the Black Canyon.

Well, it was gone now, vanished like a dream—like the fabled Garden that the Old Man of the Mountains made at Alamut. And as the Wolverines faded I stirred the fire and looked through the camp library for some book I hadn't read before ... *Scoop*, now, by Evelyn Waugh—that might be just the thing. Adam and Eve, as they crouched over their first lonely campfire after being kicked out of Eden—they must have felt the need of something cheerful, too.

26

The Finlay Rapids

At long-shadowed noon of September 10, I ran the canoe aground at the head of Pete Toy's Bar and stepped ashore. I made tea there, and for something to eat I cleaned up the last of the bannock and cheese and finished off a picking of blueberries. Then I washed the pots, dried them in the hot sun and packed them away in the load. I shed my travel-worn, much-patched ruins—which were now once more torn—and put on my shore-going pants. Lastly I changed an old leather waistcoat for a gaily beaded buckskin one of Stoney Indian construction. And, with that done and the outfit neatly stowed away in the canoe, I was ready to make my entry into the trading post.

I had awakened that morning to a heavy frost: seventeen above zero, I found later, on the thermometer at the radio station at Finlay Forks. There had been new snow on the Wolverines, and now, from my noonday halt, I could see new snow on Mount Selwyn. It was one of those gorgeous fall days, crystal clear after rain—and Marigold was somewhere up in the blue, enjoying it all from the low-flying mail plane on the way in from Prince George.

I tarped up the load and ran down past Pete Toy's Bar—and nobody saw me from the trading post. I turned into the snye and paddled silently up to the landing where I made fast to an old boat of Roy McDougall's. Nobody saw me walk up the steep bank, and I proceeded, wearing the old porcupine-quill moccasins and making no sound, along the trail towards the buildings. The first person I met was a small Indian girl who was coming from the direction of the store, absorbed in a stick of chocolate and with eyes for nothing else. We were quite close when she looked up and saw me—and in no time at all a look of amazement and distrust wiped the well-filled contentment off her chocolate-smeared countenance. With a low cry and a babble of words in Sikanni, she rushed off through the trees, leaving me standing there, wondering what had gone wrong. Apart from being dressed in my best, it seemed to me that I was looking fairly normal.

The McDougalls didn't seem to see anything odd about me, and when I told Marge about the little girl she just smiled. Presently an Indian woman appeared; she wanted something from the store, and I went over, too, to see what my chances were of stocking up for the four-hundred-mile canoe trip that Marigold and I still had ahead of us. The Indian woman didn't seem to want anything much, but she kept turning again and again to look at me, saying something to Marge in her own language.

When she had gone Marge began to laugh. "That's the mother of the little girl you scared so, back there on the trail," she said. "She just can't figure out who you are and how you got here, and all I told her was that you were a stranger in these parts—which she could see well enough for herself."

"But what's the matter with these Indians?" I asked. "Surely they must be used to having people come in on the river?"

"Sure they are. But what they now expect is to hear some engine noise long before folks get here—an inboard or an outboard, whatever it may be. And here you come in without a sound, just like old times. They can't figure that out at all. If you'd had a kicker on your canoe they'd all have been at the landing to meet you, just to see who it was. They'll see your canoe when the plane comes in—then they'll know and be happy."

The plane came in about six. It lit on the river, taxied into the snye and made its last few yards by canoe paddle. Out of it stepped Marigold, and I could tell from her colour and the way she looked that she'd had a wonderful trip. We had been given the room behind the store where Alan and I had slept—and there, among the axe hafts, the coils of rope and the bunches of traps, the moccasins and the rolls of moosehide, she told me all about it. The plane was a Beaver—but to her, after the main airlines, it was a small plane. She had rather wondered about that as they climbed into the air over Prince George; but somebody had told her that the pilot had been in the Fleet Air Arm during the war, and she remembered that and felt completely safe. If, she thought, he could land a plane on the shifting deck of a carrier, then it would be no trick at all for him to put one down in perfect weather on McLeod Lake or the Finlay River. As for the journey, it had been pure delight: flying level with the mountains, almost in them; seeing from close at hand small alpine lakes and meadows, unvisited by men; following the winding, shining waters of the Crooked River and the Parsnip with the plane's shadow speeding over woodlands that were splashed with autumn gold.

And then there was the setting down of the plane. The blue expanse of McLeod Lake came into view and, away at the north end, small pinpoints of white that were the old buildings of McLeod's Lake Fort. The plane began to lose height. Then it circled over the old post, dropping down for a landing. And the pilot began to whistle "Pop Goes the Weasel."

He whistled it very quietly, but again and again Marigold, sitting next to him, heard the little tune. The water flashed by beneath the plane: the tempo of "Pop Goes the Weasel" changed ever so slightly— and the floats hit the surface of the lake exactly on the *Pop*. Neatly done, Marigold thought, as she jumped ashore and walked up to have a look at the Hudson's Bay Company's post while the mail was being unloaded. And now, once again the plane had landed on the *Pop*, this time at Finlay Forks. It had pleased Marigold to observe this. It was clearly no accident: it was a piece of ritual, and that was the way that pilot set down a plane.

There was a second pilot on board, possibly to gain a knowledge of the route, and also the game warden and a passenger for Ware. Being already late, the plane would remain at Finlay Forks for the night, and everybody—benighted plane travellers, canoe wanderers and the rest—would be housed by these kind people, and also fed, probably in two shifts, at Marge's lunch counter. And the plane party would leave in the morning with a good breakfast inside them—and thanks would be the only currency receivable.

Marigold contemplates the serene surroundings at the meeting of the rivers, a place of quiet beauty.

Carrots greeted us that night, piled in heaps around the moose meat—carrots straight out of the garden, done to a turn and buttered. In the ordinary way of life I think a carrot is a despicable thing. But having been so long without any fresh vegetable, I couldn't have enough of these: I thought they were one of the most delicious things I had ever tasted.

The morning brought another fifteen degrees of frost and another warm, sunlit day. The plane went off to Ware, returning in the afternoon and stopping just long enough to pick up the mail for the outside. Marigold and I walked up through the woods to the head of Pete Toy's Bar. We came on a meadow there, cleared and seeded by somebody, I suppose, in the days when the settlement was flourishing. An old building of some sort stood on the meadow, and the place, ringed around with trees and looking eastward over the blue river to the Rockies, had a quiet beauty under the autumn sun. Nobody seemed to be using the meadow now, and we wondered if it might be possible to buy it as a place of our own near the meeting of the rivers. I followed that up afterwards, but it came to nothing—and now I'm thankful that whoever owned that land refused to let it go. We would have made a good landing there and built a screened camp shelter nearby, like the ones in the national parks, only better. We would have given something of our hearts to it all, only to see it destroyed, with all the other meadows, in one tremendous devastation.

That evening the Warrens dropped down the Parsnip from Scott Creek to pick up their mail and visit overnight—and Marge was delighted: for the first time in the history of McDougall's post she had, in her living room, two all-White tables of bridge.

Marigold and I departed after lunch the following day. Four miles brought us to the mouth of the Parsnip, and there the two rivers of the Trench combine to form the Peace. One mile down that mighty river saw us at the head of the Finlay Rapids, and there we landed and walked on to look things over. The last thing Roy McDougall had said was: "Maybe you can run the rapids with your little canoe. But if you line down you'll be more sure. And right close in to the south shore, mind you: that's the channel, whichever way you handle it."

And here we were, and the shore was a wide shelf of rock with cubes of pyrites embedded in it, polished by the action of the river till they shone

The Pattersons' canoe slides gently through calm water.

like an inlay of gold. Black, of course, had noticed them. "Little yellow facets" he called them. This level pavement of rock terminates abruptly at the river, dropping straight off into deep, rushing water. On the landward side it is bounded by the trees and the steep slope of the hill.

Marigold and I walked down till we reached a rock point at the foot of the rapids. Here, below the point, is the head of the eddy—one of the biggest and strongest eddies I have ever seen. Immediately offshore from this point are the big, standing waves. The water has rushed down a considerable slope, gaining speed all the way; and here, where the slope levels off, it is flung up by submerged reefs into curling, white-crested ridges that extend right across the river to some rock islets. Below these swells the rush of water tapers off into a long confusion of smaller waves, noisy but harmless, racing on towards the Rockies. And, almost touching the tail of the race, upstream comes the silent but powerful water of the eddy, travelling almost as fast. Such is the canoe channel by the south shore of the Finlay Rapids.

The big waves at our feet had soaked Swannell and Jim Alexander and half-filled their big dugout for them.[40] Could my small eggshell do any better? Beyond the rock islets, between them and the north shore, there was less force of water—a shallower, slower river, broken by reefs. That was the way Haworth and Lavoie had gone down, wiggling around amongst the rocks—and that was the way Marigold and I would go when we came again six years later. But the northern passage was slow and more like work. This canoe channel by which we were standing, if you could make it at all, was quick and exciting. As for Black,[41] he was no man to follow in a small canoe; he simply took the whole thing in his stride: "Arrived at the Rapid below Finlay's Branch which we run down." I don't suppose they even stopped to look.

"I believe I could run that," I said.

"Can we both go?"

"No, I'm afraid not. I'd have to have your weight out of the fore end of the canoe, otherwise it wouldn't climb up and down these waves and we'd swamp. I'll tell you what we'll do: we'll go back to the canoe and run halfway down the fast water together. Then you can land in that little gravelly bay that we saw as we walked down, and I'll take the canoe the rest of the way. How's that?"

"All right, if you think you can manage it. And we'd better start back for the canoe now. Look at those clouds over the Rockies: what are they going to bring?"

Nothing good, by the look of them, I thought. They might mean anything, from the inside of a chinook arch to the advance guard of a winter storm. It was time to be moving—now, while yet it was warm and still. So we went back and ran the canoe down to the little bay, and Marigold landed there. "Give me time to get down to the rock point," she said. "I want to see this. And I'll cheer when you go by." And off she went.

Feeling that this might be rather a wet performance, I fished in under the tarp, pulled out my campaigning trousers—what remained of them—and put them on. No sense that I could see in getting soaked in one's best and then having nothing dry for camp. Then I pushed things into place, tarped up the load and jammed Marigold's jacket into the nose of the canoe where it would keep dry. And, with everything seen to and the spare paddle handy, I shoved out into the current. A waving handkerchief from a small figure in the distance I acknowledged by brandishing the paddle.

The shoreline flitted past, faster and faster. There was one black submerged rock to look out for: it would be easy to see, for it was the Parsnip water that was flowing down this side, clear and green. The rivers had not mingled yet ... And there was the rock, and a thrust of the paddle sent the canoe to the outside of it. Then on again and down a green, unbroken slope of water, gathering more speed and with the solid rock of the shore just a bare six feet away. Ahead rose the first of the big standing waves ... and the canoe swept splendidly up the curling slope of water, topped the foaming crest and dropped down the far side without slewing out of the straight. By God's truth, I thought, if it'll do that again for me it'll be a miracle! But it did it again: it rose up out of the trough and took the second wave the same way—only this time the spray slapped me in the face. A shout of encouragement came from the rock point and I caught a quick glimpse of Marigold, about three yards away and tense with excitement.

Down the canoe plunged—and then it tried to rise again. But this time there was no room to level off, and, rushing on with the whole force of the Peace behind it, the little craft drove through the upper part of the third wave. The water curled solid over the bow, smote me in the chest and flooded the canoe. One more like this, I thought, and all I'll have is about an inch of freeboard—if that ... But there was no fourth wave, only a babbling turmoil and chop of whitewater.

I raced on down the river with about four inches of water swilling around in the canoe. I must have gone nearly half a mile before it was safe to turn into the eddy. Then, as I was carried back upstream on the strong current, I could see Marigold still standing on the rock point, watching—and a thought occurred to me.

She came down to the water's edge and caught the nose of the canoe as it came in. She was pleased and excited. "What a wonderful little craft!" she said as I stepped out on to the shelving rock. "The way it took those waves—absolutely marvellous!" And then, suddenly: "My God, what on earth are you wearing? *What* are those awful things on your legs?"

"My seagoing pants," I told her, shortly but truthfully.

"Do you mean you've been going around like that all summer?"

"No. I finally wrecked these things scuffling around on driftpiles up the Omineca, and I propose to hang them in a tree for the squirrels to have fun with as soon as we get down the Ne Parle Pas Rapids. I wore them here only because I thought it might be a rough passage—and it was. But never mind my pants. Do you happen to have your matchbox on you?"

"I always have it on me when we're on a trip. No—wait a minute ... No, I don't seem to have it. It must be in my jacket pocket and that's in the canoe."

"Yes—and I go careering down the rapids with that, and with your eiderdown and the grub box and everything else in the canoe. My God, what was I thinking of? Supposing I'd upset the whole outfit? And nobody due this way for a couple of weeks—not till Art van Somer goes down to Gold Bar."

We stared at each other in silence for a moment. And then, "Don't let's pull that one off again," somebody said in a small voice.

"No, we'd better not. Perhaps we should try and use our heads the next time. And now let's bail the canoe and get going. The day won't last forever."

At the end of a tough summer, Patterson stands at the foot of the Finlay Rapids clad in his "seagoing pants"—or, in Marigold's words, "those awful things on your legs."

For the last time we ran down the tail of the whitewater. Then the great river swung into the north, and continued so for a couple of miles till it turned again, this time to the eastward—and the Gap of the Peace opened up before us and we passed through.

The mountains closed in around us, and suddenly it was evening. But the narrow portal, the Gap, still stood open behind us and the river here was quiet and slow-flowing. Wishing to take farewell of the Trench and the wide country by the meeting of the rivers, we turned the canoe around and let it drift backwards with the stream. Far away in the west, and beneath the grey canopy of cloud, a band of orange light still lay across the horizon. Against it, black and clear-outlined, were hunched the summits of the Wolverines, sinking already below the curve of the earth.

Then came a bend in the river and the Gap was closed to us as if, after the last act, the curtains had been drawn across a lighted stage. We turned the canoe again, drove in the paddles and went on in the softly gathering dusk—to Wicked River and to camp below Mount Selwyn.

Appendices

A. Nicholas Ignatieff was born in Russia in the province of Kiev in 1904. His family history reaches back six hundred years, to the Metropolitan Alexis of Moscow, who was Regent during the minority of the Prince of Muscovy of that time. The family has always been of "the service aristocracy"—of those nobles who regarded their privileges as pledges to be redeemed by service to the state and to the people. The tradition in that family has always been one of hard work.

A great-grandfather of Colonel Nicholas Ignatieff was Governor General of St. Petersburg and president of the council of ministers. A grandfather, General Nicholas Ignatieff, delivered the Russian ultimatum to Turkey in 1876, and imposed the conditions of peace on Turkey in 1878 at San Stefano. His father was deputy minister of agriculture in Russia and then, in 1915, minister of education.

In 1919 the family went into exile in England. There Count Nicholas Ignatieff (he of Wicked River) completed his education, graduating in civil engineering from the University of London in 1925. Setting aside his title, he then came to Canada and worked at various jobs—on survey and in the gold mines of the Porcupine area—then on construction work as an engineer, and with the Ontario Hydro-Electric—gradually trending to academic work, writing, and, in wartime, intelligence.

He died in 1952.

B. It was not until 1927 that the Hudson's Bay Company opened up a post above the mouth of the Kwadacha. They called this post Ware, or Fort Ware, and it remained open till 1953, when the Bay closed it down. There was no trading post at Ware for three years, until 1956, when Ben Corke established a store there. He operated up to the end of 1963, dying in January, 1964. Art van Somer purchased Ben Corke's stock and interests and has run the trading post ever since.

C. Fleet Robertson. For those who may be interested in Fleet Robertson's further progress and in his analysis of his trip:

He arrived at Hazelton on September 16 in three inches of snow, having been absent from there ninety-one days and having made seventy camps.

Jack Graham was paid off there, and Robertson set out down the Skeena River in a large, Coast Indian dugout canoe such as was used at that time for freighting up to Hazelton in low water in the fall when the river was too shallow for the sternwheelers. The canoe was carrying fifteen men and a ton of baggage, and it reached Port Essington and the sea on September 20 after a most exciting run down the Skeena.

Robertson arrived in Victoria on September 24 after a trip of 2,626 miles, which broke down into: 1,455 by steamer; 612 by boat or canoe; 559 with horses.

He had not been outside British Columbia and he had thoroughly enjoyed his summer.

D. W. F. Butler. This young officer, who had fallen in love with the life of the voyageur, was no mere sportsman-traveller; had his advice been followed in the last years of the century he might well have changed the course of history. In 1897, Lieutenant-General Sir William Butler, KCB, having campaigned and served in many lands, found himself in Capetown, General Commanding in South Africa, acting governor of Cape Colony and acting High Commissioner for South Africa.

A war was being engineered against the two South African republics—the Transvaal and the Orange Free State. Butler firmly believed that a war between the Dutch and the English would be the greatest calamity that had ever occurred in South Africa. Furthermore, he warned that it would be no walkover for the English, and he gave his opinion as to the number of men that would be required—a number greatly in excess of the strength under his command. Events were to prove even Butler's estimate to be far under the mark; but needless to say, his warnings went unheeded in London at the Colonial Office.

Without direct orders from the War Office, Butler refused to bring war nearer by a policy of border incidents, or by pressure on the Boers. He was no stranger to South Africa and he felt certain that, with good will, peace could be maintained and a free people left unmolested. He was not a man to compromise with his principles: either he had to shut his eyes to the whole shady business, or else he had to resign. He resigned, and was recalled to England and given a home command. Later in that same year of 1899 the Boer War—which might never have taken place had anyone listened to Butler—began. With it, according to some historians of the present day, also began the disintegration of the British Empire. Once again Butler has been proved right—though at the time he was most unjustly blamed for the early disasters of the war.

In 1905, by then well on the road to vindication, he was placed on the retired list. In 1910, full of honours, he died at his home at Bansha, County Tipperary—and Lieutenant-General the Right Honourable Sir William Butler, G.C.B., Member of the Privy Council of Ireland, was laid to rest near his father at Killardrigh.

E. Chief trader Samuel Black spent the winter of 1824–25 at Dunvegan on the Peace River. In 1825 he went to York Factory on Hudson's Bay, returning from there later in the year to the West to take charge of the post of Walla Walla (or Nez Perces) on the Columbia River. Early in 1831 he was transferred to the post of Thompson's River (now Kamloops). In 1837 he was promoted to the rank of chief factor and was appointed to "the superintendence of the Indian Posts of the Columbia." Since his great friend, Ogden, also by now a chief factor, was at Fort St. James in charge of the district of New Caledonia, this arrangement suited the two of them very well and they made a point of spending a few weeks of every year in each other's company. Black died on February 8, 1841, aged sixty years, murdered by an Indian in the hall of the fort at Thompson's River.

Bibliography

Books

Anderson, A. C. *A History of the Northwest Coast.* Typed from the copy in the Academy of Pacific Coast History, University of California, Berkeley, California. Victoria: Archives of British Columbia, 1878.

Bowes, Gordon E., ed. *Peace River Chronicles.* Vancouver: Prescott Publishing Co., 1963.

Butler, Lieutenant-General Sir William Francis, G. C. B. *The Great Lone Land.* Reprint: London: Burns & Oates, 1910.

———. *The Wild North Land.* Reprint: Toronto: The Musson Book Co. Ltd., 1924.

———. *Sir William Butler, An Autobiography.* London: Constable & Co. Ltd., 1911.

Haworth, P. L. *On the Headwaters of Peace River.* New York: Charles Scribner's Sons, 1917.

MacGregor, J. G. *The Land of Twelve-Foot Davis.* Edmonton: Applied Arts Products Ltd., 1952.

Moberly, H. J. and W. B. Cameron. *When Fur was King.* London, Toronto: J. M. Dent & Sons Ltd., 1929.

Morice, The Reverend A. G., O. M. I. *The History of the Northern Interior of British Columbia (1660-1860).* Toronto: William Briggs, 1904.

Pike, Warburton. *The Barren Ground of Northern Canada.* London: Macmillan & Co., 1892.

Publications of historical societies

Black's Rocky Mountain Journal, 1824, with an Introduction by R. M. Patterson. London: The Hudson's Bay Record Society, Vol. XVIII, 1955.

Unpublished diary

Swannell, F. C., B.C.L.S. Diaries 1913 and 1914.

Canadian government papers

Constantine, C. "Peace–Yukon Trail." Ottawa: *Reports of the Royal North-West Mounted Police,* 1905, 1906, 1907, 1908.

McConnell, R. G. "Report of an Exploration on the Finlay and Omineca Rivers." *Geological Survey of Canada, Annual Report (New Series), Vol. VII, 1894, Part C.* Ottawa: 1896.

Moodie, J. D. "Edmonton to the Yukon." *Report of the North-West Mounted Police, 1898, Part Two: Reports of Northern Patrols.* Ottawa: 1899.

Robertson, W. Fleet. "Report of the Bureau of Mines." *Annual Report of the Minister of Mines for the Year Ending 31st December, 1908,* pp. J66-J84. Victoria: Province of British Columbia, 1909.

Selwyn, Alfred C. "Report on Exploration in British Columbia." *Geological Survey of Canada, Report of Progress for 1875-6.* Ottawa: 1877).

Swannell, F. C. "Exploration of Finlay and Ingenika Valleys, Cassiar District." *Report of the Minister of Lands for the Province of British Columbia for the year ending 31st Dec. 1914,* p. D83. Victoria: Province of British Columbia, 1915.

Periodicals

Blanchet, Guy. "Samuel Black on the Finlay." *The Beaver.* Spring 1956.

Denny, Cecil. "Down the Peace in a Dugout." *The Beaver.* March 1943.

Johnson, Patricia. "McLeod Lake Post." *The Beaver.* Autumn 1965.

Patterson, R. M. "With Butler on the Omineca." *The Beaver.* December 1952.

———. "The Strangest Man I Ever Knew." *The Beaver.* Spring 1956.

Robinson, J. Lewis. "The Rocky Mountain Trench." *The Beaver.* March, 1953.

Swannell, F. C. "Ninety Years Later." *The Beaver.* Spring 1956.

(Good photographs in all of the above, except in the Blanchet book review.)

Map of Inspector Moodie's route

Edmonton to Yukon River. Route of NWMP under Inspector J. D. Moodie, by Constables F. D. Lafferty and H. S. Tobin. 10 2/3 miles to the inch.

North-West Mounted Police Route (2 sheets). 1897-98.

Endnotes

[1] Independent—i.e., not in the employ of the Hudson's Bay Company.
[2] See Appendix A.
[3] This book (there is only one copy of it—the original) only came to light in the H. B. Co. Archives a few years ago. In this strictly private and—I seem to have heard—locked volume, the governor felt completely free to let himself go on the officers of the H. B. Co. I hope the book was locked for their peace of mind—for the results, judging from excerpts, were often rancorous, malicious, libellous, and every other kind of "ous."
[4] *Salutation to Five*, by Shane Leslie (Hollis and Carter, London, 1951).
[5] Macoun had passed that way before, in company with Horetzky in 1872. But mist and rain can obscure any mountain, however strange—and this time he was hoping, along with Selwyn, that Butler's Spire might be revealed to them.
[6] Fort Grahame (named for Commissioner Grahame of the H.B. Co.) was built about 1890. It was an offshoot of the old-established (1826) Fort Connolly on Bear Lake, and was generally known by the old-timers as Bear Lake Outpost, or more simply, BLO. Bear Lake lay approximately west-southwest, ninety miles through the mountains in a direct line from Grahame. Two trails led to it from Grahame—one starting up the Ingenika, and one up a small creek opposite Grahame. It was by this latter trail that Father A. G. Morice paid a brief visit to Grahame in 1895. Bear Lake was closed about 1900—Grahame about 1948.
[7] On the map today: Akié (pronounced Ak-eye-ee).
[8] Named by Moodie for Clifford Sifton, Minister of the Interior.
[9] See Appendix B.
[10] Now Tutachi Lake.
[11] Of the evening primrose family: fireweed, willow herb.
[12] *The Wild North Land*, p. 258.
[13] McConnell never saw those lakes. Haworth was not to see them until three years later, when he returned with a party, reaching, by way of the East Fork, the lake that is named after him.
[14] On today's map, Fox Pass.
[15] When a river is on the rise it is high in the centre and the drift tends to go to the sides. When it is on the drop it is lower in the centre than at the sides, and the drift either lodges on the bars or seeks the middle of the stream.
[16] See Chapter 11.
[17] Transcribed by Dr. Tyrrell from Black's manuscript as "Mithridates." The error was perpetuated in the Appendix to Haworth's book, and remained a puzzle to all until Black's *Journal* was published in 1955.

[18] See *Trail to the Interior* by R. M. Patterson (William Sloane, New York, 1966).
[19] On the map today as Toodoggoné Lake—on the Toodoggoné River.
[20] Literally, "the men at the ends"—i.e., bowsman and steersman. Here it seems to refer to the whole crew.
[21] See Chapter 15.
[22] See Chapter 14.
[23] Eighty feet according to Black; fifty feet according to Fleet Robertson.
[24] The Old Slave and his family had been left behind to go with Methodiates to Thucatadé River. He would rejoin Black later.
[25] See Chapter 7.
[26] See *Trail to the Interior* by R. M. Patterson (William Sloane, New York, 1966), pages 69-74.
[27] See Chapter 19.
[28] See Chapter 20.
[29] See Chapter 14.
[30] See Appendix C.
[31] See *Far Pastures* by R. M. Patterson (Gray's Publishing, Sidney, B.C., 1967), Chapter 17.
[32] Ibid.
[33] See Chapter 18.
[34] The true right bank of a river is the one on the right as one faces downstream—and so also with the left bank, always facing downstream.
[35] Jim Alexander, sometimes called Jimmy to distinguish him from Jim Nep, who was Nep Yuen.
[36] Rock islets with grass and trees on top, the bases of which have been cut away by running ice and river action till they are much narrower than the level tops.
[37] See Chapter 22.
[38] See Chapter 10.
[39] See Appendix D.
[40] See Chapter 15.
[41] See Appendix E.

Index

A__ 69-70
Abu, Frank 235
Akié (Akieka) River 86, 124, 153, 173, 297
Alberta 9, 16, 159, 161, 249
Alexander, Jim 95-96, 98-103, 116, 136-37, 139-41, 146-48, 212-13, 237, 239-41, 243-46, 249, 264, 287, 298
Alluvium 6, 8
alpine fir 164, 200, 279
American Biological Survey 165
Anderson, A. C. 54
aneroid 152, 241, 243, 259-60
Arctic Circle 81
Arctic grayling 23-24, 127, 232, 235, 277
Arctic Ocean 3, 38
Ashanti 73-74
Athabasca Landing 26
Athabasca River 4
Attichika Creek 202

Babine Lake 230
Bad Luck Mountain 141-43
Bannock 131, 174, 208, 211, 231, 236, 255, 260, 278-79, 282
Barge Camp 87, 124, 229
Barren Lands 26
Barrow, Thomas 30, 35
Bear Lake (Bear's Lake) 88-89, 297
Bear's Lake Outpost (BLO) 139, 191, 297
bear(s) 108, 152, 163-65, 199-202, 212, 215-16, 219, 221, 226, 234, 276, 279
Beaufort Sea 39, 197
beaver(s) 21, 58, 62, 70, 99, 111, 129, 137, 146, 155, 177, 190, 195, 198, 201, 207, 226, 240, 244, 247-48, 250, 262, 270, 275
Beaver (airplane) 16, 172, 174, 283
Beaver Indian(s) 62, 129, 146, 188
Benin, the 73
Berghammer, Joe (Hamburger Joe) 117, 259, 261
Big Bend, the 67
Big Buffalo Mountain 124
Bight of Benin 73
Black Canyon 40, 65, 71, 74, 79, 82, 102-3, 112, 134, 224, 253, 269, 271-78, 280-81
Black, John 54
Black, Samuel 4, 7-8, 52-55, 58-63, 87, 97, 106, 123, 125-26, 146-48, 157, 162, 176-194, 196-207, 212-15, 218-21, 230, 233, 236-40, 247-48, 256-57, 287, 294, 297-98
Black's Report 12, 125, 176
Black's Rocky Mountain Journal 54, 193, 195, 201, 218, 220, 237, 247, 295, 297
Blackwood's 54
blaze(s) 132, 141, 171, 205, 211, 222, 226, 243, 265-66
Boer War, Boers 66, 293-94
Bouché, Jean Marie 60, 125, 184
Bower Creek 110, 151, 153, 159, 169, 171-72, 174-76, 178, 190, 208-9, 213, 215, 221-22, 225-28, 234-36, 279
Bower Mountain 153, 170, 232, 236, 239
Bower, L. M. 226-28, 239
British Columbia vii, 2-3, 7, 11, 30, 41, 43-44, 69, 80, 90-91, 94, 161, 207, 218, 293
British Columbia Department of Lands 43, 95
British Columbia Provincial Police 39
Bronlund Peak 214
Bronlund, Emil 4, 214, 220-22, 226
Bronlund's cabin 221-22, 228, 247
Buffalo Head Ranch 129-30
bug tent(s) 13, 15, 17-18, 48, 116, 124, 169, 263, 267
Bulkley River 132
bully beef 235, 252
Burns Lake 133-34
Butler Range 40, 79, 82, 98-99
Butler Ridge 51
Butler, W. F. viii, 40, 64-76, 81-82, 103, 146, 208, 271-76, 293-97

cache(s) 4, 31, 33-35, 65, 82-83, 86, 126, 134, 137, 139, 141, 144, 146, 149, 155, 157-59, 166-67, 170, 175, 180, 191, 202-3, 208, 217, 222, 225-27, 232, 235, 239, 273, 276
Caesar, dog 98, 136, 140-41, 240
Calgary 26, 35
Canada xi, 8, 41, 44, 54-55, 67-68, 72, 74, 80, 96, 124, 264, 292
Canadian Board on Geographical Names 8
Canadian Pacific Railway 74, 96
Cape cart 73, 76
Cape Coast Castle 73-74
Carey 64-65

caribou 27, 61-62, 85, 165, 182, 187-88, 197-202, 205, 207, 211-12, 214, 219, 243-44, 280
Caribou Hide 132, 211
Carrier(s) 95, 189-90
Cascade Canyon 135, 180-83, 239, 247-48
Cassiar Central Railway 89
Cassiar Mountains 4, 58, 60-61
Character Book, George Simpson's 53, 207
Charlie 30-37
Chatham 68, 80
Chestnut "Pleasure Model" canoe 104
Chestnut "Prospector" canoe 12, 101
Chilkoot Pass 81, 88
chinook 29-31, 288
Chinook jargon 95, 137
chute(s) 21, 103, 151, 162, 194, 229, 233, 243, 245
Coast Range (Coast Mountains) 2-3
Collins, Collins' House 116
Collins' Flat 85, 115-16, 136, 261
Colonel, the 10-11
Columbia River 3, 6, 51, 55, 58, 60, 294
Constantine, C. 88-89, 97
Continental Divide 25, 161
Copley, George Vancouver 95, 98-103, 132-148, 150, 236, 239-41, 243-46, 248-50, 264
Corke, Ben 292
Corless, Dick 18-19, 25, 38, 41, 111
cottonwood viii, 4, 6, 30, 58, 69, 71, 99-103, 105, 111, 134-35, 148-49, 237, 249, 257-58, 262, 274, 279-80
Cournoyer, Joseph 60, 179, 189, 192, 197, 203, 248
Cowart, Slim 42
Crooked River vii, 13, 18, 20, 24, 30, 81, 104, 108, 112, 279, 284
Cust House 249
Cust, Bill 64-65
cutbank(s) ix, 26, 33, 36-37, 46, 111, 130, 148, 154, 262
Cutoff Creek 181, 221, 239

Davis, F. H. (Twelve-Foot) viii, 29-30, 35, 64, 83
Dawson, G. M. 81
Deadwater, the 112, 268
Dease Lake 13
Dease River 87
deer 183, 198, 201, 203
Del Creek 124, 129, 151, 252

Delta Creek 93, 195, 212, 226-27, 243
Deserters Canyon 108, 117-23, 125-26, 145, 147-48, 176, 203, 229, 233, 249, 252-53, 261, 264
Deserters Peak 118, 147-48, 153, 259-60
Deserters Portage 127, 146, 252
devil's club 76, 79, 266
Devil's Thumb 119
Diary, Swannell's 97, 102, 144, 148, 238, 241, 248
Dick, dog 97-98, 136, 141, 240
Dictionary of the Carrier Language, A. G. Morice's 96
Dolly Varden 24, 127-28, 138, 149, 236, 257
driftpiles 6, 98-99, 111-13, 116-17, 136, 139, 143-45, 194, 262, 269, 270-71, 289
dugout canoe viii, 4, 30, 69, 71-72, 99, 101-2, 105, 134-35, 147-48, 237, 239, 244, 248-50, 287, 293

eddy, catching the 178-79, 195-96, 203-4, 273
Edmonton 26, 85, 87-88, 104
England 67, 73-74, 149, 158, 271, 292-93
English 52, 69, 72, 171, 177, 223, 293
Europe 43, 184, 220
Evans, Ezra 83

Falls, the 92, 193, 195-96
Finlay Forks (the Forks) vii, viii, x, 6-7, 16, 18, 33, 38, 42, 46, 48-49, 51-52, 71, 92, 102-4, 108, 128, 134, 136, 232, 252-53, 282, 284
Finlay Rapids 31, 33-34, 44, 50, 63, 102, 249, 282, 286-87, 290
Finlay, John 7-9, 51, 176
Finlay's Branch 7, 9, 45, 51-52, 63, 191-93, 201, 287
Firesteel River 4, 195, 203, 205, 214
Fishing Lakes (Tototadé) 4, 52, 95-96, 178, 180-81, 184, 186-88, 190-91, 193, 212-15, 218-20, 235, 237-39, 241, 243-44
Forks of the Kwadacha (North Fork, East Fork) 156-158
Forks of the Peace 82
Fort Babine 227-28, 230
Fort Chipewyan 26-27, 55, 61, 69, 126, 130, 191
Fort Dunvegan 59, 69, 294
Fort Fraser 132, 134
Fort Garry 67, 275

Fort George (Prince George) 51
Fort Grahame (Bear's Lake Outpost) vii, 4, 40, 80, 85-89, 95, 98-101, 113, 115-16, 124, 126, 131, 134, 136-37, 139, 146, 222, 228-30, 239, 249, 260, 262, 264-65, 297
Fort Kearney 67-68
Fort McLeod (McLeod's Lake Fort) 24, 31-33, 35, 51, 72, 82, 134, 136, 228, 249, 284
Fort Nelson 154, 210
Fort Resolution 26-27
Fort Saskatchewan 88
Fort Selkirk 87
Fort St. James (Stuart's Lake Fort) 51-52, 72, 95-97, 103, 134, 136, 228, 249, 256, 258, 262, 294
Fort St. John vii, 53, 69, 85, 88-90, 97, 146
Fort Vancouver 60
Fort Vermilion 29
Fort Ware (Ware) 16, 19, 110, 118, 127, 129-32, 151-52, 169, 171-73, 211, 219, 231, 233, 235, 252, 258, 262, 265, 284-85, 292
Fox River (Tochieca) 4, 6, 8, 19, 87, 95, 130-32, 150-51, 153, 159-60, 163, 169, 173, 176-77, 180, 239, 248-49
Fox, William 86-89, 229-30
Fox Pass 297
France 149, 220
Fraser River xi, 3, 23, 51-52, 64, 81
Fraser, Simon 51, 134
French 68-69
French-Canadian xi, 59-60, 95, 104, 237
frogging 21-22, 108, 144, 196, 233

game record 96, 137
Gauvreau, N. B. 80, 124
Geological Survey of Canada x, 72, 74, 80-81, 180
George 173
German(s) 114-15, 265
Germansen Landing 64-65, 71, 83
Gibraltar Rock 119, 121, 254
Gibson, Rex 154
Giscome Portage 23, 81
glacial lake(s) 157
gneiss 65, 82
gold 30, 64-65, 83-85, 91, 109, 122, 124, 142, 144, 149, 226, 231-32, 235, 275, 280, 287, 292
Gold Bar 289
Gold Coast x, 73
Gold, Axel 97, 102

goldfields 29, 64
Graham, Jack 227-28, 230, 293
Great Glacier (Lloyd George Icefield) 154, 156-58
Great Lone Land, The, W. F. Butler's 67-68
Great Slave Lake 26

Halfway River 85
Haworth Lake 87, 154
Haworth, Paul Leland ix, 4, 10, 21, 24, 26, 36, 65, 104-6, 127-28, 137, 152-62, 164-67, 175, 178-79, 189, 199, 233, 236, 253, 287, 297
Hazelton 88, 90-91, 144, 227, 292-93
Henderson, Bob 25
History of the Northwest Coast, A, A. C. Anderson's 53
Horetzky, Charles 25, 74, 297
Hudson's Bay Company viii, 7-8, 27, 29, 36, 52-55, 58-61, 68-70, 74, 80, 86, 89, 95, 99-101, 116, 130, 134, 137, 151, 172, 176-77, 208, 218, 235, 249, 252, 264, 284, 292, 297
Hudson's Hope vii, 29, 36, 69-70, 74, 146, 250

Ignatieff, Nicholas x, 37, 41-45, 292
Ignatieff, Vladimir 43
Ingenika River 7, 91, 96, 129, 134, 137-47, 262, 266, 297
Interior Plateau 2-3, 24
Ireland 66-67, 72, 294
Irish x, 66, 228
Irish, A. M. 228-29, 234
Iron Gate, the 180
Iroquois 30, 52-53, 59, 85, 106, 125, 182, 184, 212, 237
Iroquois Cap 182-83

John 29, 32-34, 69

Kalder, William 69-70, 273
Kastberg, Victor 97, 102
Kechika Ranges 152
Kechika River 8, 87
Kerry Lake 25
Kettle Glaciers 154
Klondike (gold) rush 81, 87-88
Klondike trail (Klondiker's trail, Moodie's trail)) viii, 81, 84, 149-50

Klondiker(s) 86, 117, 124, 139, 149, 222, 229
Kodak Cascade 241, 245
Kwadacha River 6, 87, 104, 126, 128, 130, 150, 153-58, 176, 180, 238, 249, 292

L'Ence [Anse] du Sable (Sandy Bay) 178, 185-86, 188, 214
La Guarde, Joseph 59-61, 123, 179, 181-85, 187-89, 194-201, 203, 212-13, 219, 221, 237, 239, 241, 248
La Prise 59-62, 126, 181, 184, 186-88, 191, 194-95, 197-98, 201-6
La Prise's wife 59-61, 181, 186-88, 202
Lake Athabasca 27, 55, 61
latigo lace(s) 223-24, 256
Laurier Pass 85, 89-90, 112
Lavoie, Joe 4, 36, 104-6, 127-28, 152, 155-56, 158, 161-67, 253, 287
lean-to(s) 17, 209-11, 223-25, 257-58, 261, 272, 281
Leith, Mary 54-55
Lemas, Hebert 55
Leslie, Shane 66, 297
Lesser Slave Lake 35
Liard Coal Company 91
Liard River (Rivière aux Liards) 3-4, 7, 52, 81, 87, 91, 126, 153, 177, 190
lining 50, 63, 83, 103, 123, 126, 136, 144, 151, 194, 196, 204, 229, 233, 243, 247-49, 255, 269-70, 273, 286
Little Buffalo Mountain 124
Little Canyon 65, 82
London 8, 42-43, 55, 68, 76, 218, 225, 292-93
Long Canyon 152, 162, 166, 171, 179-81, 232, 234, 237, 239, 248
Long Portage 189, 191
Loving, Gunnar 279-81
Lower Post 81
Lynn Canal 81
lynx 96, 137

Mackenzie River 3-4, 9, 26, 38-39, 197
Mackenzie, Alexander 51, 82
Macoun, John 72, 76-77, 79, 297
Mannlicher 211, 216, 267
Manson Creek 64, 83
Manson, Donald 59-61, 125, 186, 196, 198, 201, 203, 205-6, 237
marmot(s) (whistler, siffleur) 160, 190, 198-99, 202, 219
Martin, Nurse 172-74

Massito (Massiter) family 171, 231, 236
McConnell Creek 91-92, 144
McConnell Pass 180-82, 221
McConnell, R. G. 4, 64, 80-83, 124, 126, 138, 152, 154, 156-57, 168, 177, 180-81, 222, 237, 239, 269, 297
McDougall, James 8, 46
McDougall, Marge 49, 109-10, 265
McDougall, Margie 109
McDougall, Roy 45, 48-49, 105, 279-80, 282, 286
McDougalls, the 23, 108, 279, 283
McDougall's trading post 16, 19, 45-46, 48, 50, 64, 112, 286
McKay, Murdo 27, 29, 32-34, 36
McLeod Lake (Mcleod's Lake) 24-25, 27, 40, 51, 82, 102-3, 134, 136, 284
McLeod Lake Indians 134
McLeod, Cpl. 89
McLeod, John 3, 7-8
McLeod's Lake Fort (Fort McLeod) 31-33, 35, 51, 72, 82, 136-37, 284
McLeod's River (McLeod River) 26, 32-33, 36, 82, 134, 136
Mesilinka River (Stranger River) 40, 94, 97-99, 102
Methodiates 184, 188-93, 195, 202, 206, 219, 298
Metsantan Lake 207, 212
micaschist 71, 79, 82, 277
Miller, Del 124
Moodie, J. D. 84-89, 149, 297
moose 18, 85-86, 129, 131, 138, 140-41, 144, 155, 166, 177, 181, 212-13, 215, 217, 226, 240-41, 243, 265-66, 279-80, 285
moosehide 33, 48, 177, 210, 283
Moose-that-Walks 146
Morice, A. G. 96, 207, 297
mosquitoes ("musquattoes") 13, 15, 18, 22, 38, 44, 92, 114, 116-17, 139, 145, 148-49, 210, 214, 263
Mount Haworth (Observation Peak) 153
Mount Lloyd George 158
Mount Robson 154
Mount Selwyn 42, 44, 50, 73, 75, 78, 176, 281-82, 291
Mount Smythe 154
Mount Yuen 154
mulligan 122, 131, 231
muskeg 85, 156, 166, 171, 186
muskox 27
Muskwa River 158

Index

Nahanni country 7, 129-30
Nation River 26, 33, 36
Necessity (raft) 4, 167, 179
Nechacco (canoe) 72
Ne parle pas Rapids 50, 285
New Caledonia 51, 58, 125, 294
North Saskatchewan River 68
North West Company 7, 51-52, 54-55, 59, 124
North West Mounted Police ix, 85-87, 234
Northwest Territories 91, 234, 258
Northwest, the x, 8, 36, 42, 54
Northwesters 51-52, 55, 58-59, 123

Obo River (Porcupine Creek) 183-84, 240
Observation Peak (Mount Haworth) 106, 153, 157-58
Ogden, Peter Skene 54-55, 58, 207, 294
Old Man, the (Split Rock) 4, 162-63, 178, 180, 239
Old Slave, the 62-63, 123, 125-26, 176-77, 179, 181-84, 187-89, 298
Omineca River viii, 29, 40, 64-65, 71, 74, 79-80, 82-83, 95, 97, 101-3, 112, 126, 134, 154, 224, 233, 253, 268-75, 279-81, 289
On the Headwaters of Peace River, P. L. Haworth's 10, 21, 104
Orange Free State 73, 293
Ospika River 85-86, 90, 112, 268
Ossin, Louis 60, 125, 184
Ottawa 8, 43, 73, 81, 158

Pacific Ocean 2-3, 51, 81
Pacific–Arctic Divide 12
Pack River (McLeod's River) 24, 26, 36, 51, 134
Pardonnet, Jacques 69-71, 273-75
Paris 67-68, 112
Parsnip River vii, 6, 8, 18-19, 22, 24, 26-27, 30-33, 36, 38, 40-41, 43-44, 51, 64, 72, 79, 102, 105, 108, 230, 249, 263, 275, 284, 286, 288
Pat 30-37
Patterson, Alan vii, viii, 11, 13, 16-17, 23-24, 27, 40, 48-49, 109-10, 117, 120, 131, 151, 167-68, 171-75, 208, 235-36, 263, 283
Patterson, Marigold viii, 11, 13, 16-17, 232, 253, 279, 282-89
Pattie, David 169
Pattie, Mr. 131, 151, 169, 174, 252
Pattie, Mrs. 131, 169, 252
Paul's Branch 149-50, 153
Peace River vii, viii, x, 3-4, 6-7, 9-10, 12, 16, 21, 23, 25, 27, 29-30, 34-36, 40, 42, 44, 48, 50-51, 53, 59, 61-62, 65, 69-70, 73, 76, 78-79, 82, 85, 102, 104-5, 108, 143, 181, 197, 249-50, 286, 289, 294
Peace River Crossing 249
Peace River Gap (Gap of the Peace) vii, viii, 6, 35, 40, 42, 49, 74, 79, 89, 276, 291
Peak Mountains 185-88, 206, 212-15, 219
Pelly Creek 266
Pelly Lakes 253, 266
Pelly River 87
pemmican (pemican) 182-83
Perreault, Antoine 59-60, 123, 186-88, 197-201, 203, 207, 219, 237, 253
Pesika Creek 252-53
Pete Toy's Bar 46-49, 64, 71, 91, 106, 109-10, 198, 282, 285
Peterborough canoe(s) 81, 83, 101-2, 126
Picket Fence, the 112-13, 268
Pike, Warburton viii, 26-27, 29-36, 52, 69, 81
placer gold 64, 141
Platte River 67
Police Trail, the 88, 90, 97-99, 112
poling 29, 46, 59, 63, 69-70, 72, 82, 98, 102-4, 106, 108, 112, 123, 133, 136, 139, 141, 144, 151, 167, 170-71, 175, 177-78, 193-94, 231-34, 241, 246, 269, 272-73
poplar 5, 8, 149, 168, 235, 280
porcupine 138, 195, 210, 225, 282
Porcupine Creek (Obo River) 238, 240, 292
Portage Mountain 51
portage(s), portaging 21, 29-30, 59, 63, 65, 81-82, 96, 120-28, 135, 147-48, 180, 182-85, 187-88, 191, 194-96, 223, 229, 232-33, 237, 241, 245, 247-50, 253-58, 270-73, 275-76
Portland, the 84
Prairie Mountain 4, 87, 130, 151-52, 154, 156, 158-59, 162-63, 166-69, 177, 235-36, 252, 261
Prince George (Fort George) 11-12, 16, 18, 38, 132, 279-80, 282, 284
Prince Rupert 132
Prussians 68

Queen Victoria 74, 76
Quesnel 30, 32, 64, 69, 72, 81-82, 86, 88, 132, 181, 275

Red Deer River 9
Red River 67-69, 73
Reed, Harper 186
Reef Canyon 186-88, 214, 219, 241-44, 246-47, 249
Report, Robertson's 228
Richards, J. 88, 90
Riel Rebellion 67
riffle(s) ix, 13, 18, 20, 98, 104, 169, 175, 180, 233-34, 246, 253-54, 262
Robertson, Fleet 91-94, 144, 226-29, 237, 254, 292-93
Rocky Mountain Canyon 250
Rocky Mountain Portage 29, 50-52, 63, 65, 71, 189, 191, 197, 249
Rocky Mountain Trench (the Trench) vii, viii, 3-4, 6-8, 24-25, 31, 39-41, 44, 48, 51, 58, 77, 79-80, 84-85, 87, 93, 129-30, 153, 158, 163, 169, 177, 249-50, 253, 259-61, 286, 291
Rocky Mountains (Rockies) vii, 3, 6-7, 10-11, 16, 18, 25, 27, 29, 31, 34, 38-43, 45, 48, 50-52, 58, 67-69, 77, 79, 85, 87, 89-90, 95, 112, 114, 116, 118, 130, 153-55, 158-59, 161, 176, 215, 249, 261-62, 265, 267-68, 276, 281, 285, 287-88
Ross 99-101, 136, 146
Rossetti 100, 103
Ruby Creek (Spinel Creek) 221, 238
Russel, H. Y. 82-83
Russian(s) 42, 58, 149, 190, 292

Salmon River 134
Saskatchewan River 8, 67-69
Scandinavian(s) 42, 280
Scoop, Evelyn Waugh's 281
Scotland 54-55, 60
Scott 38-39
Scott Creek 38-40, 286
scree 161-62, 179, 215, 239
Selwyn, A. R. C. 72, 79-80
Selwyn, Mount 42, 44, 50, 72-75, 77-78, 276, 281-82, 291, 297
Seven Mile Pool 169-70, 235
Shakespeare 245
sheep x, 10, 60, 85, 159, 162, 165, 183, 187, 214, 218-20, 232, 236, 266
Sheep Creek 163, 166

Sheep Point (Point du Mouton) 178, 181, 183-85, 189, 240, 247
shingle bar(s) 16, 44, 46, 64, 111, 113, 118, 120, 127, 144, 152, 155, 168, 171, 178, 235-36, 241, 253, 269-70
Sifton Pass 8, 87, 153
Sifton, Clifford 89, 297
Sikanni Indians (Sikannis) 7, 30, 34-35, 62, 123, 125, 131, 165, 173, 178, 181-83, 186, 188-90, 192, 195, 197-98, 202, 204-5, 207, 221, 239, 283
Silver Creek 64, 83
Simpson, George 53-55, 61, 196, 207
Skeena River 293
Smaaslet, Ludwig 109-14, 117-20, 124, 129, 131, 151-52, 170-71, 175, 208-9, 217, 225, 231-32, 252-53
Smythe, F. S. 154
snye(s) ix, x, 46, 49, 64, 109-11, 170, 175, 263, 267, 281-83
Somosierra Pass 220
South Africa 73, 293
South Nahanni River 3, 91-92, 235
spinner(s) 24, 208, 235
Split Rock (the Old Man) 4, 162, 178
Stanier, Jack 91, 144
Starke, Jack (the "Black Pirate") 91, 144
Stikine divide 62, 189, 207
Stikine Plateau 4-5
Stikine River 60, 62, 81, 90, 132, 186, 189, 207
Stikine Trail 186
Strandberg, Ed 109
Stuart Lake (Stuart's Lake) 82, 86, 97
Stuart's Lake Fort (Fort St. James) 51-52, 86
Stuart, John 207
Summit Lake vii, 10, 12-13, 17-18, 23-25, 30, 38, 81, 108, 279
surveyor general 94
survey(s), surveyor(s) 20, 29, 48, 80, 94-97, 99, 102-4, 117, 132, 134, 137-38, 141, 143-44, 148, 180, 214, 237-39, 241, 244, 249, 264, 292
Swannell, Mrs. 96
Swannell, F. C. (Frank) 95-99, 101-3, 105, 116, 132-41, 143-46, 148, 150-51, 162, 178, 180, 184, 186, 214, 220, 236-37, 239-50, 264-65, 287
Swedes 92, 98
sweeper(s) ix, 46, 113-14, 176, 262, 268-69

Takla Lake 95
Tarrangeau, Jean Baptiste 60, 197, 203
Tatlatui Lake 214
Tatlatui Range 198
Teapot Mountain 18
Teare, Mort 108
Telegraph Creek 88, 90, 163, 256
Telegraph Trail (Ashcroft Trail) 90
Teslin Lake 88
Testerwich, Baptiste 30
The Virginian, Owen Wister's 133
Thlingit 190
Thloadenni(s) 189-90, 192-93, 206, 219
Thomas, Napoleon 85-86
Thompson River xi
Thompson's River (Kamloops) 294
Three Isle Lake 161
Thucatadé Lake (Toodoggoné Lake) 188, 193, 206, 298
Thucatadé River (Toodoggoné River) 189, 191, 193, 205-7, 213-15, 298
Thudaka Creek 214, 247-48
Thutadé Lake ix, x, 4, 59, 61-62, 92, 144, 176-77, 191, 193, 195, 197, 201-2, 207, 212, 214, 236, 244
Thutadé Creek 198, 207
Tipperary 66, 294
Together, Norman Douglas' 210-11, 217, 225
Toma 265-66
Toy, Pete 64-66, 82, 275-76, 280
tracking 12, 29, 31-32, 59, 72, 136, 170, 175, 178, 194, 232, 241, 271, 273
trackline(s) 12, 22, 31, 45-46, 62, 196, 232-33, 237, 255-56, 263, 268-70
Trading Nahannis 189-90
trapline(s) 38-39, 42, 108, 110, 114, 170, 266
Triple Fugue, Osbert Sitwell's 257-58, 278
trout 18, 20, 24-25, 62, 92, 125, 138, 171, 174-75, 195, 197-99, 201, 208-9, 234-35, 252, 276-78
Tuchodi River 158
Turnagain River (Black's River, Black River, Mud River, Big Muddy, Kechika) 7-8, 87
Tutizzi Lake (Long-water Lake) 97-98
Tyrrell, J. B. 176, 297

umbrella trees 22
Upper Canada 68
Upper Canada College 41

van Somer, Art 109, 122, 252, 289, 292
van Somer, Bill 25
Vancouver Island 16, 95, 172
Victoria 2, 69, 73, 96, 275, 293
voyageur(s) 22, 50, 52, 70, 103, 105, 179, 200, 237, 275, 293

War Office 42, 68, 293
Warren family 38, 40, 286
Warren, Milton 40
Warrens' house 263
Weber, Frank (Shorty) 263-67, 280
west fork (of Bower Creek) 213, 215, 221-22, 225
Weston 39
Weston Creek 39
White Pass and Yukon Railway 88
Whitehorse 88
whitewater 4, 50, 60, 118, 159, 241-42, 246, 275, 289, 291
Wicked River 42-45, 291-92
Wild North Land, The, W. F. Butler's 67, 73-75, 103, 146, 275, 297
willow(s) 15-16, 20, 22-23, 49, 89, 111-12, 125, 136, 140, 149, 166, 168, 173, 184, 186-88, 198, 211-12, 235, 261, 263, 278, 280-81
Wolseley, Garnet 67, 73
Wolverine Mountains 40, 42, 48, 79, 103, 276, 280-82, 291
wolverine(s) 32, 152, 202, 216, 221
Wrede 139
Wrede Creek 140, 266

York Factory 58, 294
Yuen Creek 154
Yuen Lake 154
Yuen, Nep (Jim Young, Jim Nep) 96-97, 100-1, 132-34, 137-39, 141-42, 146, 149-50, 239-40, 244-46, 249, 264, 298
Yukon River 84-85, 87-88
Yukon Telegraph Line 88, 90
Yukon Territory 3, 81, 267

The Author

Raymond Murray Patterson began life in England in 1898. He attended Oxford and fought in the First World War, but in 1924 he left a predictable life behind for the unknown in the Canadian West. First he homesteaded in the Peace River country of northern Alberta. Then the lure of the fabled Nahanni gold led him on a quest into the Northwest Territories in the late 1920s.

Although he found no gold, Patterson found a way of life that suited him: pursuing adventure. After marrying Marigold Portman in 1929, he raised cattle on a dude ranch called the Buffalo Head, in the foothills of the Canadian Rockies. From this base, he spent the next 16 years exploring the high country of the Continental Divide with George Pocaterra and Adolf Baumgart.

In the late 1940s the Patterson family moved to Vancouver Island, where, over the next two decades, RMP published five books as well as numerous articles in *Blackwood's Magazine* and *The Beaver*. His vivid portrayal of the Canadian wilderness has never been surpassed.

Patterson is best known for his international bestseller *The Dangerous River*, about his adventures on the South Nahanni River. His other classics include *The Buffalo Head*, about his ranching days; *Trail to the Interior*, about the Stikine region; and *Far Pastures*, a collection of stories about homesteading in northern Alberta and his river escapades.